COMPLETE
POWERBOATING
MANUAL

COMPLETE
POWERBOATING

Tim Bartlett

Simon Collis

Tony Jones

MANUAL

NH
NEW
HOLLAND

First published in 2008 by New Holland Publishers (UK) Ltd
London • Cape Town • Sydney • Auckland
www.newhollandpublishers.com

Garfield House	80 McKenzie Street	Unit 1, 66 Gibbes	218 Lake Road
86–88 Edgware Road	Cape Town	Street, Chatswood	Northcote
London W2 2EA	8001	NSW 2067	Auckland
United Kingdom	South Africa	Australia	New Zealand

ISBN 978 1 84537 296 5

Senior Editor Sarah Goulding   **Illustrator** Stephen Dew
Editor Guy Croton   **Picture Research** Emma Brenton, PPL Ltd
Designer Neil Adams   **Production** Marion Storz
Series Design Robert Last   **Publishing Director** Rosemary Wilkinson

Designed, typeset and edited by Focus Publishing, Sevenoaks, Kent
Printed and bound by Times Offset (Malaysia) Sdn Bnd, Malaysia
Reproduction by Pica Digital Pte Ltd, Singapore

1 3 5 7 9 10 8 6 4 2

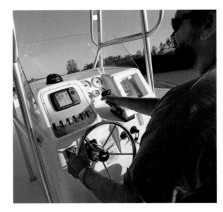

CONTENTS

INTRODUCTION

All kinds of people go motor boating, in all sorts of places, and for many different reasons. For some, it offers a chance to get away from people, while for others it's an opportunity to socialize. Some go boating for the excitement, others to relax, and some for the intellectual or physical challenges it presents. It can be an opportunity to revel in your independence, to enjoy operating as a team, or to escape from the everyday responsibilities of working life.

You can enjoy boating almost anywhere that there is water. The sea, of course, is the most obvious choice, particularly for the largest and fastest boats, but there are plenty of opportunities for inland boating on lakes, canals, rivers and even on flooded gravel pits.

It almost goes without saying that the boats designed to meet so many different expectations and to operate in such different conditions must vary enormously. The smallest are the size of a single bed, while the largest are longer than a football pitch. The slowest can just about manage a brisk walking pace, while others are faster than most family cars.

Unless you are absolutely certain that you want to get involved in one of the more extreme forms of boating, you are probably well advised to go for a reasonably middle-of-the-road kind of boat – one which will be reasonably

Above: *A typical sports boat, the 555 Commander.*

competent at most things, and which won't be too quirky to drive. It should be easy to buy in the first place, and easy to sell when you decide to move on to something bigger, or more specialized.

Most of these 'general purpose' boats are likely to be described either as sports boats or sports cruisers. There's no formal definition of either category, but sports boats are generally smaller – often small enough to carry on a trailer towed behind a large family car. They have little or no under-cover accommodation, but have relatively generous open seating areas (called cockpits). Their engines may be either petrol or diesel, either built into the boat or mounted on the back, and generally have a top speed of between 20 and 40 knots (37–74kph/23–46mph) – though some can do considerably more.

A sports cruiser is generally larger, so although some of the smallest sports cruisers are trailable, most are kept afloat. As well as a cockpit similar to that of a sports boat, a sports cruiser has covered accommodation, usually including a toilet, a kitchen area (called a galley), and at least a couple of beds. Larger

Above: *A typical sports cruiser, the Sealine 29.*

ANATOMY OF A SPORTS BOAT

The main body of the boat is called the hull; this is usually made of very strong glass-reinforced plastic (GRP). The front is called the bow (which is pronounced to rhyme with 'cow', not 'low'), and the back is called the stern. The width of the boat is called its beam, and the depth of water it requires to float is called its draft.

Hull shape

The bottom panels of the hull are angled upwards and outwards to give the boat a V-shaped cross-section. This has an important effect on the boat's ability to handle rough water: in general a 'deep vee (V)' gives a more comfortable ride than a shallow vee.

Helm console

Very small boats can be steered by means of a lever attached directly to the outboard motor, but most boats have a steering wheel. Alongside the wheel are the engine controls – usually a single lever that controls the gear and speed – and engine instruments.

Every boat should have a compass, and most owners add other navigation instruments.

Outboard motor

An outboard motor is a self-contained power unit, clamped or bolted to the back of the boat. As well as the engine, it includes a gearbox, giving a choice of ahead, neutral or astern ('reverse') thrust. The boat can be steered by turning the whole unit, so as to direct the thrust slightly to the left or right.

Propeller

Hidden below the waterline, the propeller converts the rotation of the motor shaft into useful thrust.

sports cruisers may well have an indoor 'sitting room' (called a saloon) and several separate sleeping cabins. In the UK and most of Europe, at least, most sports cruisers have twin diesel engines, mounted inside the boat under the cockpit.

Types of boat

DINGHY AND OUTBOARD

One of the cheapest and most convenient ways of getting afloat, an inflatable dinghy and outboard can be carried to the water's edge in the boot of a car, and inflated in minutes. Don't confuse a proper inflatable dinghy with a beach toy: it is actually a tough little vessel that will last for many years, and is ideal for exploring rivers, for adding a new dimension to family picnics, or for introducing children to powerboating. However, size is a serious limiting factor.

LARGE OR SMALL?

The size of boat to buy is inevitably determined at least partly by your budget. A large boat not only costs more to buy than a smaller one, but is also considerably more expensive to run. Not only do fuel, maintenance and insurance cost more, but as soon as you have a boat that is too big to be kept on a trailer at home, you will need to find somewhere to keep it.

However, although the average size of 'entry level' boat has increased considerably over recent years, you won't necessarily get five times as much pleasure if you pay five times the price for your boat.

Big boats are generally more comfortable, both in harbour and at sea. They can carry more people, are generally capable of covering longer distances at higher average speeds, and are less affected by poor weather. A big boat is not necessarily any more difficult to drive than a small one: they tend to be more docile, and most people adapt very quickly to their size and weight. However, the consequences of getting a manoeuvre wrong are considerably worse: what would be a minor bump in a boat that weighs a ton can cause serious damage in one that weighs twenty tons.

It is often said that smaller boats are more fun. They can certainly be more exciting, and they can go to places that larger boats cannot. They are more easily managed by one or two people, and boats that are small enough to be trailed can be taken to a different stretch of water whenever the fancy takes you.

Above: An inflatable dinghy with an outboard motor.

Above: *A rigid inflatable boat (RIB).*

RIBS

Inflatable side tubes mean that a small RIB may easily be mistaken for a biggish inflatable dinghy. But the initials stand for Rigid Inflatable Boat – so called because it has a rigid bottom, like a conventional sports boat. Now more popular than conventional sports boats, RIBs offer similar performance, but are widely regarded as more 'seaworthy' – better able to handle rough water and with a huge reserve of buoyancy in the tubes.

SPEEDS ON WATER

Compared with the speeds we are used to driving at on the road, the speeds achieved by even a high-performance boat can seem modest.

This is partly because water speeds are usually given in knots, rather than in miles per hour. A knot is a nautical mile per hour, but a nautical mile is about 15 per cent longer than a statute mile, so 40 knots is the same as 46mph (74kph).

Even more significant is that our perception of speed over a ruffled water surface is very much faster than on a smooth road. It is hard to quantify this, especially as a small boat usually feels as though it is going very much faster than a big one at the same speed. However:

• The world water speed record is 220mph (354kph), whereas the world land speed record is 763mph (1,228kph).

• River and harbour speed limits are usually about 6 knots compared with road speed limits in town which are usually 30mph (48kph).

So it is fair to say that a boat capable of 30 knots feels roughly equivalent to a car capable of 120mph (193kph).

Galley

The whole point of a sports *cruiser*, as opposed to a sports *boat* is that you can live on board. Consequently, the kitchen area, or 'galley' (see below), is an important part of this floating home-from-home, even if it is seldom used for much more than storing beer or making coffee!

ANATOMY OF A SPORTS CRUISER

Saloon

There is generally much more space in a sports cruiser than a sports boat, providing an under-cover seating and eating area (see bottom left).

Aft cabin

If possible, builders always like to offer a private sleeping cabin, and designers are remarkably good at finding room for them to do so (see above right).

Helm console

The console of a sports cruiser (see below) is similar to that of a sports boat, but may have more sophisticated instrumentation and communications equipment.

Bathroom

Any sports cruiser will have a toilet compartment – often known by the traditional term 'heads' (see below right). It usually includes a washbasin and shower, using freshwater that is stored on board and heated by the engine.

Engine

Although there are outboard motors available that will produce over 200hp, most sportscruisers have diesel engines (see bottom right) inside the boat (usually under the cockpit floor), with an outdrive transferring the power to the propeller.

Outdrive

An outdrive looks very much like the bottom half of an outboard. Like an outboard, it transfers power from the engine to the propeller through a gearbox, and it can be turned easily in order to steer the boat.

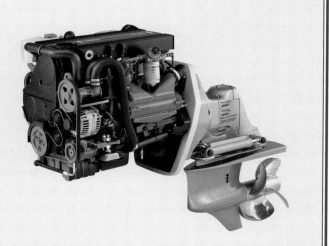

Above: *A bass boat, popular in the USA.*

A 5m (16ft) RIB can easily be trailed behind a family car, and RIBs of that size have gone all the way around Britain, while slightly bigger RIBs are used by diving clubs, as lifeboats, and by the armed forces. However, RIBs are generally quite heavy, and the thickness of their tubes makes them fairly bulky, whilst limiting the amount of space available to the passengers on board.

BASS BOATS

Bass boats are light, low and are fitted with very powerful engines that give them dramatic acceleration and a very high top speed. When they stop, they are very stable on the water. This makes these boats ideal for fishing. However, bass boats are specialist flat-water machines which are not good in rough conditions, and they are almost unheard of outside the USA.

AIRBOATS

Called airboats because they use an aircraft-style propeller instead of a water propeller, airboats generally have shallow, flat bottoms that allow them to operate in very shallow water and even to slide over mud banks, dense weed, or ice. This makes them popular in places such as the Florida Everglades and in parts of Canada. However, the air propeller is very noisy, and they are only rarely imported into Europe.

NARROWBOATS

The industrial heartland of England is criss-crossed by a network of over 2,000 miles (3,218km) of man-made canals. Built over 200 years ago, they were essential to the industrial revolution, because – long before the development of railways – they allowed goods and raw materials to be moved around the country. Now, canal boating is a popular activity, using very specialized narrow boats. The

Above: *An airboat in full flow.*

name speaks for itself: a narrow boat is never more than 2.1m (7ft) (usually 2.07m/6ft, 10in) wide, but may be anything up to 30m (72ft) long. They are slow and totally unseaworthy, but perfectly adapted to the very narrow locks and low bridges of a canal network.

PERSONAL WATERCRAFT

Apart from some dinghies, personal watercraft (sometimes, wrongly, referred to by Kawasaki's trade-marked name 'jet ski') are generally in the smallest category of powerboats. Originally designed as a self-propelled waterski, the idea has evolved into something more like a waterborne motorbike: a very small boat, with a motorcycle seat, and handlebar steering, propelled by a small but powerful engine and a waterjet drive system.

Above: A narrowboat, specially designed to cope with the narrow locks and bridges of Britain's canal network.

ZAPCATS

Developed from simpler inflatable catamarans that were used by surf lifeguards in South Africa, Zapcats are fast, seaworthy, and exciting racing machines that weigh less than 150kg (330lb) yet are driven by 50hp motors. Their low prices – in 2007 you could buy a new, race-ready Zapcat for £8,000 – has made

Above: A Kawasaki Jet Ski.

TRY BEFORE YOU BUY

Self-drive hire – usually referred to as 'charter' in the marine world – might seem to be the ideal way to try boating before you commit to the expense of buying a boat of your own. Unfortunately, however, although many companies offer self-drive motorboats on inland waters such as canals, lakes and rivers, opportunities to charter sports boats or sports cruisers on coastal waters are very much more limited, and companies generally expect some proof of competence

from would-be charterers before they will hand over a boat.

For the complete novice, a much better bet is to take a short course at a recognized training centre.

In the UK, the Royal Yachting Association runs several training schemes, for different types of boats.

For powerboaters, the most appropriate courses are those operated under the Powerboating scheme, which is concerned mainly with small, open powerboats without

accommodation or cooking facilities. Additionally, there is the Motor Cruising scheme, which is more appropriate for larger boats, and more extended cruising. Both schemes include courses at several different levels, all run by independent training centres.

The Level 2 Powerboat course can be completed by most people in about two days, and gives a good basic level of powerboating knowledge – certainly enough to 'go solo' in daylight in reasonable weather conditions.

Above: A ski boat moving at high speed.

Left: A Zapcat is a cheap way to enjoy the excitement of racing.

them very popular as funboats as well as for more serious racing in many parts of the world.

SKI BOATS

It is quite possible to ski behind almost any sports boat that is more than about 5m (16ft) long. However, although it may look like an 'ordinary' sports boat, a dedicated ski boat is a very specialized machine. Its hull will have been designed to give a soft, flat wake; it will probably have a 'shaft drive' system instead of an outboard or outdrives, and it will have a tow post somewhere near the middle of the boat.

HARD-TOPS

Putting a lid on a sports cruiser changes its character completely; it is like the difference between an open-top car and a conventional saloon car. However, there are good practical reasons for having a hard-topped boat: whilst it may not be as appealing when the sun is shining, the hard top comes into its own when the weather is less than perfect, and the enclosed wheelhouse becomes a welcoming 'indoor' space.

NEW OR SECOND-HAND?

Of course the idea of buying a brand new boat is appealing. You will get the boat of your choice, clean and shiny, with the upholstery and accessories that you have personally selected, all covered by a warranty that may last for anything up to five years. In many cases you will be welcomed on board your new acquisition with champagne, flowers, and various 'goodies' such as towels, cutlery, or branded jackets and baseball caps.

However, you pay a lot for the privilege: just like cars – though to nothing like the same extent – boats lose value as soon as the first owner steps on board. The rate of depreciation soon levels off, but a second-hand buyer can usually expect to pay slightly less for a ten year-old boat than the original owner bought it for when it was new. You won't get the warranty, or the goodies, but you will get a boat that has been tried and tested, and had most of the inevitable new-boat snags put right, and it will probably come complete with a lot of useful equipment acquired by previous owners – everything from rope to electronic navigation equipment.

Above: A hard-top sports cruiser.

Above: A typical river cruiser.

RIVER CRUISER

Some river cruisers look very much like their sea-going counterparts, though their average size is smaller. They are more likely to have single engines (instead of twins) and the engine is likely to be less powerful, as it is only required to operate at river speed limits. Lower speeds require less aqua- and aero-dynamism, meaning that the whole boat can often be rather more box-like in appearance. This is an advantage in that it makes the most of the accommodation in the boat whilst keeping the depth, height, and width as small as possible to fit into locks and under bridges.

MOTOR CRUISER

Motor cruisers vary enormously in size, style and function. They are generally bigger than sports boats, often with considerably better accommodation, as well as the engines and fuel reserves that are required to travel hundreds of miles at high speeds.

DISPLACEMENT MOTOR YACHT

Most powerboats achieve high speeds by skimming across the water like a waterski or a surfboard, rather than cutting through it. However, some owners and naval architects are quite prepared to sacrifice high performance in exchange for low-speed efficiency. They go for 'displacement' boats, that carry enough fuel for fourteen days and nights of continuous operation, during which time it could cover 2,500 miles (4,023 km).

Above: A displacement motor yacht.

Above: A motor cruiser in full flight.

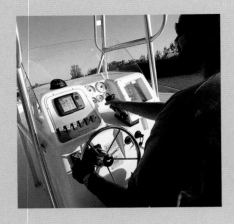

BASIC BOAT HANDLING

Most powerboats have a steering wheel, just like that on a car. That is where the similarities to a car end, however. A boat does not have brakes, nor does it have four or five forward gears: it has just one forward gear and one reverse – usually called 'ahead' and 'astern'.
However, the most important difference between a boat and a car is that a boat doesn't have wheels and tyres that give it a positive grip on a firm surface. A boat can slide through the water in almost any direction, while the water itself may be moving. Adapting to the differences between a boat and a car is what makes boat handling a rewarding challenge, but it is a challenge that millions of people have enjoyed overcoming.

The five forces

The best boat handlers are constantly aware of five forces that can affect the way a boat moves at any time. Two of them are external factors over which the helmsman (driver) has no control, while the other three are all governed by the steering and engine controls.

The external factors are:
• the wind
• the tidal stream or current (the movement of the water)

The controllable factors are:
• thrust – ahead or astern
• steering
• the paddlewheel effect

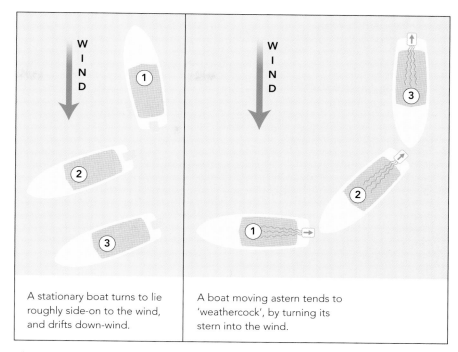

A stationary boat turns to lie roughly side-on to the wind, and drifts down-wind.

A boat moving astern tends to 'weathercock', by turning its stern into the wind.

Above: The effects of wind on a powerboat.

There is just one other important factor to bear in mind, which is that a boat has a characteristic known as inertia. If you try to make a stationary boat move, it resists you: and if you try to make a moving boat stop, it resists you. If you try to turn a boat around, or if you try to stop a boat from turning once it has started, it resists you. This isn't necessarily a problem, and it can be very useful. It certainly shouldn't come as a surprise – after all, a car doesn't stop instantly when you touch the brakes – but it is something that novice sailors often underestimate.

WIND
Except in a flat calm, the wind always has some effect on a powerboat.

A drifting boat will be blown along by it. The boat may take a little while to pick up speed, and it won't always move in exactly the same direction as the wind – it may move forwards or backwards, as well as directly down-wind – but it will always move. And it will usually turn so as to present one side to the wind. This may also take anything from several seconds to a few minutes to happen, but it is generally quicker if the boat is pointing into the wind to begin with.

When you are moving forwards, the effect is often barely noticeable, especially if the wind is behind you. A side wind tends to make the boat turn away from the wind, and to drift sideways, but the turning effect is easily counteracted by steering into it.

The wind is always much more noticeable when you are going astern (backwards). The bow of the boat (the front) is blown downwind much more quickly than the stern (the back), so the overall effect is that the boat swings her stern into the wind.

TIDAL STREAM OR CURRENT
In some parts of the world, such as most of the Mediterranean and the Baltic, and on most lakes, the water is generally still. The surface may not necessarily be smooth, but at least the water itself stays in one place. However, there are plenty of other places, particularly around the UK and the Atlantic coasts of Europe, where the rising and falling tide makes huge quantities of water move from place to place, while the

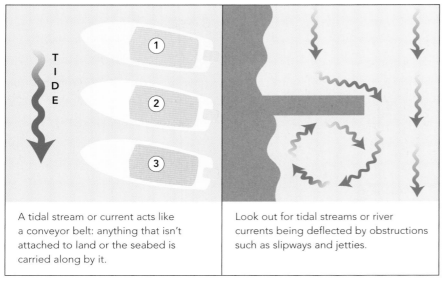

A tidal stream or current acts like a conveyor belt: anything that isn't attached to land or the seabed is carried along by it.

Look out for tidal streams or river currents being deflected by obstructions such as slipways and jetties.

Above: The effect of a tidal stream or current.

water in any river is constantly moving downhill towards the sea.

Whatever its cause, moving water is always a force to be reckoned with, and its effect is often more significant than that of the wind. Fortunately, it is generally easy to predict and allow for, because it doesn't make the boat turn around.

In effect, the water acts like a giant conveyor belt, on which everything that is not attached to the land or to the seabed is swept along, all moving in the same direction and at much the same speed. The only problems occur around obstructions, which can create swirling eddies, or set up cross-currents at an angle to the main flow.

THRUST

Most boats use a propeller to convert the power produced by their engines into useful thrust.

You can visualize this either as the propeller screwing itself through the water like a woodscrew being driven into wood, or as the propeller pushing water away from itself, like a fan creating a cooling breeze in a hot office.

Most sports boats and sports cruisers have either outboard motors or outdrives, in which the propeller is mounted on the bottom of a drive leg. The leg includes a

gearbox, so the thrust can be directed forwards or backwards.

There are two types of control in common use, known as 'single-lever' and 'twin-lever'.

As the name suggests, a single-lever control uses a single lever to control both the gear selection and the engine speed. Starting from the neutral position, if you push it forwards, it first selects ahead gear. Pushing it further forwards increases the engine speed. If you pull it back from the neutral position, it engages astern gear. Pulling it further back increases the engine speed.

Single-lever control is highly intuitive: move the lever the way you want to go, and push it further to go faster. Some single-lever controls have a safety latch that prevents the lever from moving out of neutral unless the latch is released – usually by squeezing a lever built into the under-side of the handle or by pressing a button on the end of it.

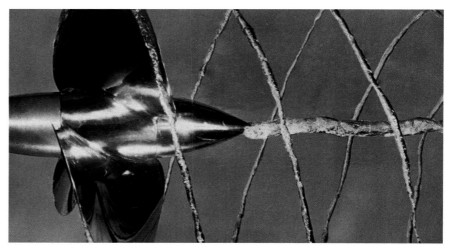

Above: The rotation of a propeller sets up a circular swirling motion in the water.

Above: *Twin-lever controls for a twin-engined boat.*

Left: *A single-lever control.*

Twin-lever controls are becoming increasingly rare, although some people still prefer them for bigger boats or particularly powerful engines. A twin-lever arrangement has one lever to select the gear, and a second lever to control the engine speed. The gear lever selects ahead gear when you move it forwards, and astern when you pull it backwards, but the speed control only works one way: pushing it forwards increases the engine speed.

In a boat with twin engines, each engine has its own set of controls, so a twin-engined boat with twin-lever controls actually has four levers.

Using twin-lever controls is more complicated and calls for more dexterity. Experienced boat-handlers may find that twin levers operate more smoothly and allow more precise control, but they are not recommended for novices.

Always reduce the engine speed to tick-over before changing gear . Then move the control lever boldly to select the new gear without allowing the gear box to 'chatter'.

STEERING

On an outboard or outdrive powered boat, the whole drive leg can be swivelled, directing the thrust anything up to about thirty degrees either side of straight ahead or astern. It is this directional thrust that steers the boat, usually controlled by a steering wheel.

When you are moving forwards, in open water, the steering wheel seems to have much the same effect as in a car: if you turn it to the left, the boat turns left: and if you turn it to the right, the boat turns right. However, in close-quarters manoeuvring, there are two important differences:

The steering works by directing the thrust, so it only works when there is thrust available to direct. It has very little effect when the gearbox is in neutral.

Above: *A single-lever control is easier to use than a twin-lever set of controls.*

The steering works on the back of the boat, not the front. So if you are in ahead gear, and turn the wheel to the left, it looks and feels as though the boat turns left, but what actually happens is that the stern (back) swings out to the right.

PADDLEWHEEL EFFECT

As well as creating thrust, the rotating propeller sets up a circular, swirling motion in the water, the effect of which is to push the stern (back) of the boat sideways. It is called 'paddlewheel effect', because its effect is rather as though the propeller were acting as a paddlewheel: almost all outboards and most outdrive propellers turn clockwise in ahead gear, so they push the stern of the boat to the right. In astern gear, of

Above: Even in gentle conditions, a boat is affected by five forces: nature controls the wind and water, while the helmsman controls the other three.

course, they turn the opposite way, so they push the stern to the left.

Paddlewheel effect, when going forwards, is barely perceptible. It becomes much more of a force to be reckoned with when going astern, particularly with very high performance propellers that are optimized for driving the boat forwards.

Basic manoeuvres with a single outboard or outdrive

Outboards and outdrives both steer the boat by swivelling the drive leg, to alter the direction of the propeller thrust. Of course there are big differences between them, but so far as boat handling is concerned, they can be treated as being almost indistinguishable from each other.

FORWARD AND REVERSE SLALOM

A slow forward and reverse slalom – zig-zagging between a line of posts or buoys – has almost no practical value whatsoever, but it is

Above: To the helmsman of this boat, it feels as though the bow (front) is swinging left. What is really happening is that the stern (back) is being pushed to the right.

a great way to get the feel of a boat and to experiment with the effect of the wind, tide and controls.

It is best to start by trying the boat forwards, keeping the speed down to about 3–4 knots – equivalent to a brisk walking pace.

You will see that the tidal stream or current (if there is one) will make quite a noticeable difference to the speed at which you pass each buoy or post: you will travel much faster when the current is flowing in the same direction as you are moving. As you pass through the gaps between the posts or buoys, you will see that they appear to be moving through the water. You obviously don't want to be mown down by one of these moving posts, so it makes perfect sense to aim for the up-tide end of each gap, allowing yourself to be swept harmlessly down-tide as you are swept through it.

If there is any wind, its main effect will be on the way the boat responds to the steering: she may seem slightly reluctant to turn into the wind and correspondingly eager to turn away from it.

Most people find repeating the exercise backwards rather more tricky. To start with, you probably need to use more power, because boats and propellers are both designed to be most efficient when they are moving forwards. Even if there is no wind, the boat is generally less responsive to the steering, and if there is any wind, its effect is more pronounced.

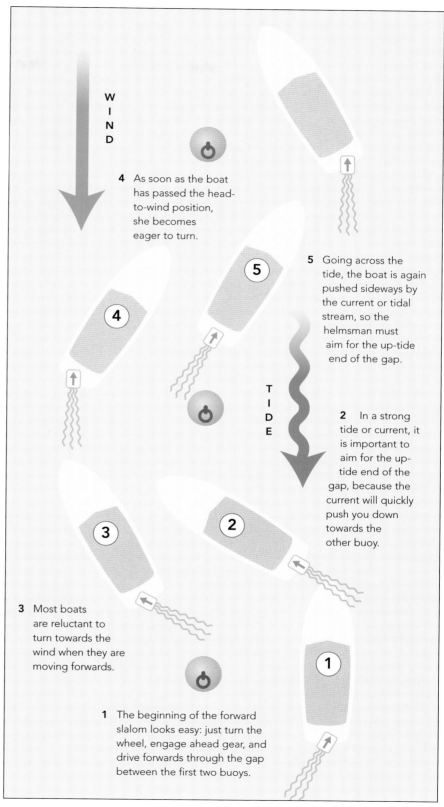

WIND

4 As soon as the boat has passed the head-to-wind position, she becomes eager to turn.

5 Going across the tide, the boat is again pushed sideways by the current or tidal stream, so the helmsman must aim for the up-tide end of the gap.

TIDE

2 In a strong tide or current, it is important to aim for the up-tide end of the gap, because the current will quickly push you down towards the other buoy.

3 Most boats are reluctant to turn towards the wind when they are moving forwards.

1 The beginning of the forward slalom looks easy: just turn the wheel, engage ahead gear, and drive forwards through the gap between the first two buoys.

Above: The forward slalom.

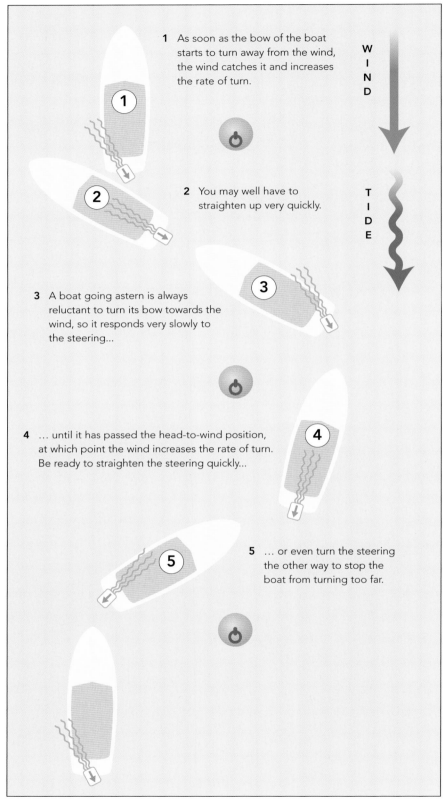

1 As soon as the bow of the boat starts to turn away from the wind, the wind catches it and increases the rate of turn.

2 You may well have to straighten up very quickly.

3 A boat going astern is always reluctant to turn its bow towards the wind, so it responds very slowly to the steering...

4 ... until it has passed the head-to-wind position, at which point the wind increases the rate of turn. Be ready to straighten the steering quickly...

5 ... or even turn the steering the other way to stop the boat from turning too far.

WIND

TIDE

Above: The backward slalom.

MOORING BUOYS

A mooring buoy is probably the easiest way to 'park' a boat: you just tie the boat to the buoy, and when you want to leave, you just untie it. From the harbour master's point of view, mooring buoys waste a lot of space because they can't be packed as close together as the pontoons in a marina, but they are cheap. From the point of view of the user, there is the slight problem of getting between the moored boat and the shore. Some harbours have a water taxi service, but most motor cruisers and many sports cruisers carry a small inflatable dinghy for the purpose.

LEAVING A MOORING

Leaving a mooring, with any boat, is probably the easiest manoeuvre there is in powerboating.

Just let go of the mooring, and allow the wind, tide or current to push you away from it. When you are about half a boat's length clear, motor gently away.

If there is no wind, tide or current – or if there is so little that allowing the boat to drift away from the buoy seems to be taking a long time – it is safe to use a gentle nudge of astern power to move the boat clear of the buoy and its associated ropes and chains.

PICKING UP A MOORING

Picking up a mooring in the first place is only slightly more complicated.

As in almost every boat handling manoeuvre, it pays to begin by assessing exactly what you are trying to achieve. In this case, you are aiming to end up with the bow of the boat tethered to the buoy. The direction she ends up pointing in is decided by the wind and tide or current. If there is a strong tide, but no wind, she will end up pointing straight into the tide; if there is a strong wind and no current, she will end up pointing into the wind. In most situations, though, she will end up pointing somewhere between the two.

The ideal approach is made in a straight line, pointing in the same direction but aiming for a spot a metre/foot or two to windward of

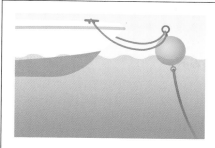

To moor a small boat for a short time, the simplest method is to lead a rope from the bow of the boat, through the ring on top of the buoy, and back to the boat.

Do not use this method for a big boat or if the boat is to be left unattended.

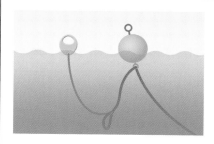

Mooring arrangements vary: the only standard part is the rope or chain riser, which connects the mooring to the seabed.

A common arrangement has a length of strong rope or a chain with a loop in it that can be attached to the boat, hanging down below the buoy. To make it easy to get hold of the loop, a smaller pick-up buoy is tied to the loop with a length of thinner rope.

Never secure to the pick-up buoy!

Above: Mooring buoys.

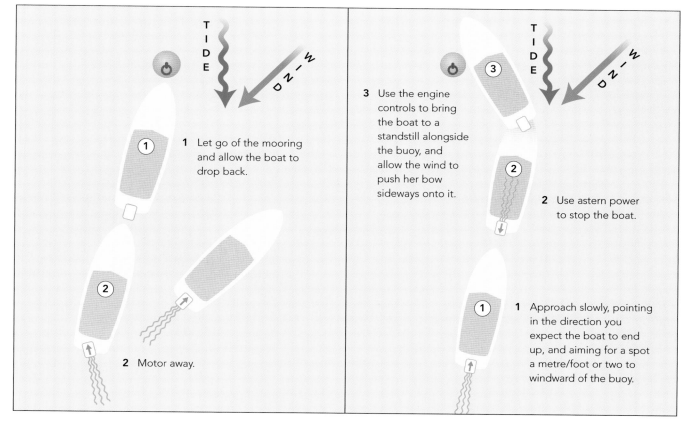

1 Let go of the mooring and allow the boat to drop back.

2 Motor away.

Above: Leaving a mooring.

3 Use the engine controls to bring the boat to a standstill alongside the buoy, and allow the wind to push her bow sideways onto it.

2 Use astern power to stop the boat.

1 Approach slowly, pointing in the direction you expect the boat to end up, and aiming for a spot a metre/foot or two to windward of the buoy.

Above: Picking up a mooring.

HOW BOATS ARE TIED UP

Very small boats, such as dinghies and the smallest sports boats, are often tied to pontoons and harbour walls with just a single rope.

Bigger boats need rather more sophisticated arrangements, not to stop them drifting away, but to stop them moving around.

The classic way to secure a boat to a quayside or pontoon uses four ropes. In general, a rope that attaches a boat to something else is called a 'warp', but each of these four warps has a specific purpose and name:

1 The head rope stops the bow of the boat from moving away from the pontoon.

2 The stern rope stops the stern of the boat from moving away from the pontoon.

3 The back spring stops the boat from moving backwards.

4 The fore spring stops the boat from moving forwards.

Ideally, each rope would be fastened to its own cleat, ring, or bollard on the pontoon, and to its own cleat on the boat, but in real life there are never enough cleats, rings, or bollards to go around, so ropes often have to share. It doesn't matter too much if the warps aren't laid out in exactly the same pattern as in the illustration, so long as there is one warp doing each of the four jobs.

Inflatable fenders – usually sausage-shaped – are used to stop the boat from bumping into the wall or pontoon.

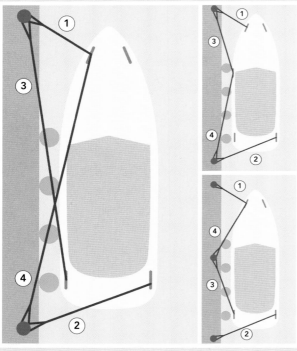

1 Head rope
2 Stern rope
3 Back spring
4 Fore spring

Above: Warps.

Above: Fenders.

the buoy. By the time you are about four boat lengths from the buoy, you should be moving very slowly – only just fast enough to keep control of the boat. A boat length or two from the buoy, you should be in neutral, then going into astern gear in order to bring the boat to a standstill alongside the buoy.

The idea is that as the boat slows down and stops, the wind gradually begins to take control, pushing the bow of the boat sideways, towards the buoy.

With the boat stationary, and the wind pushing it against the buoy, it should be reasonably easy to get a boathook and then a rope onto the buoy. It is made easier still if the helmsman (driver) has managed to get the right part of the boat alongside the buoy:

- In most sports boats, aim to pick up the buoy just forward of the mid-point.
- In most sports cruisers, aim to pick up the buoy a few feet back from the bow.

If there is no wind or tide – or not enough to make any real difference – you can still achieve much the same effect. Start the approach, again aiming for a point a few feet to one side of the buoy. Just before engaging astern gear to stop the boat, turn the wheel away from the buoy. As well as slowing the boat down, the astern thrust from the engine also makes her start spinning, turning her round to rest her bow against the buoy, just as the wind did.

TURNING ROUND IN A CONFINED SPACE – THE 'THREE POINT TURN'

Most outboard or outdrive powered boats are surprisingly manoeuvrable, but there are occasions – especially when visiting unfamiliar marinas – where you might find yourself in a dead-end

<table>
<tr><td colspan="2">SAFETY TIP</td></tr>
<tr><td>Never try to stop a boat from bumping into something by pushing with your hands or feet, and never use any part of your body to cushion the impact. This is a mistake that is commonly made by novices. However,</td><td>even a small sports boat, with two people on board, can easily weigh more than a ton. You will not stop it just by putting a hand or foot in the way, but you will get hurt, and could end up with serious crush injuries.</td></tr>
</table>

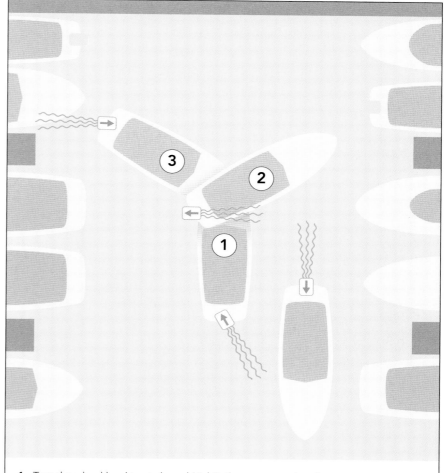

1 Turn the wheel hard to starboard (right), then engage ahead gear.
2 Before the boat has time to start moving forwards, disengage gear, turn the wheel hard in the opposite direction, and engage astern gear.
3 Before the boat has time to start moving backwards, disengage gear, turn the wheel hard in the opposite direction, and engage ahead gear.

Above: The three point turn.

channel, without enough room to do a U-turn. If the same thing happened in a car, you would execute a three point turn.

Exactly the same applies in a boat.

LEAVING AN ALONGSIDE BERTH

Leaving and returning to a pontoon or a quayside are probably the most common of all boat handling manoeuvres: if nothing else, they are the ones you will probably use whenever you refuel.

For a very small boat, it may be possible to get away with simply undoing the rope that holds it to the shore, and pushing off, but anything much bigger than a dinghy requires rather more finesse.

Planning and preparation are the keys to a successful getaway, because the manoeuvre is largely governed by the combined effects of the wind and any tidal stream or current. If they are tending to push the boat backwards – in other words if the back spring is tighter than the fore spring – then it is generally best to leave the berth in a forwards direction.

If the wind and tide or current are tending to push the boat forwards, so that the fore spring is tighter than the back spring, then it is best to go out backwards. And if in doubt, reverse out!

Preparation involves removing any warps that are slack – because in this state they are not doing anything useful. The other warps can then be re-rigged as 'slip ropes'. This involves attaching one end of the rope to a cleat on board, and taking the other end around a cleat or bollard on the pontoon, before leading it back to the cleat on board. This makes it easy to let go from on board simply by letting go of one end, and pulling the other.

Assuming that you are going to be leaving forwards, this probably means that the head rope and back spring will be rigged as slip ropes, and the stern rope and fore spring are removed. Release the headrope, and the action of wind and current should swing the bow of the boat out. If they don't, you can always give nature a helping hand, either by pushing the front of the boat out or by giving a gentle nudge of astern power.

When the bow of the boat is well clear of the pontoon, check that the outboard or outdrive is in the straight-ahead position, let go the stern rope, and motor gently away.

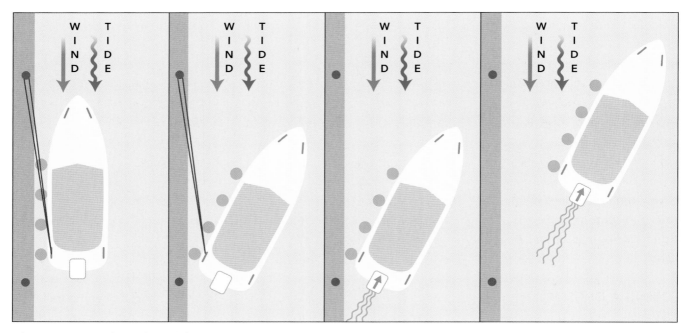

Above: *Leaving an alongside berth forwards.*

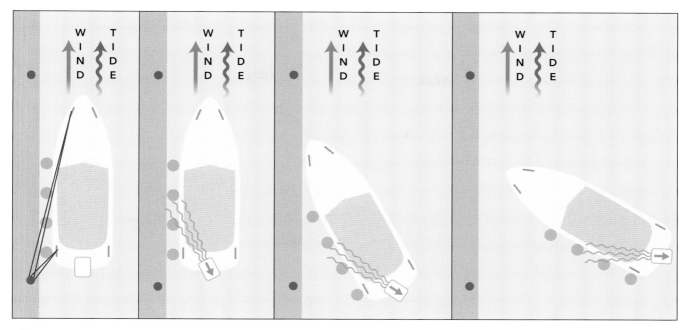

Above: *Leaving an alongside berth astern.*

It is particularly important not to try to steer yourself out of a berth when you are going forwards. If you give in to temptation, by turning the wheel away from the pontoon, then as soon as you engage forward gear, the thrust of the engine will cause the stern of the boat to push sideways, into the pontoon.

If, instead, you go for a stern-first departure, then you will probably remove the head rope and back spring first, leaving the stern rope and fore spring in place until the last moment. When you are ready to leave, turn the wheel hard away from the pontoon, let go both of the remaining ropes, and engage astern gear.

COMING ALONGSIDE

Planning and preparation are even more important when you are trying to get into an alongside berth as when you are trying to leave it: after all, it's no good reaching the pontoon only to find that the warps are still in the locker!

The classic approach to an alongside berth is made heading into the tidal stream or current. This will dictate which side of the boat is going to be alongside the pontoon or wall, so that the crew can start getting the warps and fenders ready in good time.

Assuming a gentle current and not too much wind, the ideal approach to make is at an angle of about twenty or thirty degrees to the pontoon, aiming for the spot at which you would like the bow of the boat to end up. In an ideal world, you would be lined up for the approach at least four boat lengths from the berth, with the engine still in ahead gear, but only just ticking over. Knock the gearshift into neutral a couple of lengths from the berth.

About one boat length from the berth, it is quite likely that you will lose sight of the pontoon, under the bow of the boat.

At this stage, turn the wheel quickly towards the pontoon, and engage astern gear. Turning the wheel towards the pontoon – rather than away from it, as you might expect – means that when you use astern power it not only stops the boat's forward movement, but also pushes the stern in towards the pontoon.

Ideally, and if you have judged everything correctly, the boat ends up perfectly stationary, parallel to the pontoon, and close enough to it for the crew to be able to step off

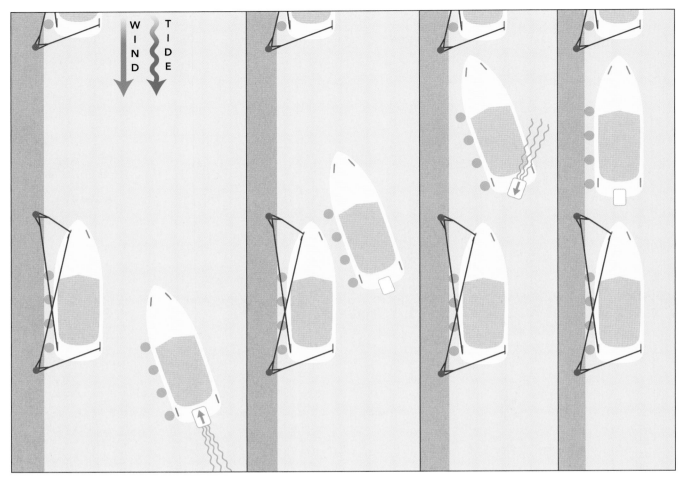

Above: *Coming alongside.*

onto the pontoon to secure the warps.

One of the most common mistakes made by beginners is to forget to take the engine out of gear once they've arrived, so the boat starts moving backwards.

It does take a little practice, and the standard formula needs to be adapted slightly to take account of different conditions.

If the wind is blowing onto the pontoon, it is much easier: just drive up alongside the intended berth, parallel to it, and stop, to let the wind push the boat sideways. If the tide is very strong, the approach is much the same, but you will need to aim for a point slightly further along the pontoon than normal, and may well need to use more ahead power to overcome the tide. You will not be able to use as much astern power, either, so the boat may end up at an angle to the pontoon, but moving backwards. In this situation, the cure is to turn the wheel away from the pontoon and to give a little nudge of ahead power.

In very strong winds, it is often worth considering a stern-first approach. Travelling stern first gives the helmsman great control over where the back of the boat goes, because if you turn the wheel left, the back of the boat goes left, and if you turn it right, the back of the boat goes right, but it is extremely unlikely that you will be able to get the boat nicely lined up, parallel with the pontoon. This doesn't matter too much: once you can get the stern secured, the bow can be pulled in by hand. It doesn't look very slick, but it works!

BASIC SAFETY

Despite the fairly obvious hazards associated with boating, its safety record is generally very good. However, there are risks, so it makes sense to take a few simple precautions to minimize the chances of something going wrong in the first place, and to stop it becoming serious if it happens anyway.

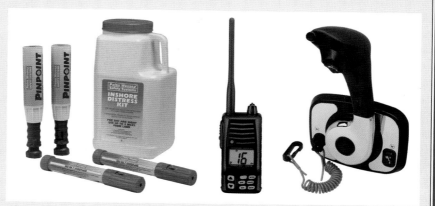

Above: Kill-cords (the coiled red wire above right) save lives, while distress flares and a marine VHF radio allow you to call for help if things go badly wrong.

Plan your journey

Know where you are going, how far you expect to travel, and be aware of any hazards on the way. For all but the very shortest journeys, have a contingency plan.

Be aware of the weather forecast

The most important factors affecting boating safety are wind strength, sea state and visibility.

Make sure you have enough fuel

Estimate how much fuel you are likely to use, and aim to keep at least 20 per cent of your tank's total capacity in reserve.

Tell a responsible person where you are going and when you will be back

Make sure that they have a description of the boat and the number of people on board, and instructions on how to raise the alarm if you have not made contact by a certain time.

Carry suitable communications equipment

Mobile phones are all well and good, in their place, but they are no substitute for a proper marine VHF radio and distress flares.

Use a kill-cord

One of the greatest dangers is of falling overboard and either being run over by your own boat, or left behind. A 'kill-cord' attached to the helmsman's leg or lifejacket, is intended to switch the engine off if the helmsman falls overboard.

Carry or wear lifejackets

A lifejacket is your last line of defence. Whether you carry one or wear one is a matter of individual choice, but modern, automatically inflating gas lifejackets are compact enough to wear all the time. Smaller versions are available for children.

Above: Wear or carry lifejackets, and ensure you have enough fuel for your journey.

ADVANCED BOAT HANDLING

Once you have mastered the basics, you should be well-equipped to start enjoying your boat and life on the open waves. However, some advanced boat handling skills will stand you in excellent stead as your interest in, and passion for, powerboating increases (as it undoubtedly will).

Engine size

There are practical limits to the size of an outboard or stern drive. At the time of writing, the biggest outboard in production produces 300hp, while the most powerful outdrive goes up to 475hp. So if a boat builder wants to install any more power than that, he either needs to go for a 'shaft drive' system, or for more than one engine.

However, multiple engines are not confined to very big or very powerful boats: even in boats as little as 6m (20ft) in length, there are advantages to having two small engines instead of one bigger one. Twin engines provide a built-in back-up if one engine fails; they may make the boat more manoeuvrable, or more efficient at low speeds; or they may allow the designer to make better use of the space available.

Above: Weigh up the pros and cons of twin engines carefully before buying your boat – added manoeuvrability generally comes at the cost of efficiency at high speeds.

It almost goes without saying that twins have their drawbacks, too. They are generally heavier, less efficient at high speeds, and more expensive to buy and to look after than a single engine of the same total power.

Nevertheless, twin engine installations are very popular, particularly in boats over about 8–9m (26–30ft) in length, and are almost standard in boats over 10m (33 ft).

A boat with twin engines has two sets of engine controls and instruments, so that the two engines can be operated independently of each other. They share one steering system, however, so the boat has only one steering wheel.

Handling twins: outboards or outdrives

Handling a boat with twin outboards or outdrives is very similar to handling one with a single engine. The only real difference is that neither of the two engines is on the centreline, so when just one of the pair is in gear, the thrust is lop-sided.

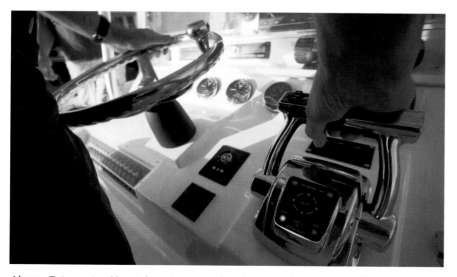

Above: Twin-engined boats have two sets of engine controls operated independently of each other, but only one steering wheel.

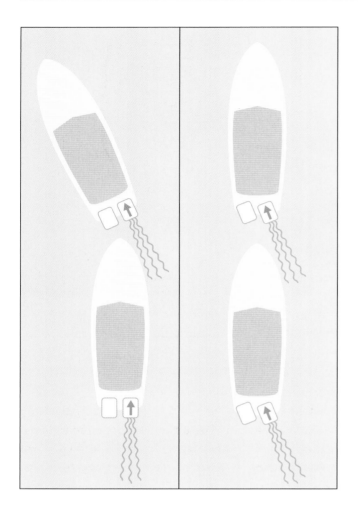

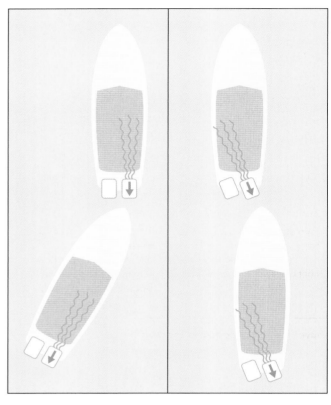

Above: *The boat will quickly pivot going astern with one engine.*

Left: *With starboard engine ahead, the boat will turn to port. Turning the wheel slightly to starboard will counteract this.*

This means that if you put the starboard (right hand) engine into ahead gear, the boat will turn to port (left). In order to go straight, the wheel will have to be turned slightly to starboard. In practice, the effect is often surprisingly small, and most people counteract it almost without thinking.

The effect of lop-sided thrust is much more noticeable when you are using astern power. Going astern with one engine will quickly make the boat pivot. Again, you can stop the turn by turning the steering wheel, but this time it will require a much bigger movement, so the thrust will be at a more pronounced angle. The overall effect is that the boat may move diagonally, rather than straight backwards (see above).

This may seem awkward, especially when you are trying to go in a straight line, but are forced to use one engine in order to stick to an unrealistically low speed limit. However, there is a big payback when it comes to manoeuvring.

Suppose, for instance, that you want to spin the boat to port (left) on the spot. It begins in just the same way as if you were doing it in a boat with one engine – by turning the wheel hard in the direction you want the bow of the boat to move. The difference is that in a boat with twin engines, you use only one of its two engines – the one that will be on the outside of the turn. Having the thrust offset, as well as angled, means that the boat will turn very quickly indeed.

Every manoeuvre in a boat with twin outdrives or outboards is exactly the same as it would be with a single engine, so long as you remember two golden rules.

Twin engines, both offset from the centreline, can be used to turn around in a confined space by putting one ahead and one astern.

Turning the wheel at the same time will reduce the effect: here, the starboard engine is driving the turn, but the angled thrust of the port engine is opposing it.

The quickest way to turn a boat with twin outdrives or outboards is to turn the wheel one way and use the opposite engine.

If the boat moves forward too far, reverse the wheel and go astern with the opposite engine to continue the turn.

Above: The 'rule of opposites' in action.

The first one is just as valid for single engines: 'steer then gear'. In other words, make any big movements of the steering wheel while the gear selector is in neutral.

The second is specific to twin engines. It's sometimes called the 'rule of opposites', because it says that if you turn the wheel to starboard (right) you use the port (left hand) engine, and vice versa.

There's one exception to the rule of opposites, which is when you are leaving a berth alongside a wall or pontoon. The object of the exercise

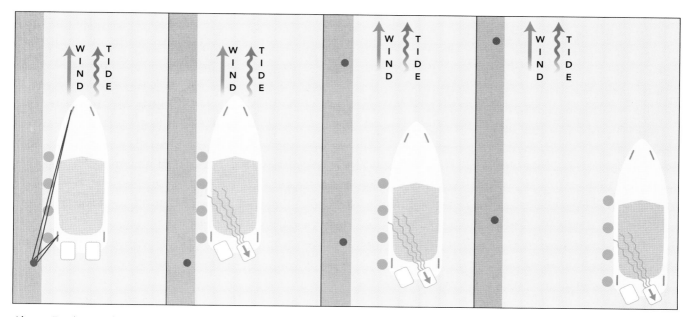

Above: Disobeying the rule of opposites in order to leave a berth alongside a wall or pontoon with minimum turning effect.

35

here is not to turn the boat around. In a perfect world, it wouldn't turn at all, but would move sideways, out of its berth. Directly disobeying the 'rule of opposites' achieves almost exactly that: turning the wheel to starboard and going astern will pull the boat away from the pontoon on the port side, but by choosing the starboard engine, the turning effect is reduced to a minimum

Coming alongside, in a boat with twin outboards or outdrives, is really not much different from the same manoeuvre in a boat with just one outdrive or outboard.

Assuming a gentle current and not much wind, approach at an angle of about thirty degrees to the pontoon, aiming for the spot where you want the bow of the boat to end up.

A couple of lengths from the berth, put both drives in neutral.

About one boat length from the berth, turn the wheel quickly towards the pontoon, and engage astern gear on the engine furthest from the pontoon. The astern power stops the boat and swings the stern towards the pontoon.

Remember to put both drives' engines in neutral when the boat has stopped: do not allow it to start moving backwards!

Shaft drives

Outdrives are a relatively recent development. For many years, the standard arrangement was for the gearbox to drive the propeller via a straight, rigid shaft, which protruded, at an angle, from the bottom of the boat. It's an arrangement that is still popular now, particularly in working boats, where simplicity, reliability, and low maintenance costs are important, and in large motor boats that need more power than can be transmitted by outdrives. Taking this to extremes, ships' engines, developing tens of thousands of horsepower apiece, are almost

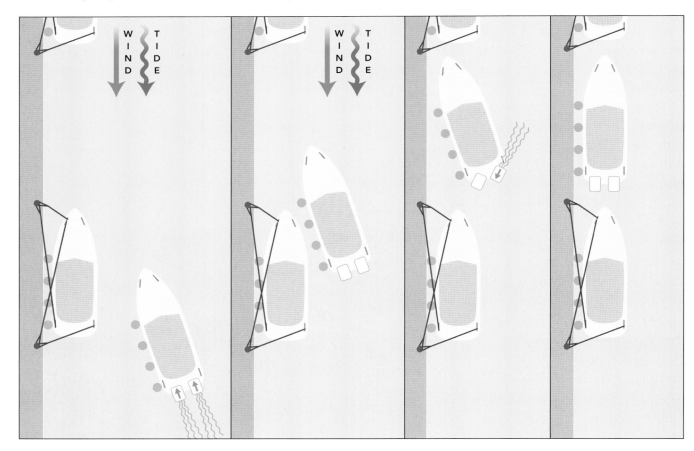

Above: Coming alongside.

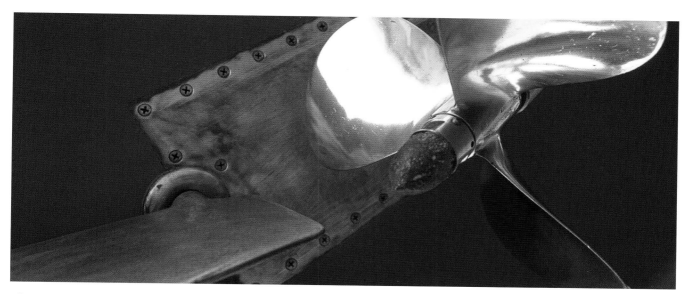

Above: *A rudder mounted just behind the propeller enables you to steer.*

invariably turning propellers on rigid shafts – often just one engine driving one propeller per ship.

But big ships seldom have to be parked without the assistance of tugs, and they can expect, as a bare minimum, to have the help of someone on the quayside to take their ropes. Handling a boat with a single shaft-driven propeller is a much more tricky proposition than one with a single outboard or outdrive, so a single shaft arrangement is something of an oddity amongst private pleasure craft.

The principle of manoeuvring with a shaft drive is very simple. You can't change the angle of the shaft, so the propeller, in principle, can only drive the boat forwards or backwards. You steer it by means of a rudder mounted just behind the propeller. When the propeller is driving the boat forwards, it sends a stream of water past the rudder,

so when the rudder is turned one way or the other, it deflects the thrust sideways. The effect, in some ways, is rather like an outdrive.

The picture changes, however, when you take the engine out of gear. Assuming that the boat is still moving forwards, there will still be water flowing over the rudder, so it will still work. How effectively it works depends on the boat: sailing boats often have huge rudders, which will work at speeds as low as

half a knot (1kph/0.6mph) while very high performance boats have tiny rudders that achieve hardly anything.

If you then engage astern gear, the situation changes again. The propeller is pulling water in from all around the rudder, effectively stopping the orderly flow that the rudder must have if it is to work. At the same time, the paddle wheel effect (see page 22) becomes much more significant.

If the boat does, eventually, start

Above: *High performance boats have tiny rudders, making them hard to manoeuvre.*

moving backwards, then the rudder may start working again, but few single shaft boats can be steered accurately or reliably astern.

MANOEUVRING WITH A SINGLE SHAFT

Paddlewheel effect isn't always a nuisance. In fact, in some situations it is a powerful asset, so long as you know what it is going to do.

Most single-engined boats have 'right handed' propellers that are designed to push the boat forwards when they are turning clockwise. In other words, if you had a glass-bottomed boat and could look down on the top of the propeller, you would see the top blade moving from port to starboard when going ahead.

When you go astern, the propeller turns the other way, with the top

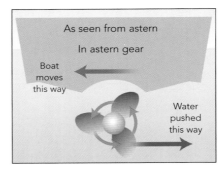

Above: *Single-engined boats usually have 'right handed' propellers.*

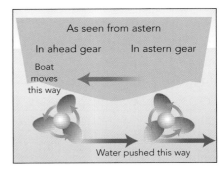

Above: *Propellers on twin-engined boats can make the boat turn on the spot.*

blade moving towards the port side, and the bottom blades moving to starboard. By doing so, it pushes the back of the boat to port.

So, if you want to come alongside a pontoon which is on your port side, the paddlewheel effect is helpful: all you need to do is to approach the pontoon, at an angle of about twenty degrees or so, taking the engine out of forward gear a couple of boat's lengths

before you reach your chosen spot.

You can afford to let the boat drift for a few seconds, knowing that the rudder still works if you need to fine-tune the final few feet of the approach. Then, when you put the engine astern in order to stop the forward movement, the paddlewheel effect takes command and kicks the stern in.

The problem with a single shaft is that you don't always get to choose which side the pontoon or wall will be – and if you have a right-handed propeller, getting alongside a pontoon on your starboard side can be very difficult, because as soon as you apply astern power, the paddlewheel effect will kick the stern away from the pontoon. If you really must do it, the best idea is usually to make the approach very, very slowly, so that you have to use as little astern power as possible.

MANOEUVRING WITH TWIN SHAFTS

A twin shaft installation is very different, because the propellers are designed to rotate in opposite directions, almost invariably with a

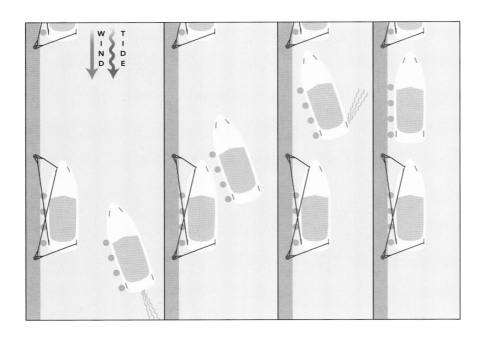

Above: *Coming alongside a pontoon on your port side.*

right-handed propeller on the starboard side and a left-handed propeller on the port side.

The beauty of this arrangement is that when both engines are in ahead gear, their paddlewheel effects cancel each other out, so the boat goes in a straight line.

When the starboard engine is in astern gear, its paddlewheel effect pushes the back of the boat to port, while having the port engine in astern gear pushes it to starboard.

The most dramatic effect of this arrangement is when you have one engine in ahead gear, and the other in astern. To achieve this, both propellers must be turning in the same direction, so their paddlewheel effects are both pushing the stern the same way, making the boat turn on the spot. Having one engine driving astern while the other is driving ahead would make the boat spin, anyway, just as it would with twin outdrives, but with paddlewheel effect kicking in as well, a twin screw

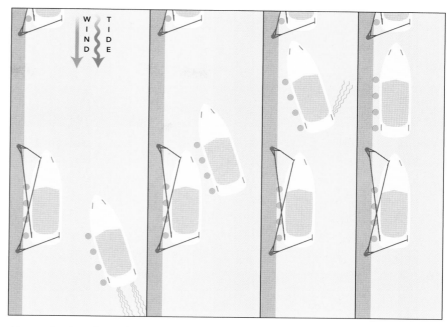

Above: *Coming alongside with twin shafts with the pontoon on your port side.*

boat really can turn in its own length.

Unlike an outdrive-powered boat, you can even speed up the rate of turn by turning the steering wheel. It will move both rudders, just as the wheel on an outdrive boat moves both outdrives, but the rudder on the engine that is running astern will

achieve nothing. The other one, however, will receive a good flow of water so it will work to help complete the turn as quickly as possible. And if you find that the boat isn't spinning on the spot, but is moving forwards or backwards, you can always hold it in one place by increasing the speed of one engine slightly.

COMING ALONGSIDE WITH TWIN SHAFTS

The beauty of twin shafts is that you have a choice about which way the paddlewheel effect works.

So, if you want to put the boat alongside a pontoon on your port side, you approach at the usual angle and knock the engines out of gear a couple of boat lengths from the pontoon in the usual way. Unlike an outdrive – but just like a

Above: *Coming alongside is easier when the pontoon is to port.*

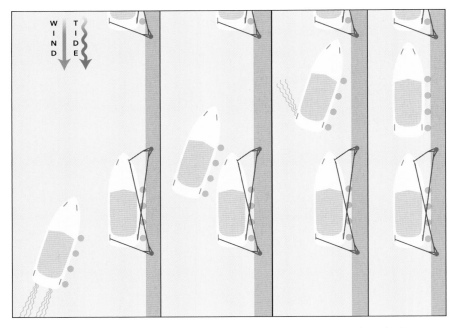

Above: *Coming alongside with twin shafts with the pontoon on your starboard side.*

single shaft – the rudders will still work, to fine tune the last few metres/feet of the approach, as the boat's momentum carries her towards the berth. Then, using your skill and judgement, a touch of astern power on the starboard engine – the one furthest from the pontoon – serves to stop the boat, while its paddlewheel effect kicks the stern in.

Coming alongside a pontoon on the starboard side, instead of being almost impossible as it might be with a single shaft, is now just a mirror image of the port side manoeuvre: approach the berth at an angle of about twenty degrees or so, knock the engines out of gear a boat length or two away from the berth and use the rudders to fine tune the last few metres/feet of the approach. Then, nudge astern with the engine furthest from the pontoon to stop the boat and swing her stern in.

Handling boats in open water

Handling boats in open water is generally easier than in the confines of a river or harbour, especially as you are likely to be trying to make progress from one place to another, rather than to achieve some particular manoeuvre, such as coming alongside a pontoon. However, there are a few tricks of the trade that are specific to open water.

WAVES

Waves are a fact of life in almost any water – and in a suitable boat, small

---

DON'T JUMP!

Never allow or encourage your crew to jump from the boat to a wall or pontoon.

1 It is counter-productive: as they push themselves away from the boat, they are applying an equal and opposite force to it, pushing it away from the pontoon.

2 It is an insult to your boat handling, because it implies that you can't

park the boat without their brute strength.

3 It achieves nothing that can't be achieved just as well when the boat reaches the pontoon, a second or two later.

4 It is dangerous: the jumper is taking off from a moving vessel, and landing on a surface which

may be slippery or unstable, with obstructions such as cleats or rings. In a worst case scenario, they could fall between the boat and the pontoon and be crushed or mangled by the propeller. Or, over many years of jumping about in boats, they could gradually crush the cartilage in their knees.

Above: *Breaking waves are caused by the wave reaching the shore, which blocks the circulation of water at the bottom of the wave and causes the top to spill over.*

waves are all part of the fun. However, in the open sea or on large lakes you may encounter waves that are big enough to be uncomfortable or even dangerous.

The best way of dealing with really big waves is to go and sit under a tree – in other words, don't be caught out amongst them in the first place. That isn't as difficult as it sounds, because the overwhelming majority of waves you are ever likely to encounter are generated by the wind. So if you listen to the weather forecast, and a strong wind is forecast, it is quite reasonable to expect big waves.

We can refine this rather obvious generalization quite a bit.

For instance, if the wind is blowing off the land, there is likely to be an area of relatively smooth water close to the shore, but it will get progressively rougher further out.

However, when established waves run into shallow water they tend to get higher and steeper. That is why you often see breaking waves or 'white horses' on a beach, where the sea further out looks relatively smooth. This means that if the wind is blowing towards the land, the very worst place to be is close to the shoreline.

Even in calm weather, waves can also be caused by moving water flowing over a shallow or uneven seabed, such as you often find off headlands and at the mouths of rivers.

Even lifeboats have been lost in harbour entrances when a strong onshore wind met an out-going current over a patch of shallow water, but such conditions are unusual. Waves are a hazard, but they are a hazard that most boats are designed and built to cope with.

Preparing for bad weather

If you can't avoid rough water altogether, there are a number of tactics that can be used to minimize its effects. They will be all the more effective if you can prepare for it in

Above: *In rough conditions, close any hatches and port lights to prevent the ingress of water.*

Above: Matching your speed with that of the waves means that you ride along with the wave, while staying just behind its crest.

advance, by shutting any hatches and port lights (windows) that might let water into the boat, securing any loose equipment that might be thrown about, and making sure that the boat at least starts off as dry as possible.

How you actually deal with the sea depends mainly on the direction in which you are attempting to travel compared with the movement of the waves.

Down-sea
Travelling in the same direction as the waves is easy, and can be very fast and remarkably comfortable, so long as you are sure that there is either shelter or a safe harbour entrance somewhere ahead.

If your boat has trim tabs, raise them as far as they will go, and if you have outboards or outdrives, tilt them up slightly, so as to lift the bow of the boat. Then, in moderate conditions, you can go as fast as you like.

If it gets sufficiently rough that you are starting to 'fly' off the crests of waves, then it's worth slowing down slightly as you overtake each crest, because if you don't take off from the crests, then you can be certain that you won't crash land in the troughs.

As an alternative, particularly as the waves get bigger still, try to match your speed with that of the waves, so that you effectively ride along with the wave, but just behind its crest.

Whatever you do, don't let the waves overtake you. If this seems likely, then change your plans, and go in a different direction.

Across the sea
Travelling across the direction of the waves can also be fast and surprisingly comfortable. The golden rule is not to allow yourself to get caught broadside-on to a large breaking wave. The best place to be is in the troughs between waves, or on the gently sloping windward side of a big wave. If you have to cross the line of the wave, wait until the crest alongside you breaks, then drive through the smooth but slightly frothy patch it will have left behind.

Above: If travelling across the waves, stay in the troughs.

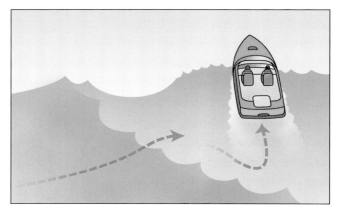

Above: If travelling up-sea, cross waves at an angle.

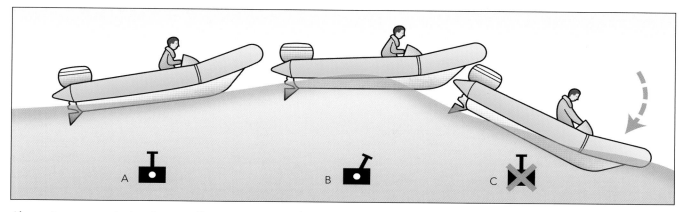

Above: A common mistake when travelling up-sea is to cut the power too late, causing the boat to belly-flop. Instead, put the power on as soon as the bows start to dip over the crest.

Up-sea

Trying to make progress into the waves can be hard work and uncomfortable, though a skilled helmsman can do a lot to give his passengers a smoother ride by steering round the biggest waves, or reducing their effective slope by crossing them at an angle, in much the same way as a skier reduces the slope of a mountain by zig-zagging.

One solution, good for short distances, is to trim the outboard or outdrive leg out, raise the trim tabs, and slow down until the boat has her nose in the air. On paper, it seems as though you are doing everything wrong, but so long as you keep the speed down, it works.

Otherwise, the more conventional advice is to trim the outdrive or outboard leg in and lower the trim tabs so as to make the boat as level as possible. Then, keeping one hand on the throttle all the time, use plenty of power as you climb up towards the crest of each wave. Take the power off just before you reach the crest, so that the boat's momentum carries her

TRIM TABS

Many sports boats and most sports cruisers are fitted with trim tabs – flat metal plates hinged onto the bottom edge of the transom, and moved up and down by an electric or hydraulic ram.

Trim tabs work rather like the ailerons and elevators on the wings and tail of an aeroplane, or the hydroplanes on a submarine: when both tabs are lowered, they press downwards on the water rushing past the hull, so they tend to lift the stern of the boat – giving the impression that they are lowering the bows. When just one tab is lowered, it tends to lift just one side of the boat, either making her lean over, or correcting a lean.

Above: Trim tabs.

up to the top and allows her to flop over the peak. Put the power back on again the moment the bows start to dip, going over the crest. This will lift the bows, to stop the boat from 'stuffing' – driving into the front of the next wave.

A common mistake is to cut the power slightly too late, just as the boat takes off from the crest. Cutting the power at this stage means that she will belly-flop into the trough.

MAN OVERBOARD

Someone falling overboard, particularly in open water, is probably one

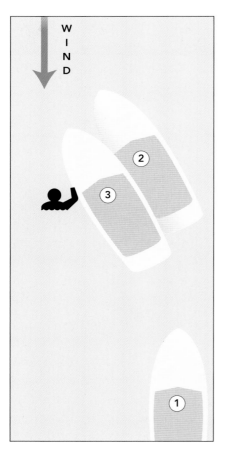

Above: *Be sure to practise your routine for rescuing a man overboard.*

of the scariest things that can happen on a motorboat. And although you may think that the victim can swim ashore, or tread water and wait to be picked up, it accounts for most of the fatal motor boating accidents that happen each year.

Of course, prevention is better than cure, so get into the habit of sitting down, except when you really have to move around. Also, hold on to the boat whenever you can, and be alert to the possibility of sudden movement. However, if someone does go overboard in spite of your precautions, their best chance of survival is if you have a practised routine ready to deal with the situation.

On a sports boat or sports cruiser you are likely to know, very quickly, that someone has fallen overboard. Don't waste that advantage by driving away from them, but slow down or stop as quickly as possible, and assess the situation.

The tide or current will affect the boat and the casualty equally, so your main concern must be the wind. Circle the casualty, keeping them in view but making sure you have room to manoeuvre, until you are down-wind of him or her (1). Then turn up-wind, aiming for a spot about a boat's width to one side of the casualty, and moving slowly (2). Just before you reach the casualty, turn the bow of the boat towards him or her, and give a nudge of astern power to stop the boat (3). If you are using an outdrive or outboard, remember to turn the

THE SKI-BOAT RECOVERY

Ski-boat drivers deal with people in the water all the time, so they make it look easy! The ski-boat recovery only works for conscious and uninjured casualties, but for them, it is quick and easy.

A ski-boat uses the ski-rope. Non-skiers will have to prepare a substitute, such as tying a fender so that it is at right-angles to a long piece of rope. Then, drive in circles around the casualty, trailing the rope behind. Eventually, and inevitably, the end of the rope will reach the person in the water, who will be able to hold onto it while you pull them back to the boat.

wheel away from the casualty as you nudge astern: on a shaft drive boat, turn the wheel towards the casualty before the boat comes to a halt.

The idea is to stop the boat with the casualty somewhere just forward of the middle and on the down-wind side.

Take the engine out of gear and – unless it would be dangerous to do so – stop it. The last thing you want to do is risk getting your casualty chewed up by the propeller!

A conscious casualty can probably climb aboard, perhaps with a bit of help, either by using a boarding ladder or by standing on the outboard or outdrive leg. An unconscious casualty may have to be lifted or rolled onto the bathing platform or over the side. And if you can't do any of those things, then tie him or her to the boat, and use the radio to call for help.

Stopping a boat

CRASH STOP

Boats don't have brakes, so the obvious ways to stop are either to take the engine out of gear and let the boat drift to a standstill – which can take a long time and a lot of distance – or you can use astern power to stop more quickly.

The trouble with using astern power is that the waves which have been created by your own boat's movement don't stop as soon as the boat does. They carry on moving, and smack into the back of the boat; on a small boat, they can quite easily lap over the transom.

A very effective 'crash stop' is to quickly spin the boat through ninety degrees, and then apply astern power. The boat may try to carry on moving in the same direction as before, but boats aren't very good at moving sideways, so it will stop remarkably quickly. The gentle nudge of astern power that is all that's required is much kinder to the engine and transmission, while the sudden change of direction means that the stern wave passes harmlessly by.

There's just one drawback to the crash stop – it's too good. As a way

Above: You need a secure anchorage if you want to be able to fish in peace.

of making people fall out of sports boats, there's nothing to touch it!

ANCHORING

Most boat builders' adverts fall into one of two categories: they either show their boat powering along across a wide expanse of smooth blue water, or they show it anchored in some idyllic spot.

Powering across smooth blue water is very easy! Anchoring in the idyllic spot calls for a bit more expertise.

The first step may sound obvious, but you need to make sure that you have the right equipment with you: an anchor (of course), and a length of rope or chain.

Anchors

Anchors come in a wide variety of different shapes and sizes, with conflicting claims made by their respective makers. In general, though, there are three main types: those with flat blades, those with plough-shaped blades, and those that are shaped like scoops. It would be very difficult, if not impossible, to say that any of these three is 'better' or 'worse' than the others, although the ploughshare type is probably the most consistent performer across a wide range of conditions.

A fourth type, known as a grapnel, is popular in small boats because it folds up to occupy very little space.

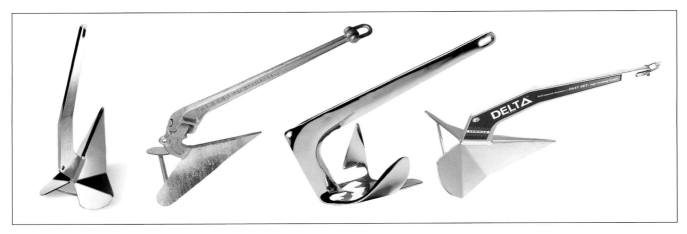

Above: *Anchors come in all shapes and sizes.*

Unfortunately, like the traditional 'fisherman's' anchor on which it is based, it really doesn't work very well.

Cable

What all anchors have in common is that they only work if they are being pulled along the seabed, not upwards away from it. To achieve that, you need a surprisingly long length of rope or chain.

Chain is generally regarded as the most effective option, because its weight tends to drop it down towards the seabed, so you only need about four times as much chain as the depth of water in order to be reasonably certain that the anchor will be subjected to a horizontal pull. It also has the advantage of being unlikely to be damaged by anything that it might come across down there.

Some big-boat owners prefer rope to chain because it is more resilient. However, it is so much lighter than chain that you need

much more of it – typically about six times the depth of water – and it's still worth having a few metres/feet of chain between the anchor and the rope. Having said that, rope is cheaper, lighter, kinder to the hands and much easier to stow than chain, and can be used for other purposes.

For boats up to about 7m (30ft) long, there's a third option, which is webbing. It has most of the strengths and drawbacks of rope, except that because it's flat, it lends itself to being stowed on a reel, where it is very compact and virtually guaranteed not to tangle.

Planning an anchorage

Making sure that an idyllic anchorage lives up to expectations is all about planning, but rest assured that it is not rocket science.
1   Make sure it is sheltered from the wind and waves, and ideally out of the tidal stream or current. Bracing yourself against the movement of a boat that is leaping from wave crest to wave

crest may be fun, but not when you are anchored and trying to eat lunch!
2   What is the seabed like? In clear, still water, you can sometimes see whether you are anchoring on sand (which is good) or weed (which is not). If not, then look on the navigational chart for the little letters that indicate the nature of the seabed, or for the anchor symbol that indicates recommended spots. Anchors hold best in seabeds into which they can penetrate easily, such as sand, clay and mud.
3   Make sure that there is enough water, both in terms of depth (remember that the tide may go up or down – see page 108) and in terms of space around you.
4   Be considerate to other people: don't anchor close to slipways or jetties, or in marked approach channels.
5   Remember what you came for. If you want peace and quiet, don't

anchor off a popular bathing beach or near a waterski area; similarly, if you want to swim ashore for ice creams, don't choose an isolated cove!

Anchoring

When, after all that preparation, you come to actually anchor, the main thing to bear in mind is that the object of the exercise is to make sure that the rope or chain cable attached to your boat is exerting a horizontal pull on the anchor itself. If you can achieve that, then a decent anchor will usually make its own arrangements about digging in.

The way to anchor correctly is to motor up to your chosen spot rather as though there were a mooring buoy available. Once the boat has stopped, instead of grabbing hold of the non-existent buoy, lower the anchor to the seabed.

Whatever you do, don't just drop it. Lower it, counting the number of armfuls of rope or the time the anchor winch has to run before the anchor reaches the bottom. This gives you an accurate check on the depth of water.

By the time the anchor has reached the bottom, the boat should be starting to drift away from the spot, so the anchor cable will pull away from the boat at a slight angle. So long as the cable is not vertical, it is safe to let more cable out, because you will be laying it out along the seabed. However, don't let out more cable if is hanging straight down from the bow of the boat, because you will just be dropping it in a heap.

Eventually, when you have let out the right amount of cable (four times the depth if you are using chain, or six times the depth for rope), you can secure the rope or chain and, if you really want to, give a gentle nudge of astern power to 'dig the anchor in' and make sure it is holding. The emphasis here, though, is on the word 'gentle'.

Weighing anchor

Weighing anchor or 'unanchoring' is even easier.

Essentially, it is just a matter of pulling the boat back up to the spot at which she is directly over the anchor, and then, with the anchor being in its weakest possible condition (with the pull straight upwards), simply lift it away from the seabed.

The helmsman can make life a lot easier for his crew by motoring the boat up to the anchor, rather than forcing the crew to pull it, and the crew can make things easier for the helmsman by keeping a gentle tension on the anchor cable and indicating which way the cable is leading.

Once you are directly on top of the anchor, it should come up reasonably easily, though you may find yourself lifting a great ball of mud or long streamers of heavy seaweed as well as the anchor.

If the anchor has really buried itself, the best way to get it free is to motor the boat up to the anchor – at which point the chain or rope will be hanging straight downwards – and pull the cable as tight as you can get it. Then use engine power to move the boat around, so as to wriggle the anchor free.

Above: The ideal anchorage is sheltered from the wind and the waves.

TRAILERS AND LAUNCHING

Keeping your boat on a trailer brings with it numerous advantages, from the freedom of being able to begin your day's boating from anywhere you choose, to the cost savings involved in not requiring a marina berth. Although at first you might be daunted by the prospect of getting your boat on and off the trailer, with practice launch and recovery will become second nature to you.

Having said that, when you begin launching your boat you should do so with care. Once the boat is in the water, everything can happen quite quickly, so it is important to do as much preparation as you can on dry land. The thought of messing your launch up can be quite frightening, but in reality, if you take your time it's quite straightforward. The same goes for recovery, when strong wind and tide can make staying calm absolutely vital.

Easy launch and recovery requires three things: the right trailer, the right technique, and the right conditions for your boat. Let's begin by working through the basic launch procedure.

Proper preparation

Most of the time, you will be aiming to launch and recover at a slipway, where you can use a ramp to simplify the procedure. Whenever you use a ramp for the first time,

Above: Enlist the help of a friend when you are learning to launch – ideally one with some previous experience – and choose a clear day when the conditions are calm.

ideally you will have the opportunity to visit the launch spot beforehand – without your boat. Take along a boating companion and spend a morning or afternoon at the site. You will learn more in half a day than you would in three days of doing it wrong by yourself! It is best to visit at low tide, which is when you will see any obstructions that might be

hidden below the waterline in other conditions. You will also see if there are any kinks or peculiarities in the shape of the slipway.

On this first fact-finding trip, you also need to find out whether the slipway is public or privately owned. Are there restrictions – either by regulations or by the conditions – on the times of day or states of tide when you can launch? Do you know where you can park your car after you've launched? Will the gradient of the slip cause you any problems? Is there a speed limit in the area where you'll launch, and will any cross-currents or tidal factors come into play? If you can, speak to other ramp users, or any officials, about anything that's worrying you.

The first launch

For your first launch, aim for a quiet time, if at all possible. Take along a friend – if you know someone with some experience,

Above: Be sure to buy the right trailer for your boat – it will make life easier.

all the better. And if you can, select your day and time so that you can launch in calm conditions, with the tide high enough to make this particular slipway as easy to use as possible.

When you arrive, there is plenty to do before the boat goes anywhere near the water. Remember, there is no hurry, and besides, you need to allow your wheel bearings to cool before the trailer goes anywhere near the water.

Begin by removing, folding and stowing the boat's travelling covers. Take off the lighting board, electrical cable and prop cover from the rear of the trailer (putting them in your car rather than leaving them on the ground to be driven over!). Remove the transom tie-downs securing the boat to the trailer and remove the bow and back chains, leaving the winch cable attached. Attach the bow rope, or painter, to the bow eye. If you are going to dock the boat straight after launching, fit mooring ropes to the bow and stern cleats, and rig the fenders at the correct height on the appropriate side.

It might sound obvious, but check that your bung plug is closed. This will often be left open to allow rainwater to drain while the boat is not in use – but launching a boat with a hole in it is a very bad idea!

Now turn on the fuel cut-off and the battery. Put the key in the ignition but don't turn it yet – your engine needs water flowing through it, or you will break the impeller.

If your engine has a trim-tilt mechanism, you can trim the engine/gearbox down a bit, but you must maintain a safe clearance from the ground. You can always lower the engine further once the trailer is in the water.

Depending on the size of the boat, only the driver and at most one other person should be aboard during the launch. Don't load any extra weight until the boat is safely in the water.

HAND LAUNCH

The easiest launch of all is a hand launch, used when the combined weight of the craft and its trailer can be handled by one person. Simply detach the trailer from your car and walk it into the water until you can float the craft off. Even though one person can handle the boat and trailer, you will need someone to help return the trailer to the shore.

The golden rule for hand launching is to make sure you have the painter (bow rope) in your hand when you push the boat off the trailer. If you don't, you could be in for an embarrassing swim as you leap into the water to 'catch' your boat, while your trailer runs down the ramp and disappears into the water! It also makes sense to attach a vehicle's towrope between the trailer and hitch – just in case it gets away from you.

Additionally, bear in mind that ramps are often wet, so suitable footwear is essential.

Above: Keep a firm grip on the painter when conducting a hand launch.

Launching

Once you have completed the basic preparations, check one last time to make sure that there are no ropes securing the boat to the trailer, except the bow winch line. Do you have fuel, oil and water? Is there a lifejacket for everyone who will be getting on board?

Let's start with launching an outboard-powered boat. Pump the fuel primer bulb until it resists firmly. If you smell petrol fumes then abort the launch until you locate the problem. Never take a chance with petrol fumes on a boat.

Before you launch, make one last check of the wind and tide conditions. The way the water flows around any buoys in the water will give you a clue as to current; flags will do the same job for the wind. If possible, it's best to launch into the wind or tide (whichever is stronger), which will stop you getting swept sideways. If this isn't possible, then at least be aware of how the

Above: Check the direction and force of the wind by observing any flags in the harbour.

conditions will affect your boat as you launch.

Now reverse the trailer until the water pickup on the outboard is submerged. Start the engine and set it to a fast idle for a couple of minutes to ensure that water is circulating and flowing smoothly out of the tell-tale. Reduce the fast idle slowly until the engine is running smoothly and steadily at normal rpm (revolutions per minute).

TIPS FOR SAFE LAUNCHING

- Prepare thoroughly before you get onto the launch ramp.
- Don't rush the launch or the recovery.
- Communicate loudly with your crew, giving instructions clearly and warning them before making any move.
- Make sure helpers' hands are clear of winches, ropes or moving parts before you set the boat in motion. Insist that each person confirms loudly that they are clear.
- Ensure safety by going to the transom and checking that no one is near the propeller before you start the engine.
- Check that the water astern or ahead is clear before you move in either direction.
- If you are in any doubt, abort the launch.

Above: Take your time during the launch procedure.

Make sure that you are launching into water deep enough for your boat and engine. Then release the bow winch line and gently reverse off the trailer. As you get into deeper water, trim the engine all the way down. Keep your speed to a minimum and make for the jetty or boarding dock, where you can tie up until you have loaded your equipment and crew.

The tow-vehicle driver, meanwhile, should have cleared the ramp and parked up. To protect your trailer he or she should give it a quick hose down, particularly if you have launched into salt water and you are going to be away for more than just the day.

If your boat has an inboard engine, then launch and recovery are slightly different.

Trailers for boats that have shafts through the hull have slots in them for the drives and propellers. Depending on the trailer chassis, the boat has to be docked absolutely straight or floated on and off the trailers. This is much easier if three guide posts per side are fitted to the trailer.

Remember also that when you reverse a fixed-propeller boat, it 'walks' in the opposite direction to the propeller rotation, so your approaches are more difficult, unless your speed is absolutely right. Most boats have excellent rudders that react well, even at low speeds, but they don't deal well with impacts. Neither do the propellers and shafts, so it is best to use the minimum of power to get the boat as close to the trailer as possible and then winch it into place.

LAUNCHING ON A ROPE

If you are launching at low tide and on a gently sloping slipway, then you may find that submerging your trailer far enough to launch your boat could mean submerging your car more than is sensible! In this case, you will need to use a rope between the car and the trailer.

The principle is quite simple. With the boat on the slipway, put the trailer's handbrake on, and chock the wheels for extra security. Now unhitch the trailer, and tie a rope from the trailer to the hitch on your car. Next, edge the car up the slipway to take up the slack on the rope.

When you are ready, take the handbrake and chocks away, then reverse the car and launch the boat as usual.

Above: Launching on a rope is a straightforward operation.

Recovery

When it comes to recovery, the key, once again, is to take careful note of the conditions. As you near the trailer, it is easy to panic – especially if there is a queue for the slip – so prepare properly, and don't be tempted to rush. The advantage over launching, however, is that you are already on the water, so judging the conditions is much easier than speculating from dry land.

The key, as ever, is to use the conditions to your advantage. There are no hard and fast rules – that's where experience comes in – but there are numerous techniques you can use. If you are approaching directly into the conditions then that is easy, as the conditions will act as a brake to keep you in control at all times. In a crosswind, you will need to approach on the windward side (or uptide, depending on whether the wind or tide is stronger), and allow the conditions to drift you into the right position and alignment.

In difficult conditions, it is important to be decisive, and you will certainly feel the pressure to act quickly. However, remember that one decisive action can abort the recovery altogether. If you are making a hash of it, just move away and begin your entire approach again. On your second attempt you will have knowledge of the conditions that will make recovery much easier; trying to produce a safe recovery from a poor position, on the other hand, is a very advanced skill.

Above: *Most of us have to be careful of how far we submerge our vehicles when launching and recovering. The owner of this truck probably isn't so worried!*

The other difficult part is working out how far the trailer should be submerged. When you launch your boat, make a mental note of how much of the trailer is underwater, which will give you a rough guide to where it will need to be when you recover. The supporting hull bed and front half of the trailer should be dry. The water on the hull will provide sufficient lubrication for it to slide on these beds if the trailer is so equipped.

Distribute the weight in the boat evenly so it is on an even keel (not leaning to one side or the other)

Above: *Rollers on the trailer will help when you winch your boat out.*

Left: *The recovery process begins. Sometimes it is best to approach at an angle and allow the conditions to bring the stern around.*

Below left: *Idle the boat towards the trailer and attach the painter or winch strap.*

Below right: *Activate the winch when the boat is properly aligned.*

Bottom: *Slowly pull the car and trailer clear of the water.*

Above: *The same principles apply when launching and recovering on a beach as on a slipway. Make sure that you make a note of your launch position for when you return.*

and idle the boat towards the trailer. Align the centreline of the boat with the centre of the trailer, then drive the boat between a third and halfway up. Now the winch strap should be attached and the boat pulled up to the bow snubber. If the boat sticks, the tow-vehicle driver can slowly back the trailer into the water while you apply moderate throttle to push the boat up the trailer.

SURF LAUNCH AND RECOVERY

For your first experience of launching a boat, it certainly makes sense to find a slipway rather than attempt to launch from a beach. Every such launch is different because of the local conditions, and a bit of experience goes a long way in working out how best to counter these variables.

Apart from checking the weather report, your first step before you put the boat into active surf is to study the waves to determine the pattern and timing of the sets you will be facing, even if the breaks are away from the launch site.

Soft ropes can be rigged from the bow, looping along the side to a cleat aft, for the crew to hang on to as they manoeuvre the boat, and as aids to climb aboard. The ropes must never be long enough to foul the boat's propellers.

Immediately the craft is off the trailer and in the water, turn it bow-on to the oncoming surf and move it out into deeper water.

As soon as the stern is deep enough to get water into the intakes, start the engines (alternatively, fire them up on the shore beforehand using muffs, so that there is water in the system) as the crew clambers aboard, with everyone well clear of the props. The crew then need to get forward as quickly as possible, apart from one person assigned to each motor.

Before you head out to sea, look back and get a picture in your mind of what the shore looks like, noting any reference points that you can use on your return. On a flat coastline it is not always easy to find any. Launch sites can also be marked with flags or similar markers where local identifying features are absent. You should mark the point on your GPS, if you have one.

When returning, the best technique is to wait for the biggest single wave at the back of the current set of waves and ride in on the back of it. However, when you think you have found the biggest wave, always check behind you. Another one can form that is bigger than the one you are riding and, when you hit the beach, the bigger wave could land on top of you. Ideally you would come in on the back of a friendly wave on a falling tide.

Above: *If there isn't much of a queue for the slipway, then you can secure your boat fully while you're still on the slip.*

SECURING THE BOAT

No matter how you recover your boat, when the boat and trailer are still on the ramp, remove the bung plugs to allow water to drain out. Then clear the slip and, before you go anywhere, fasten the boat to the trailer.

To do this, tie down the bow using adjustable ties or strops. A propeller bag must cover the lower half of the engine, which should be locked into a raised position.

Ensure that the boat is very tightly secured. A few bits of carpet or rag where the strops meet the hull mean you can tighten the bonds without damaging your boat.

When you leave, it is good practice to travel a few miles and then stop to check that the strops are still holding the boat firmly.

Trailers and the law

The legal situation regarding towing varies throughout the world and is quite complicated. If you are in any doubt as to whether you comply, check with your country's driver and vehicle licensing agency (for licensing queries) or department for transport (for trailer specifications).

In general, the key figures in towing law refer to maximum authorized mass, or MAM. For a trailer, the MAM is the maximum permitted mass, so it doesn't change according to what is actually being towed – even when the trailer is unladen, its MAM remains the same. Confusingly, MAM is also called the gross vehicle weight (GVW).

What you are permitted to tow depends largely on when you passed your driving test. In the UK,

if this was before 1 January 1997, then you can drive a vehicle and trailer combination with a MAM of up to 8,250kg (18,233lb).

If you passed your test on or since 1 January 1997, your ability to tow is more restricted. You can drive a car with a MAM of up to 3,500kg (7,735lb) with a trailer of MAM up to 750kg (1,658lb). You can also tow a heavier trailer, as long as the combined MAM of the towcar and trailer does not exceed 3,500kg (7,735lb), and the MAM of the trailer does not exceed the unladen mass of the towcar. If this isn't sufficient for you, you will need to take an additional driving test to gain a 'Category B+E' licence. Holders of provisional licences may not tow trailers.

Your trailer may be legally required to have its own brakes. This applies if the trailer's MAM is greater than 750kg (1,658lb), or if the laden weight of the trailer (that is, the weight of the trailer plus its load) is more than half your car's kerbweight.

A few other items are compulsory. Your trailer must be fitted with a 'breakaway cable' or chain, which will activate the brakes if the trailer comes free from the towcar. You must have an adequate view to the rear, either via your ordinary mirrors or extended versions. The registration mark of the towcar must appear at the back of the trailer, on a standard number plate. You also need third-party insurance cover for your boat (as well as for your towcar).

There are also restrictions on the maximum length of trailer that you can tow, though the regulations are a bit of a minefield. If your towcar has a MAM over 3,500kg (7,735lb) then your trailer can be up to 12m (39ft, 4in) long and 2.55m (8ft, 4in) wide; if the towcar has a MAM of 3,500kg (7,735lb) or less, then the length of the trailer should not exceed 7m (23ft) and the width 2.3m (7ft, 6in). These lengths do not include the drawbar or the coupling device. The total length of the car/trailer combination should not exceed 18m (59ft).

Finally, towing also affects your speed limits – you must not exceed 50mph (80kph), or 60mph (100kph) on motorways or dual carriageways. When towing, you are also prohibited from using the outside lane on three- or four-lane dual carriageways or motorways, unless there are lane closures restricting the road to two carriageways or less, or you are instructed to do so by the police.

Choosing a trailer

A new boat will probably come with a purpose-made trailer, but if you have bought a boat 'off the water', you may be in the market for a new or second-hand trailer. Normally your choice will depend on the launching facilities you are most likely to encounter, but you should also opt for a trailer that can do the job efficiently with the least inconvenience, and will endure.

A trailer must be structurally strong – a good safety margin is at least twice as strong as required to carry your boat. Most trailer manufacturers construct units for specific boats, but there are universal trailers that can be adapted to carry boats of different dimensions.

Trailers are rated according to the weight of the load. Clearly, your trailer's MAM must be higher than the weight of the boat you are planning on towing, which in reality will include any equipment on board, any fuel or water and any other bits and pieces you may be carrying.

If you buy a complete rig from a reputable boat manufacturer, the trailer is likely to be properly rated. With a second-hand trailer, inquire whether its original specifications have been modified, or have it checked by a marine surveyor or a mechanic who knows

Above: *A simple two-wheeled trailer like this one will be easy to manoeuvre, but ensure that it is rated high enough to carry your boat.*

trailers and understands how yours will be used.

Bear in mind that while a double axle (four-wheeled) trailer will take a greater weight, and will probably be easier to tow over soft sand than its two-wheeled counterpart of the same loaded mass, it may be more difficult to manoeuvre by hand.

SALT OR FRESH WATER?

Trailers used in fresh water can be made of mild steel, either painted or epoxy coated. Those for salt water launches should be constructed from hot-dip galvanized mild steel or stainless steel, to prevent rust. Coated or sprayed galvanization is not as effective as hot dip; hot dip should meet British Standard BS

Left: Your trailer may be specifically designed for your boat, or it may be universal.

Below left: Double-axle trailers will be able to take more weight.

Below right and bottom right: Check that moving parts are in good condition on a second-hand trailer, and always keep them well lubricated.

729. Box sections should be sealed by plastic caps for added protection.

Aluminium trailers are lightweight and don't rust, but they need to be made by a specialist as the welding requires proper equipment and experience.

Trailer beds

Trailer-bed designs include timber-covered steel beds on which the boat sits; keel rollers fitted to metal brackets on which the boat's keel rests; and fully hinged roller bogies placed strategically on the frame. Rollers have pretty much taken over as the standard choice, because they are more flexible and easier to use. You should have 24 rollers (six sets of four) for every 1,000kg (2,210lb) your boat weighs.

Modern swing-beam trailers can be adjusted for the best support, or for different boats, so they may be a better investment if you are thinking of changing boats in the near future.

Above: *Aim for 24 rollers for every 1,000kg (2,210lbs) of boat weight.*

Trailer brakes

Most braked trailers are fitted with over-run brakes. This involves a sprung, damped hitch that operates a steel arm connected to a cable attached to the brake shoes (in a similar fashion to most vehicle handbrakes). Alternatively, it may have disk brakes operated through overrun arms; both types have some form of reverse lock that has to be engaged before you back up the rig. (A system is available that automatically disengages the brake shoes when reversing.)

Salt water is a major enemy of braking systems, causing them to corrode rapidly and become ineffective. Drum brakes are particularly adversely affected. This

Above: *Hose down brake calipers with fresh water to prevent rust.*

Above: *Your boat should fit securely on the bed.*

is one of the reasons why disk brakes have gained popularity, as the workings are always exposed and can be properly hosed off after use. It is difficult to do this with drum brakes, unless they are fitted with a special flushing adapter through which you can introduce fresh water inside the drums.

Extension bars

An extension bar lengthens the gap between the vehicle and the trailer, reducing the potential for the tow-vehicle to come into contact with corrosive seawater.

Most trailers are built out of rectangular or square tube and comprise a backbone that runs the length of the trailer, forming an A-frame with cross members at the widest point and the rear forming the rigid rectangle on which the boat bed is mounted. A smaller-diameter tube is inserted down the backbone, through which two holes have been drilled and collets inserted. A matching hole is drilled near the front of the outer tube. The tow hitch is mounted on the inner tube.

When preparing to launch using an extension bar, find a level piece of ground. Drop your jockey wheel until the weight is off the bar, then unhook the safety chain and disconnect the electric coupling. Reattach the hitch to the tow vehicle's and remove the locking pin holding the inner tube to the outer tube. Move the tow vehicle forward until the second hole in the inner

tube lines up with the hole in the outer tube and drop in the pin to complete the extension.

Choosing a tow vehicle

Matching the weight of your boat rig to your tow vehicle will reduce the likelihood of the boat overtaking the car on steep declines or in tight bends. You don't need a monster truck to tow a typical trailboat, but do check your owner's manual for information on your car's towing limits – and remember that the weight you will be towing includes the weight of the trailer and any onboard equipment, not just the boat itself. In some cases, the car's manual may refer to 'gross train weight'. This means the total weight not just of the laden trailer, but your car, luggage and passengers as well. It is easy to ignore all this extra weight, but it does add up, so be careful.

Caravanners habitually refer to the '85 per cent rule', by which the weight of your laden trailer should not exceed 85 per cent of your tow car's kerbweight. Although this is not a legal requirement, it is a good rule of thumb.

Your car's manual will also specify a maximum noseweight, which is the vertical downward force applied by the laden trailer on your car's towball. Clearly this should not be exceeded, but a certain amount of weight is a good thing, because it adds to the overall stability of your rig. As another rule of thumb, the noseweight should be around seven per cent of the actual laden weight of the trailer (i.e. its 'real' weight with the boat on it, not its MAM). Between 25 and 75kg (55 and 165 lb) is usually about right, depending on the rig and tow vehicle's springing. The only way to test the noseweight is with some scales, using a piece of wood to spread the load and protect the scales.

Before you hitch up the trailer, you should inflate your towcar's tyres to allow for the extra load, and ensure that you have sufficient pressure on

Above: Your car's owner's manual will provide its towing limits.

Above: High ground clearance is an advantage when launching, which is why 4x4s are the preferred choice for many.

the tow bar. Again, your vehicle manual should offer advice on the correct parameters; if not, speak to the trailer supplier.

Trailer maintenance

Modern trailers don't need a huge amount of maintenance, but there are some potential problem areas that you should check before the start of a new season.

In terms of your trailer's chassis, look for any cracks or damage, particularly where these may have penetrated the outer protective layer, exposing the steel to damage. Also take a look at your suspension, paying particular attention to shock absorbers, if you have them. If there is any leakage, then these need to be replaced.

Make sure that the lightboard and reflectors are firmly attached, and test the electrics and lights. The jockey wheel and winch should be

properly lubricated and operate smoothly. The jaws of the coupling should clamp firmly onto your car's towbar, and again this whole area should be lubricated.

Give your trailer's tyres a once-over to make sure they are in good condition. It is illegal to have cross-ply and radial tyres on the same axle, there should be sufficient tread to comply with legal minimums, and all your tyres should be inflated to the correct pressure. In double-axle trailers, always check the tyre pressures, because one tyre could be flat and not appear to be so until you take it on the road.

If you find a tubeless tyre regularly losing pressure, it is probably due to a bad valve or leaking 'beading'. The beading is the section on the inside diameter of the tyre that seals against the shoulder of the wheel rim. If it is a steel rim, the problem is likely to be that the rim has corroded. When

tyres are fitted or refitted after a puncture repair, the repairer should clean that section of the rim with fine sandpaper to ensure a tight seal. Many don't. If you can't get them to do their job properly, and unless you keep an air compressor at home, have a tube fitted.

Above: Ensure that the jockey wheel and winch operate smoothly.

Above: Even a large boat isn't hard to tow once you're used to it.

Check for play in the wheel bearings by jacking up the trailer and spinning the wheels. Listen for any unusual rattling or scraping noises. Rock the trailer from side to side – the wheels shouldn't really move horizontally. If they do, have the problem attended to before using the trailer.

Finally, check that your brakes are working well enough to lock the wheels, and check all mechanisms for the inevitable build-up of dirt from the roads.

Road handling

Driving with a heavily laden trailer can be a nerve-wracking experience at first, but don't let it overawe you. If caravanners can do it, you certainly can!

To begin with, be aware of your limitations when you are towing. Your car will accelerate, decelerate and turn more sluggishly than usual. You're supposed to be enjoying yourself, so just accept that you will need to drive more slowly and carefully than you might otherwise feel necessary. Also, concentrate –

when you relax you'll find that, at least once in your trailboating career, you forget that you have a boat behind you at all, and end up bouncing it down the motorway at a speed in excess of what it should be doing!

For the best handling on the road, begin by loading up your equipment properly. Ideally, the majority of the weight should be over the axle(s). Load as much equipment into your car (rather than your boat) as you can. What you do put in the boat, try to keep central, and as low as possible, to maintain a low centre of gravity. Make sure that the items are properly secured so that they can't come free and disturb the trailer's balance when you are underway.

REVERSING

Often the thing that causes the most consternation for novice

---

SNAKING

If your trailer has been properly maintained, your speed is under control and your boat's contents have been sensibly stowed, it is unlikely that you will encounter any 'snaking' or swaying while you are underway.

Having said that, there may be a small amount of swaying if you are driving in high winds or passing high-sided vehicles. If you do feel your boat snaking, stay calm. The worst thing you can do is panic or tense up. Here

are a few do's and don'ts for dealing with the situation.

- **Do** gradually reduce your speed.
- **Do** steady the steering wheel.
- **Don't** slam on your brakes – this could lead to jack-knifing.
- **Don't** try to steer out of it – you're likely to over-correct and make the situation worse.
- **Don't** increase your speed.
- **Don't** continue for a prolonged period, or if the problem recurs.

trailboaters is having to reverse the rig. Really, though, it's just a matter of practice and patience, as long as you remember that you need to take extra care and can't ever reverse without giving it your full concentration.

If you are reversing straight back, then do so slowly and watch your mirrors. If the boat appears on either side, turn the wheel towards that mirror to correct.

When you are reversing around corners, the trick is to begin by turning the steering wheel the opposite way to the way you want to go. Now slacken off on the wheel and gradually turn the other way, which will allow the car to follow the trailer as desired.

If you turn too suddenly, the trailer could jack-knife, potentially damaging your car, trailer and boat or causing an accident. If

Above: When reversing straight, do so slowly and with care.

you feel this happening, stop immediately, pull forward in a straight line, and try again.

When you are starting out, it is always easiest if you have someone to help you, who can tell you if the

trailer is jack-knifing or if you are cutting a corner. Soon, however, you will be fine in 99 per cent of situations, and reversing your rig will barely be harder than reversing your car on its own.

Above: Space to park a boat and trailer outside a pub is a rare treat indeed!

ENGINES AND DRIVES

How much do we need to know about a boat's engine? The engine is obviously the core of any powerboat, so naturally there is constant debate about engines and drives, who does what best amongst the manufacturers and the pros and cons of individual products. For the newcomer, it can all be very confusing.

Assessing your options

One could argue that all this is purely academic. After all, if you are buying a new boat you will have to accept what the manufacturer offers you, although there may be more than one horsepower option. Practically all second-hand craft come with an engine already installed, the exception being outboard-powered sports boats and RIBs, which are sometimes sold without engines.

However, a basic appreciation of marine engines is useful, not least because it can influence our choice of boat and affect our buying decision. For example, faced with two very similar sports cruisers, one with twin inboards and the other with sterndrives, some people will opt firmly for the former, others for the latter. That's because for different sorts of boating in different places, each has its own particular advantages and disadvantages – which we will come to later on.

The basics

The majority of marine engines intended for the recreational market are conventional petrol or diesel internal combustion engines, in most cases converted (marinized is the correct term) car or commercial vehicle units.

Electric power and hybrid diesel/electric are used almost exclusively in small river and lake launches. Those are specialist subjects which are not our concern in this book.

Above: A traditional speedboat with 1930s styling.

Unlike cars, in which front wheel drive, rear wheel drive and 4WD are really minor variations on the same theme, boats employ many different ways of getting the power of the engine into the water, although the final step is most often a propeller or a waterjet. Transmission and drive systems (basically anything between the engine and the propeller) include

the outboard, sterndrive, shaft drive and pod drive, while PWCs (personal water craft) are invariably waterjet-powered. We examine each variant in the following pages.

Match-making

In most cases, the type of engine is dictated by the size and type of vessel. For example, you don't see big flybridge motor cruisers

Above: A lot of fun can be had from an inflatable dinghy and a small outboard motor.

powered by outboards, or ski boats with large inboard diesels. However, between 7.6m (25ft) and 13.7m (45ft) you can find boats with outboards, sterndrives, inboards and sometimes waterjets. This is because the 100hp to 400hp power bracket is catered for by all four types. Below 7.6m (25ft) is generally regarded as outboard territory, and above 13.7m (45ft) is the domain of the inboard. However, the most powerful outboards and sterndrives are nibbling at the margins.

Small inboards up to 150hp are predominantly found in displacement (non-planing) craft such as steel cruisers and narrow boats. Little diesel inboards as small as 12hp are favoured by some fishermen due to their simplicity of operation, reliability and miserly fuel consumption. Petrol inboards are rare in the UK, apart from waterski boats operating on reservoirs and lakes, but they are sometimes found in small river and harbour launches. For sporting use, the bottom rung of the inboard ladder is around 180hp, with the sky the limit.

In the USA you see quite large game fishing boats with three or even four 200–350hp outboards bolted to the back. A well-known American expression is 'There's no substitute for inches' – the inches in this case being the cubic capacity type. Engine capacity in the USA is measured in cubic inches; in Europe, in cubic centimetres.

British boatbuilder Sunseeker has sometimes offered a choice of outboard or sterndrive power on specific models, and at the time of writing, the 34 Thunderhawk could be had with twin or triple 315hp Yamaha 'Hydradrive' diesel sterndrives. At the other end of the scale, Sea Saga offer a 7.5m (24ft, 6in) displacement wheel-house cruiser with a single 88hp inboard diesel.

Within this 7.6–13.7m (25–45ft) bracket, the type of engine will

Above: Alternatively, a 100mph raceboat might be more your style.

Above: Speed, luxury and status combine in this Sunseeker flybridge motor yacht.

Types of engine

So let us consider the basic types of engine and transmission in turn and then see which is most suited for which job. Then we will discuss petrol versus diesel, old and new 2-stroke outboard technology, and 4-strokes – inboard and outboard.

INBOARD MOTOR

We will start with the inboard motor, as it is by far the simplest to understand. Even non-boaters can picture the conventional inboard shaft drive layout in which the power unit sits roughly in the middle of the boat, driving the propeller via a long shaft that exits the hull through a watertight gland-cum-bearing somewhere near the stern.

The engine normally has a gearbox bolted directly to the back of it, as in a car. However, partly because it operates over a much smaller speed range and partly due to the characteristics of the propeller, a boat does not require several forward gears like a road vehicle. So a marine gearbox just offers forward, neutral and reverse (f-n-r) – or ahead, neutral and astern

depend a lot on the nature of the boat. Sporty versions feature outboards and sterndrives, whereas more sedate vessels often have inboards. This raises an important, but often overlooked, point: it is essential to consider your boat and engine as a package. If the hull and power unit are not closely matched and working together, the boat will be poor. If you are buying a new boat complete, the manufacturer will have sorted this out for you, but if possible read a magazine boat test

before parting with your cash. The least powerful version of a given model is sometimes only available just so that the boat builder can quote a low starting price. If you are buying second-hand, it is fairly unusual to come across a sterndrive or inboard boat that has had its original power unit replaced, but it is worth checking. You would be surprised how many second-hand outboard-powered boats get retro-fitted with unsuitable engines by less knowledgeable owners.

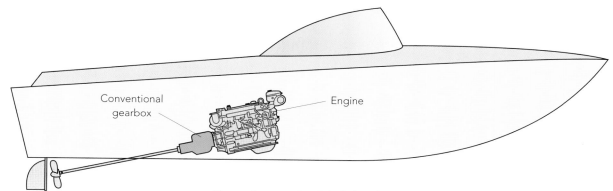

Above: A conventional shaft drive layout, with the engine and propshaft precisely in line.

if you want to be properly nautical. (Some race boats are the expensive exception to this rule.) It also reduces the speed of the propshaft compared to that of the engine (known as a reduction ratio), as engines like to turn fast and propellers more slowly.

There is a variation of the conventional inboard/shaft drive in which the engine is mounted much further aft in the boat, facing the 'wrong' way. The shaft coming out of the reduction gearbox is connected to what's known as a vee-drive gearbox, either bolted directly to it or via a short shaft. The output from the vee-drive box is directly below the input and on the same face, so it effectively 'folds' the drive train back under the engine. From here a short propeller shaft runs aft and out of the bottom of the boat, as in a conventional shaft drive. In some cases the reduction gearing and f-n-r are all built into the one box.

The basic advantage with the vee-drive is that it gets the engine out of the middle of the boat where accommodation space is at a premium, and puts it under the cockpit floor, much like a sterndrive. This can also benefit weight distribution on fast-planing craft. A slight disadvantage is additional mechanical complexity, weight and cost.

With shaft drive and vee-drive, steering is by rudder(s) behind the propeller, which deflects the prop wash from side to side.

OUTBOARD MOTOR

Originally developed as an alternative to oars, the outboard motor of today ranges from 1.5hp to over 350hp. The biggest are among some of the most advanced internal combustion engines to be found anywhere in the world.

All recreational outboards are petrol-powered. It is usual to refer to the 'engine' itself as the powerhead. Smaller motors are portable, and are fixed to the transom by screw clamps. 10hp is about the largest that can easily be lifted on and off a transom single handed, but 25hp is just about feasible for two fit adults if the boat is more or less level with a pontoon or landing stage. So that is your limit

if you need to take the engine home with you at the end of the day.

Above that size, it is more usual for the motor to be semi-permanently fixed to the transom with through-bolts. Tiller steering is possible up to 50hp; any bigger than that and you need a proper seat and console with remote control (mechanical or electrical) throttle and gearshift. The latest big outboards such as the 275hp Mercury Verado and Yamaha F350 have 'fly-by-wire' electrical controls which do away with awkward mechanical cables, and this trend is likely to continue.

The motor and leg are connected to the transom mounting plate by a lateral horizontal pin, allowing the drive angle to be altered. A minor change to assist in acceleration or get the best top speed is called trimming, while lifting the motor to a much greater angle (up to 60 degrees), for trailing or shallow water use, is called tilting.

Engines below 25hp are usually trimmed and tilted manually, with the disadvantage that trimming cannot be done when the boat is underway. Above that size, power

Below: A vee-drive layout, with the engine now facing aft. The gearbox is remote from the engine and reverses the direction of drive.

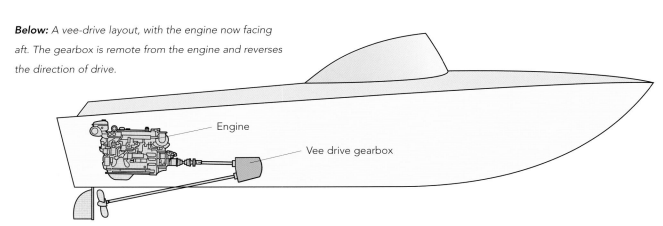

Engine

Vee drive gearbox

trim and tilt is often standard. In this case, electro-hydraulic rams worked by a rocker switch on the dash move the leg in and out through about 10 degrees for trimming. Another rocker switch – or a 'tilt override' function – fully extends them to bring the engine right up.

The Americans may favour monster triple engine 1,200hp rigs, but in Europe twins are more common, normally starting at the 40hp mark. An 8m (26ft) RIB might sport 2 x 150hp rigs, especially if it is used frequently for either diving or rescue work.

There are three basic types of outboard powerhead: the carburetted 2-stroke, the direct injection 2-stroke and the 4-stroke. The first is no longer available new in the US and Europe, due to environmental regulations, and much debate rages over the pros and cons of the latter two. This is discussed later in this chapter.

The output from the powerhead, which is mounted upright, (cylinders horizontal) is taken by the vertical driveshaft down the leg to a bevel gear at the bottom, which drives the horizontal propeller shaft. Reduction gearing is incorporated in the bevel gears and the f-n-r clutch is normally immediately behind it.

At the bottom of the leg casing are water intakes, which feed cooling water up to the powerhead and out again just below it. The leg also contains passages that either release the exhaust gases via a

Above: *Rocker switches are used to control trim tabs and sterndrive legs.*
Right: *The steering tiller and mounting clamps can clearly be seen on this 25hp Yamaha outboard.*

Above: *Larger outboards are controlled remotely from a helm station, as in this fast RIB.*

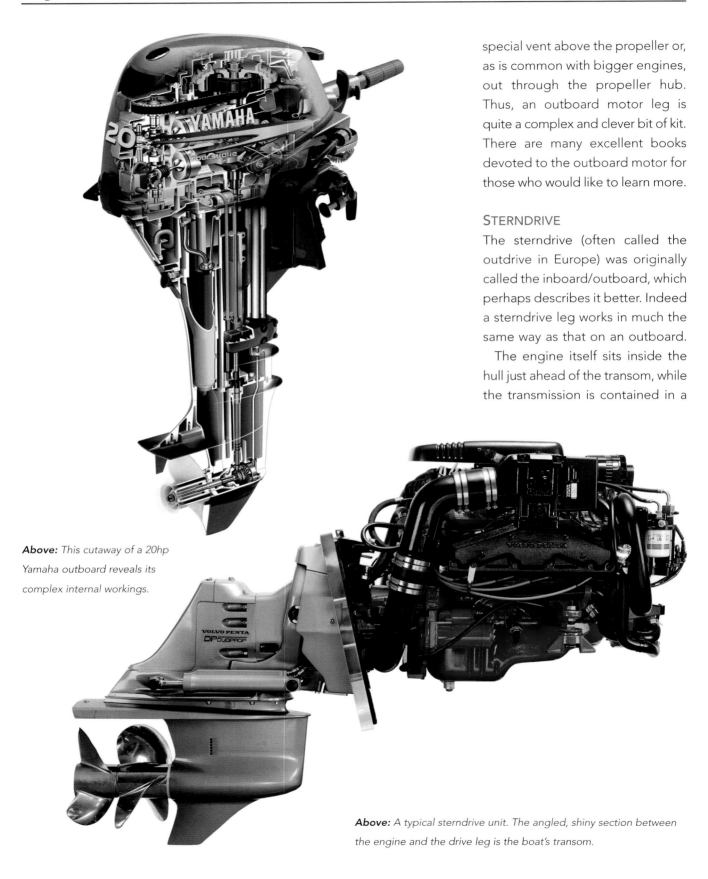

special vent above the propeller or, as is common with bigger engines, out through the propeller hub. Thus, an outboard motor leg is quite a complex and clever bit of kit. There are many excellent books devoted to the outboard motor for those who would like to learn more.

STERNDRIVE

The sterndrive (often called the outdrive in Europe) was originally called the inboard/outboard, which perhaps describes it better. Indeed a sterndrive leg works in much the same way as that on an outboard.

The engine itself sits inside the hull just ahead of the transom, while the transmission is contained in a

Above: This cutaway of a 20hp Yamaha outboard reveals its complex internal workings.

Above: A typical sterndrive unit. The angled, shiny section between the engine and the drive leg is the boat's transom.

leg bolted on the back. A short shaft connects the two. One or more universal joints in this shaft allow the drive to swivel and tilt.

A vital component of the sterndrive is the 'transom shield'. This is a multi-purpose casting bolted to the outside face of the transom to seal the large hole that must be cut for the drive shaft, exhaust and cooling water pipes, and controls between the drive and the engine. It also acts as the mounting point for the leg and provides pick-up points for the steering and tilt/trim rams.

Like the outboard, the sterndrive steers by swivelling its leg. (The technical term for this is thrust vectoring, whereas conventional rudders work by thrust deflection). It has similar trim and tilt facilities and similarly takes care of water pickup and exhaust functions.

Even the simplest sterndrive leg is a complex piece of engineering. Not only does it have to provide forward-neutral-reverse gears and a reduction ratio, but also takes the output from the engine and turns it through 90 degrees twice. Complexity is even greater in the case of legs with twin counter-rotating propellers like Volvo Penta's Duoprop, Mercruiser's Bravo III and Yamaha's TRP.

Most sterndrives come as an integrated engine/leg package from a single manufacturer, but it is possible to buy drive legs and engines separately, along with the necessary coupling parts.

Above: A closeup of a Volvo Penta Duoprop sterndrive leg, *clearly showing the hydraulic rams used to adjust the trim angle.*

However, this more advanced approach is definitely not recommended for the novice.

Sterndrive power starts at 120hp and in production diesel form goes on up to 370hp, matching the very biggest outboards. In the USA 500hp gasoline sterndrives are not that unusual and 1,000hp is normal for racing.

Race boats often use a variation on the sterndrive, in which the engine is mounted further forward and has a f-n-r reduction gearbox attached, like a conventional inboard. A somewhat longer shaft then connects to the top of the leg, whose sole job is to transfer the power to the propeller. Such simplified legs are very rugged, and usually known in the USA as 'drives' – which can be a little confusing.

Multiple sterndrives usually have their steering arms coupled together so that both turn through the same angle in response to the wheel. However, advanced joystick-controlled docking systems such as CMD's Axius employ computerized, independent leg operation.

Please note that although the sterndrive's engine is inside the hull, it is not referred to as an inboard – see below for more on this.

POD DRIVE

The pod drive is a relatively new system that combines the benefits of sterndrive and shaft drive to deliver unparalleled speed, efficiency and manoeuvrability. Volvo Penta started the ball rolling with its IPS (Inboard Propulsion System) in 2004 and Cummins Mercruiser Diesel announced the competing Zeus system a year later. As you can see below, the unique feature of IPS is the forward-facing propeller arrangement. At first sight, these look awfully vulnerable, but Volvo say they cope with debris as well as rear-facing versions.

At the time of writing, pod drives were available for boats between 10.6 and 18.2m (35 and 60ft), but by the time you read this may have migrated upwards or even downwards. Downwards is less likely, as the sterndrive is a much less expensive option for smaller boats.

The integrated pod drive package consists of an inboard engine mounted a bit further forward in the boat than with a sterndrive, coupled to a leg that extends vertically through the bottom of the hull and swivels like a sterndrive for steering. The gearbox sits atop the leg.

An essential advantage of IPS and Zeus is that the pods are electrically steered via a computer that takes its instructions from a sensor in the steering wheel hub. When underway, the pods steer together, but when

under joystick control at slow speed, they adopt independent angles to ensure that the boat goes in the desired direction.

WATERJET

The layout of a waterjet is shown to the right. As you can see, the water is picked up through a grille in the bottom of the boat, accelerated by an impeller running in a tunnel and ejected through the transom.

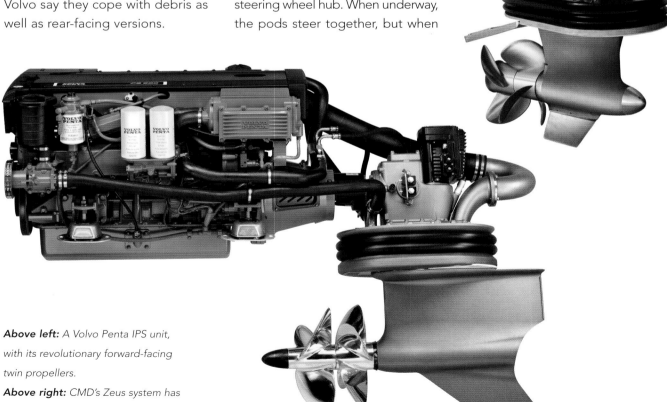

Above left: A Volvo Penta IPS unit, with its revolutionary forward-facing twin propellers.
Above right: CMD's Zeus system has more conventional rear-facing props.

Above: A small inboard jetdrive. Note the buckets that pivot downwards to reverse the water flow for going astern.

Waterjets are ubiquitous in PWCs and very common in small 'fun boats'. Their advantage in these applications are obvious: a totally smooth hull bottom, no propeller to endanger people in the water and very simple trailer launching and recovery. Their exceptional manoeuvrability is partly due to their wide-angle thrust vectoring and partly to the smooth hull bottom.

For bigger boats, the waterjet comes into its own when shallow draft is important, or when a shaft and rudder, sterndrive leg or outboard motor would be awkward or inappropriate for some reason. Waterjets are only efficient at relatively high speeds and the engine and jet drive must be very carefully matched if it is to work properly. It is something of a specialist propulsion system that does not lend itself to DIY fiddling at all!

SURFACE DRIVE

Surface drive is a specialized system for large, high speed craft. Basically, an inboard engine drives a shaft that exits not through the bottom of the hull but through the transom. In the cruise, only the lower half of the propeller is submerged. To compensate for this, the propeller

is about twice the normal diameter and its blades are specially designed to cope with smacking the water surface as they rotate. It may sound absurd, but it gets rid of the drag that would otherwise be

Above: A surface drive unit with an angled ram that adjusts the thrust angle. At speed, only the lower half of the propeller is in the water.

MAKING A CHOICE

So which type of engine/transmission is best suited to which sort of boat and boating?

Outboard motor		Outdrive		Inboard with shaft or vee-drive		Waterjet	
Pros	*Cons*	*Pros*	*Cons*	*Pros*	*Cons*	*Pros*	*Cons*
• Enhanced safety, as it is easy to clear a fouled prop • Enormous range of power outputs • Portable up to 15hp • Does not take up room inside the boat • Very good propulsive efficiency • Excellent manoeuvrability • Easily changed • Easily accessible powerhead	• Small outboards easily stolen • Engine and transmission system exposed to the elements • Aluminium alloy casing prone to corrosion	• Enhanced safety, as it is easy to clear a fouled prop • Excellent propulsive efficiency • Excellent manoeuvrability • Available from 100hp to over 350hp • Takes up less room than a conventional inboard with shaft drive	• Mechanically complex • Less robust than inboard with shaft drive • Requires meticulous maintenance for reliability • Aluminium alloy casing prone to corrosion • Maintenance is more expensive than other systems	• Mechanically very simple • Inexpensive components • Submerged sterngear offers good 'grip' on the water at low speed	• Poor propulsive efficiency at high speed due to drag of shaft and supporting brackets • Fouled prop cannot be cleared except by lifting the boat or employing a diver • Requires separate rudder • Sterngland a critical safety item • Long drive train prone to vibration	• Good propulsive efficiency at high speed • Normally smooth and vibration free • No sterngear drag or maintenance requirements • Normally reliable and light on maintenance • Safe shallow water operation	• Expensive, specialist drive system • Must be carefully matched to boat and operating regime • Very poor performance if not properly matched • Expensive if things go wrong • Not amenable to DIY maintenance or modification

caused by a submerged propeller shaft and its support brackets. Steering is either by vectored thrust or a conventional rudder.

CONCLUSION

The most important message in all of the above is that success depends on treating your boat, its engine and its transmission as an integrated package. Mixing and matching needs care and an understanding of each component's strengths and weaknesses. It's something best left to an expert. When buying a new boat, you can be fairly confident that has been taken care of by the builder. When buying second-hand, particularly if the boat or its engine have been modified in any way, a lot more caution is needed.

The type of boating you do will influence the sort of boat you buy and the type of engine you decide on. Your choice will also be influenced by whether you are interested primarily in performance, or more in economy, low maintenance and reliability.

Inside your engine

Understanding the basics of marine engines and transmissions helps not only in making a sensible buying decision, but can also lay the groundwork for more detailed familiarity with the most important mechanical components of your own boat. It may not be essential, but it's highly recommended.

With boats, as with cars, there are two basic choices when it comes to

engines: petrol or diesel. However, whereas all car engines are 4-stroke, the outboard motors used to power smaller boats are often 2-strokes. These can be further subdivided into the 'conventional' (old-fashioned) type and the much newer direct injection variety.

All inboard and sterndrive power units, whether petrol or diesel, are 4-strokes, and in recent years this technology has become increasingly popular for outboards. At the time of writing, only two manufacturers, Mercury and Evinrude, were producing new generation 2-strokes using direct injection (DI) fuel systems. Diesel outboards are few and far between, and limited to commercial applications – so we can safely ignore them.

In the USA and Europe, emission legislation means that virtually all new 2-stroke outboards are of the direct injection type. However, there are many thousands of conventional 2-strokes still in use. This is perfectly legal as emission and noise legislation isn't retroactive, and in those parts of the world with less stringent emission standards, 'old-fashioned' outboards are still available. Let's look first at the 4-stroke petrol engine, then at the two types of petrol 2-strokes, and finally at the diesel.

BACK TO BASICS

It is important to be quite clear what all three types of engine have in common, which is that they are all reciprocating internal combustion engines. This means that they all have pistons that go up and down inside cylinders, with the reciprocating movement converted into rotational movement by a connecting rod and crank. Internal combustion simply means that burning takes place inside the engine rather than outside, as is the case with the steam engine. The pivots that allow the connecting rod to swing from side to side as the crank goes round are called the big end (crank) and little end (piston) bearings.

You can see from the diagram below that if you push down on the top of the piston, the connecting rod linkage causes the crankshaft to rotate. When the 'push' – known as the power stroke – is over, the engine continues to rotate until the next push, partly because at least one piston is pushing at any point in time, and partly because of inertia – or flywheel effect.

The energy comes from fuel that is mixed with a much larger volume of air. This mixture is compressed into the top of the cylinder by the upward movement of the piston. When the piston is at the top, the mixture ignites.

The method of mixing the fuel and air, and causing it to ignite, differs between the petrol engine and the diesel – as we are about to see. However, the basic principle is exactly the same. In both cases, contrary to popular belief, combustion is not an explosion; it is a very rapid burning, lasting just a few milliseconds.

In each case we will consider a hypothetical single-cylinder engine. Multi-cylinder engines simply consist of several identical cylinders built into one big lump. Each cylinder works in exactly the same way, although at any one time each is at a different stage of the power producing process – or 'cycle' as it is commonly known.

VIVE LA DIFFERENCE

Now to the differences. Although the 4-stroke engine is the more mechanically complicated, its basic operation is actually easier to follow than that of the 2-stroke.

Let's start with our piston at the bottom of the cylinder. Technically, this is known as being at the bottom of its stroke or at bottom dead centre (BDC). Let's also assume that the cylinder is somehow full of that highly combustible mixture of fuel and air just referred to.

Above: The basic components of a 4-stroke petrol engine.

Labels: Cylinder head, Inlet port, Valve system, Cylinder block, Piston, Water cooling passages, Piston 'skirt', Big end bearing, Oil, Spark plug, Valve spring, Exhaust port, Valve head, Water cooling passages, Piston crown, Little end, Connecting rod, Crankshaft balance weight, Oil sump

Something to note is that when you see the term stroke followed by a measurement, it refers to the total vertical movement of the piston. The bore of the cylinder is self-explanatory, and when used as a measurement, refers to its diameter.

As the piston rises (either because the engine is already running, or because it is being turned over by the starter motor or pull cord) it compresses that mixture (also known as the charge), into that small area at the top of the cylinder called the combustion chamber. In some engines, that chamber is actually a hollow in the top of the piston, but it serves the same purpose.

In the top of the cylinder there are two rather special valves. Think of a hotel wash basin with one of those plugs that is pushed up by a lever and rod linkage to let the water out. Now imagine a basin with two of those plugs and you've got a very large, upside down version of a 4-stroke combustion chamber.

While the piston is moving up the cylinder and compressing the mixture, both these valves remain closed. A few milliseconds before the piston reaches the top of its stroke (top dead centre or TDC), the spark plug does its job and ignites the mixture. As it burns, it tries to expand, enormously increasing the pressure in the cylinder. And because the valves are closed it can only do so by pushing the piston back down the cylinder – or blowing the engine apart. The former is generally deemed preferable. The connecting rod converts this vertical movement into rotation of the crankshaft and we are up and running. Or at least ticking over.

Very logically, the upward movement of the piston is called the compression stroke, and downward movement, the power stroke.

We are now halfway through the 4-stroke cycle. The piston, having completed its power stroke, is now at the bottom of the cylinder (BDC). The crankshaft has gone round once and the cylinder is full of burned gas – which we must now get rid of. As the engine continues to turn, the piston starts back up the cylinder and one of those valves – equally logically called the exhaust valve – opens. So the burned gas, instead of being recompressed, is expelled down the 'plug hole' – more properly known as the exhaust port – and out into the exhaust system. We will come to the mechanics of valve operation a little later on. Ports are simply the holes in which mixture or exhaust gas get into or out of the cylinder.

With the piston now at the top of what's called the exhaust stroke and the burned gas expelled, the exhaust valve closes and the other one (the intake valve) opens. This valve's port is connected to the outside world by a tube called the intake manifold. So, as the piston descends on its intake stroke, it sucks in air.

This air has just the right amount of fuel in it, courtesy of either a carburettor or a fuel injection system. When the piston gets to the

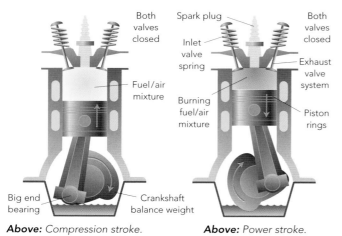

Above: *Compression stroke.*   **Above:** *Power stroke.*

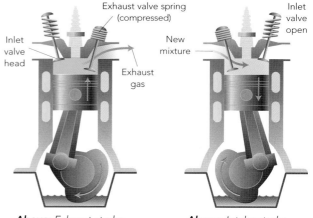

Above: *Exhaust stroke.*   **Above:** *Intake stroke.*

bottom of the cylinder it has completed four strokes, the crankshaft has rotated twice, and we are back to where we started.

On many 4-stroke sterndrives and outboards, full throttle is around 6,000rpm, so that sequence is happening 100 times per second, which equates to a great many ups and downs and round and rounds.

VALVE OPERATION

But what makes those plug-like valves open and close, and how do they do it in the right sequence? Let's go back to the hotel basin analogy. The plug is pushed up by a rod connected to a lever, usually located somewhere near the taps. Our intake and exhaust valves are operated in a surprisingly similar manner, but the 'plug' and the 'rod' are formed from a single piece of very hard metal. The plug bit is known as the valve head and the rod part as the stem. The circular ring in the combustion chamber against which the valve head sits when closed (the rim of the plug hole in basin-speak) is called the valve seat and is often a specially hardened insert to stop the head being worn away by the valve head banging against it and red hot gases rushing past it.

Instead of our fingers, the mechanism operating the rod is another shaft which is gear- or chain-driven from the crankshaft. It is known as a camshaft because it has two eccentric lumps (or cams)

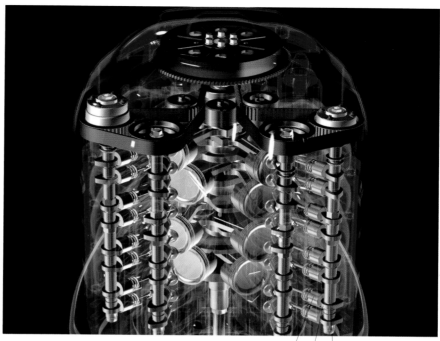

Cam follower / Camshaft
Camshaft lobe

Above: A cutaway of a multicylinder outboard motor, showing how the valves and twin overhead camshafts are arranged above the pistons.

on it: one for the intake valve, the other for the exhaust. The diagram above shows the position of the four overhead camshafts (two per cylinder bank) in relation to the cylinders on a 300hp V6 Yamaha outboard. The humpy bits of the cams are called lobes and are carefully arranged relative to the shaft itself. As the camshaft goes round, these lobes operate the linkage connected to the valves (valve gear in technical speak), pushing them open at just the right time during every revolution. The valves are spring-loaded to the closed position, so only open when forced to do so by the cam lobes. These days it is common for each cylinder to have two inlet and two

exhaust valves per cylinder, as this arrangement makes for better gas flow. Such engines are said to have 'four valve heads'.

There are numerous designs of valve gear, but high performance outboards usually have two separate camshafts, one working the exhaust valves and the other the intakes, with the lobes acting directly on the end of the valve stems as shown overleaf. It sounds like the obvious method, but is surprisingly expensive to engineer for reasons we won't go into here.

At this point we must mention lubrication. A pump picks up oil from a reservoir in the bottom of the engine known as the sump, passes it through a filter and then forces it

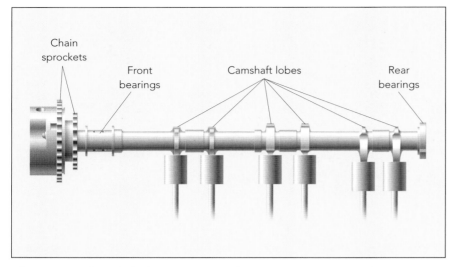

Above: A typical camshaft, showing the lobes that actually open the valves by pressing down on them as the shaft rotates.

through various drillings and passages to the crankshaft main bearings, the small and big end bearings, and any other parts such as the valve gear that need lubrication. Once it has done its job, the oil drains back into the sump where it has a chance to cool before being asked to go round again. And again, and again, and again...

THE 2-STROKE – SIMPLE AND DIFFICULT

And so to the 2-stroke. As you will have guessed, this type of engine is so called because a complete engine cycle is somehow fitted into just two strokes of the piston and one revolution of the crankshaft. Could it be that more than one thing is going on at once? Absolutely.

In many ways, the 2-stroke is more difficult to understand than the 4-stroke. In the latter case, all the

action (other than lubrication) takes place above the piston and each aspect of the cycle happens individually. With the 2-stroke, what is going on below the piston is equally important as what is going

on above it, and while there are only three moving parts, the cylinder block and crankcase casting is actually more complicated.

There are a number of subtle variations of the 2-stroke principle, most relating to how fresh mixture finds its way into the cylinder. However, as before, let's start with a basic, bare one piece, combined cylinder and crankcase. Cast into the cylinder block are a number of air 'transfer' passages (normally two or three around the circumference of the cylinder) that are open to the crankcase at their lower ends. These passages extend about halfway up the cylinder, and the tops match up with holes, known as ports, cut out of the cylinder wall. Closer to the top, there is another hole, known as

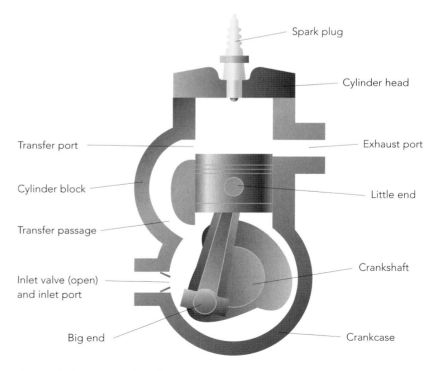

Above: Basic parts of a 2-stroke motor.

the exhaust port. The exhaust port leads directly into the exhaust system.

Initially we will examine what happens below the piston during one revolution of the crankshaft, then look at what is going on above it at the same time.

Intake

Let's start in the same place we did with the 4-stroke, with the piston at the bottom of its stroke (BDC). As the piston rises up the bore it produces suction inside the crankcase. Fuel/air mixture starts to enter through the inlet valve, which is basically a simple spring-loaded flap that can only open inwards.

By the time the piston is close to the top of its stroke, both the crankcase and that part of the cylinder below the piston are full of the new charge. Let's follow this charge through its very short lifespan.

Clearly, it can't do much good where it is. To do any useful work – for it to be compressed and ignited by the spark plug – we need it above the piston, not below it. And here comes the clever bit.

Transfer and exhaust

As the piston descends from top dead centre (TDC), the intake valve snaps shut and the mixture in the crankcase is compressed. As the piston crown or top passes the transfer ports, the fuel/air mixture rushes up through the transfer passages, then through the ports

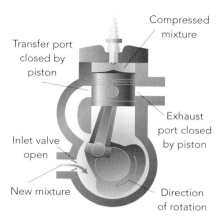

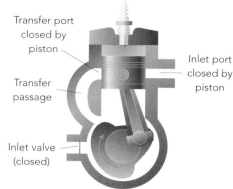

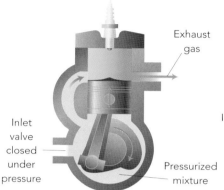

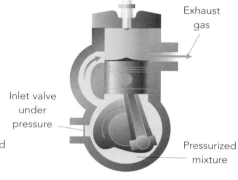

Top left: 1. Intake/compression stroke.

Above left: 3. Transfer/exhaust stroke.

Top right: 2. Power stroke.

Above right: 4. Exhaust/compression stroke.

and into the cylinder. (You can see how the passages get their name).

However, when our new charge first starts entering the cylinder, it encounters exhaust gas from the previous cycle. Fortunately this is busy piling out of the open exhaust port on the other side of the cylinder. The new charge just gives it an encouraging shove, and the rising piston also helps it on its way.

Compression

Shortly after this, the piston closes both the transfer port and the exhaust port. This diagram shows this about to happen. So our nice fresh mixture is now trapped and

gets compressed into the combustion chamber. A few degrees before TDC, the spark plug fires, the mixture burns and the piston starts back down on the power stroke. Our nice new fuel/air charge is now just a mass of red-hot burning gas. The moment the exhaust port opens it gladly escapes out into the wide world – assisted by a shove from its replacement entering through the transfer port opposite.

It's important to note that when our new mixture was flowing into the cylinder and pushing out the previous exhaust gas, a little of it also escaped. The 2-stroke's poor emissions performance is due as much to the escape of this unburned fuel (free hydrocarbons) as it is to noxious substances in the burned exhaust gas.

So, as you can see, it is the early part of every downward stroke that is a power stroke and a transfer stroke. Every upward stroke is not only an induction stroke but partly an exhaust stroke, and – once the piston has closed off the exhaust port – a compression stroke as well. That is five things happening in just one revolution of the crankshaft, with a power stroke every time – an impressive feat.

The lubrication of a 2-stroke is fundamentally different to that of the 4-stroke. If a 2-stroke's crankcase was also an oil reservoir, a lot of oil would get transferred into the cylinder along with the fuel/air mixture and be consumed in short order – with lots of nasty exhaust smoke. So instead, rather amazingly, it makes do with a very small amount of oil deliberately injected into the fuel/air mix just before it enters the engine. Most of this clings to the bearing surfaces but a certain amount gets transferred into the combustion chamber and burned. (On very basic engines the oil is manually added to the fuel in the tank in a certain proportion.) Part of the reason this apparently primitive system works is that a 2-stroke's oil is always cold, whereas the 'permanent' oil in a 4-stroke can reach 100°C (212°F). It is also absolutely clean, which helps a lot.

This is technically known as a 'total loss' lubrication system.

Before we move on to the direct injection type of 2-stroke, let's clear up any possible confusion between EFI and DI. Electronic fuel injection is simply a more accurate method than using a carburettor to mix the fuel with the intake air before

entering the crankcase of a conventional 2-stroke. Direct injection is an entirely different system – as we shall shortly see.

One of the most common variations mentioned right at the beginning of this section is Schneurle porting. In this case, the transfer ports are much higher up

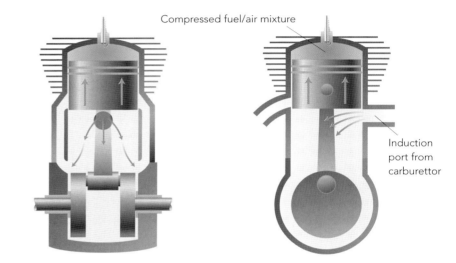

Compressed fuel/air mixture

Induction port from carburettor

(a) Induction and compression stroke showing crankcase induction

Side view

End view

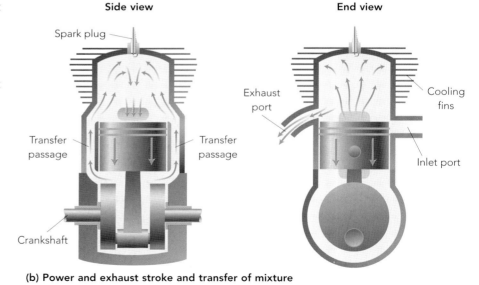

Spark plug

Transfer passage

Transfer passage

Crankshaft

Exhaust port

Cooling fins

Inlet port

(b) Power and exhaust stroke and transfer of mixture

Side view

End view

Above: A Schneurle-ported 2-stroke. Note the different position of the intake port and twin transfer passages.

and so feed fresh mixture into the cylinder above the exhaust gases. However, the basic principle remains the same: the whole engine is involved in the induction, compression, power and exhaust cycle and there is one power stroke per revolution.

DIRECT INJECTION

It may come as bit of an anticlimax to find that the direct injection 2-stroke works on exactly the same basic principle as its predecessor. The only real difference is that the fuel is not mixed with the intake air as it is drawn into the crankcase. Instead, it is injected directly into the combustion chamber just before the spark plug fires. However, this apparently minor difference changes everything.

For a start, by the time fuel is added at the top of the piston's compression stroke, the exhaust gases have all been expelled and the exhaust port is now completely closed off by the piston. So there is no loss of unburned fuel. That dramatically reduces the engine's fuel consumption and hydrocarbon emissions. Additionally, far less oil is needed to lubricate the bottom end bearings, as it is no longer diluted by petrol. Modern bearing materials and oil technology help to reduce it even further. The tiny amounts of oil that do make their way into the combustion chamber produce very little pollution.

Fuel consumption is further reduced because the electronically

Above: A direct injection 2-stroke, showing the fuel injector at the top of the combustion chamber.

controlled injectors can measure the required amount of fuel far more precisely than a carburettor or conventional electronic fuel injection (EFI). But to do so, they depend on a sophisticated, computer-controlled engine management system.

However, injecting fuel into the highly compressed air trapped in the combustion chamber when the piston is at the top of its stroke is far more difficult than simply mixing it into the airflow just before the intake valve. Not only does the fuel itself need to be highly pressurized, but the injector must be capable of standing up to the incredibly high temperatures in the combustion chamber.

So, direct injection drastically reduces those aspects where the conventional 2-stroke has always lost out, but the advanced

MAKING A CHOICE

So what are the basic pros and cons of these different technologies?

The four-stroke

Pros	Cons
• Smooth and quiet	• Larger and heavier and than the 2-stroke
• Good power to weight ratio	• More mechanically complex than the 2-stroke
• Available as petrol or diesel (except outboards)	• Maintenance costs can be steep, especially for outboards
• Economical	
• Long life if properly maintained	

The conventional 2-stroke

Pros	Cons
• Simplicity	• Suitable only for outboard motors
• Light weight	• Poor fuel consumption compared to the 4-stroke
• Good power to weight ratio	• Very dirty emissions
• Cheap to buy	• Consumes considerable amounts of oil
• Low maintenance costs	• Faster wear due to lack of a pressurized oil system
	• Not available new in USA and Europe

The direct injection 2-stroke

Pros	Cons
• Relatively simple compared to 4-stroke	• Suitable only for outboard motors
• Excellent power to weight ratio	• Not quite as smooth as 4-stroke at low rpm
• Fuel efficiency on par with 4-stroke	• Fewer makes and models available than 4-strokes
• Emissions on par with 4-stroke	• Faster wear than a 4-stroke due to lack of a pressurized oil system
• Consumes less oil than conventional 2-stroke	
• Reasonable maintenance costs	
• Wear rate less than a conventional 2-stroke	

The petrol engine

Pros	Cons
• Smooth and quiet	• Fuel is extremely flammable compared to diesel
• Lighter than equivalent diesel	• Electrical ignition system required
• More 'sporty' power delivery	

The diesel engine

Pros	Cons
• Fuel much less flammable than petrol	• More expensive to buy than equivalent petrol engine
• Robust and long lasting	• Generally heavier than equivalent petrol engine
• Very economical	• Generally more noise and vibrations than equivalent petrol engine
• No electrical ignition system	• Not suitable for outboard motors
• Modern diesels almost as powerful, smooth and quiet as petrols	• Modern diesels will not run without electronics to control the injection system

technology adds cost, thereby diminishing one of its historical advantages: reduced price.

CONCLUSION

Some people quite happily go through their entire boating lives without any idea of what goes on inside their engines – or even what type of engine they have. However, many boaters find this sort of background information useful as part of their general boating knowledge. And for the enthusiast

who wants to maintain their own engine, it's a good idea to know what's inside their engine before they start taking it apart.

Fuel systems

Motorboat fuel systems are generally more complex and require more attention than those on cars. The latter is partly due to the rather more arduous marine environment, partly due to more intermittent use and partly down to storage methods. Cars have just one engine and one fuel tank, connected to its filler by a single, fairly short pipe. Also, unless the vehicle is laid up or unused for an extensive period, it is replenished with fresh, clean fuel on a regular and frequent basis.

In contrast, a boat may have twin (or more) engines and multiple fuel tanks with quite complicated piping. Also, unlike most cars, it may not be used for several months at a time, particularly during the winter. This seasonal pattern also means that waterside fuel can have been standing for some time before it is sold. To make matters worse, small boats are often fuelled from jerry cans and other containers that may not be as clinically clean as desirable. The combined result is that the majority of so-called engine failures are caused by blockages or fuel contamination. Royal National Lifeboat Institution (RNLI) statistics show that the majority of their call-outs are to boats with engine problems and that most of these are fuel related.

OUTBOARD FUEL SYSTEMS

Outboards up to about 10hp usually have an integral fuel tank under the hood holding about two litres (0.5 gallons). The supply to the engine always runs through a filter that can be easily disassembled and cleaned. Problems with outboard fuel are usually caused by careless storage by the owner of their bulk supply.

Bigger motors take their fuel from external tanks. The red 25 litre (1.5 gallon) portable fuel tank is ubiquitous and often abused, spending its life in the bottom of the boat with water sloshing around it. Whenever possible, these tanks should be filled directly from a forecourt pump rather than a larger storage can.

The filler cap has a bleed screw to allow air to enter as petrol is consumed. If air can get in, so can other 'substances' – and the air will, in many cases, be very damp and laden with salt. Corroded or blocked bleed valves are a frequent cause of engine stoppages, and a remarkable number of 'won't start' problems are traced to the owner forgetting to open the thing in the first place!

The removable 'snap on' fuel line between the tank and the engine – normally fitted with a priming bulb to get fuel to the engine's own fuel pump following a tank change – is another source of problems. Damaged or dirt and salt contamination of the end fittings stops them sealing properly, resulting

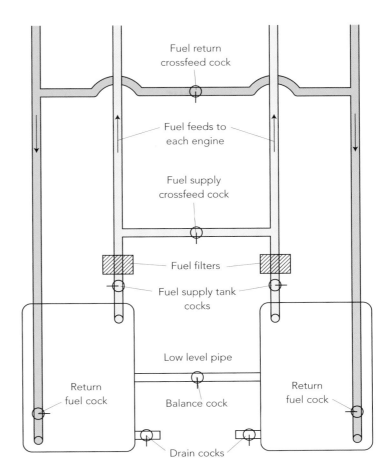

Above: A comprehensive twin engine/twin tank system capable of drawing and transferring fuel from either or both fuel tanks.

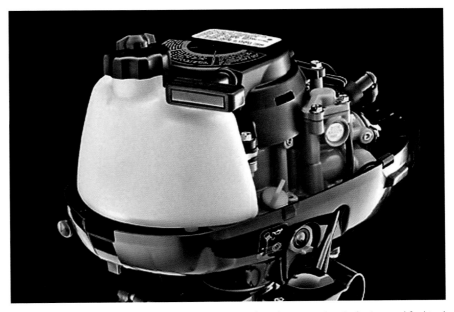

Above: The powerhead of a small outboard motor. The white container is the integral fuel tank.

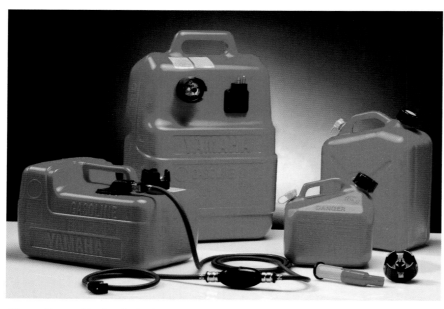

Above: External fuel tanks for larger outboards come in a variety of shapes and sizes. Note the fuel primer bulb in the fuel supply line in the foreground.

in fuel starvation, as the engine's pump obviously finds it much easier to suck in air than the much heavier fuel. The same goes for the slightest pin prick hole in the bulb or line itself.

On larger outboard-powered boats, the fuel tanks are usually built in and 'inboard' considerations apply.

If petrol is stored through the winter, it should be in an absolutely airtight container which is as full as possible to minimize the risk of internal condensation. Modern petrol has a limited shelf life, however, and it is best to arrange things so that you start with fresh fuel at the beginning of each season. And don't forget that in many countries, the amount of petrol you can legally store at home is limited.

INBOARD FUEL SYSTEMS

The same basic principles as above apply to inboard petrol and diesel fuel tanks. The fuel supply line to the engine(s) will be fitted with what's called a primary filter – see below for a typical example. These filters normally have a replaceable paper element to catch any fine dirt, and a bowl to separate out any water. The best bowls are transparent for easy visual inspection and have a drain tap to remove any water that settles out in the bottom. Frequent and careful attention to your primary fuel filter(s) will go a long way to ensuring trouble free operation. The engine itself may well be fitted with a super-fine secondary filter. Read the owner's manual to check.

Twin-engined boats usually have twin fuel tanks and these are sometimes interconnected. (See the diagram on page 83, top.) The very best have quite sophisticated systems that allow the transfer of fuel from one tank to another, and twin primary fuel filters so that one can be serviced without having to stop the engine. Your owner's manual will have full details.

All commercial vessel fuel tanks have what's known as a sump –

Above: A simple fuel filter, as fitted to many petrol-engined powerboats.

Above: A twin cartridge diesel fuel filter. The changeover valve allows one side to be serviced without having to stop the engine.

essentially a small bulge – at their lowest point. It is here that water and dirt will accumulate and be trapped when the boat is not being used. A cock in the bottom of the sump allows such contaminants to be drained off on a regular basis.

Not many leisure craft fuel tanks are fitted with sumps or even drain cocks, but some are. Unfortunately many owners are unaware of their existence. On boats that are not, but which are fitted with twin tanks with a low level 'balance' pipe between them, it is very worthwhile and usually quite a simple matter to remove the pipe and have a drain cock fitted.

CONCLUSION

Your boat's fuel system is it's potential Achilles heel. Modern carburettors and fuel injection systems just don't tolerate contaminated or dirty fuel. Your first

step should be to fuel up, whenever possible, from suppliers with a high level of turnover. Be particularly careful when off the beaten track. Boat fuel tanks are rarely spotlessly clean. Two stage – coarse then fine – filtration is the answer, but only if the filters are maintained properly.

Look after your fuel system: your engine expects nothing less.

Cooling systems

Unsurprisingly, all modern marine engines are water cooled. With unlimited access to cold water, it would be absurd if they were anything else. Cooling systems come in two types: direct and indirect. Outboards and some petrol sterndrives have direct cooling, whereas all diesel inboards and sterndrives are indirectly cooled.

INDIRECT COOLING

Let's take the car as a starting point. Technically, this is an 'indirect' cooling system. Water circulating around the engine removes heat, which in turn is removed from the water by air flowing through what is universally known as the radiator. In fact, 'air/water heat exchanger' is a far more accurate description, as most of the heat is dispersed through conduction with the air flowing across its fins – not through radiation.

An indirectly cooled marine engine works in a very similar fashion. As

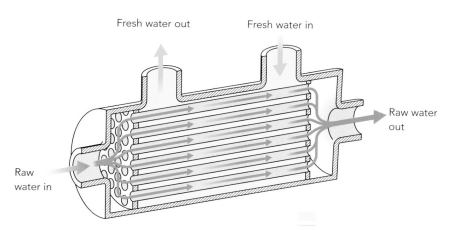

Fresh water out   Fresh water in

Raw water out

Raw water in

Above: A water-to-water heat exchanger that allows outside (or raw) water to remove heat from the engine's closed circuit cooling system.

with the car engine, a pump – which is an integral part of the engine – circulates water around the block and head and through a heat exchanger. However, in this case, the heat exchanger is a water/water device in which the tubes carrying the circulating water pass through a 'can' which has raw (outside) water flowing through it. The raw water is sucked in by a separate impeller pump, and when it has passed through the heat exchanger, dumped overboard again – usually via the exhaust system. See below for the general layout.

The big advantage with indirect cooling is that the inner cooling circuit is sealed just like a car's, so can contain antifreeze and anti-corrosion additives. Salt water only comes into contact with the heat exchanger, its associated piping and the exhaust system components. The latter are usually made of silicon tube and glass-reinforced plastic and are therefore corrosion proof. They are also much cheaper to replace than the complete engine.

All recreational diesel engines are indirectly cooled. This is due to the greater popularity of diesel fuel in Europe, where a much greater proportion of boating is done at sea compared with the USA. Petrol engines, especially those found on boats built in America, are often directly cooled.

DIRECT COOLING

Direct cooling is when the raw (outside) water is fed into what would otherwise be the sealed inner cooling circuit around the engine block and head. Once it has done its job, it is disposed of overboard – again via the exhaust. Direct cooling is clearly simpler, cheaper, and lighter than indirect, and is common on American marine petrol (gasoline) engines, as so much of their boating is done on inland lakes where corrosion is much less of a problem.

A big disadvantage is that coastal use involves salt water passing through the cooling passages of the engine itself. This can be partly alleviated on outboard and sterndrive-powered trailer boats by flushing the system through with fresh water after each trip. This is usually done by placing 'water headphones' over the water intakes in the leg and connecting to a hose. All directly cooled engines used in salt water should have replaceable, sacrificial anodes fitted, which are intended to corrode in place of the engine's cast iron parts. However, direct cooling and salt water really don't mix.

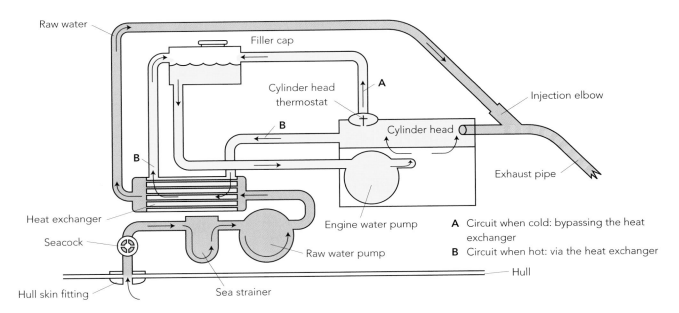

Above: A circuit diagram of a marine engine, with closed circuit cooling and water-to-water heat exchanger.

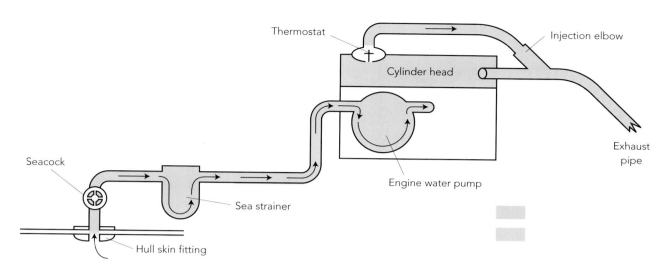

Above: The much simpler 'raw water' cooling system in which outside water flows directly through the engine's cooling passages.

Exhaust systems

The vast majority of recreational marine engines have what's known as 'wet' exhaust systems. The raw (outside) water that has been used to cool the engine is got rid of by squirting it into the exhaust pipe, just behind the exhaust manifold. The universal term for the bit that connects the cooling pipe to the exhaust is a 'water injection elbow' – largely because it is often a 90 degree fitting. However, it is no more than that; the word injection does not imply any extra activity in this case.

INBOARDS

This is not just a matter of convenience. Unlike that on a car, the exhaust system of an inboard-powered vessel runs inside rather than outside, so the water – even though it is fairly warm, having passed through the engine block or heat exchanger – helps to keep the pipes and silencer(s) reasonably cool. This is important as they often have to run in cramped spaces – frequently alongside cabins or other accommodation. The water also plays a silencing role. In boats with relatively small engines, this is often enough on its own, making additional silencers unnecessary.

However, planing motor cruisers with powerful engines usually have quite complicated exhaust systems incorporating 'water lift mufflers' or other silencing devices. Whole

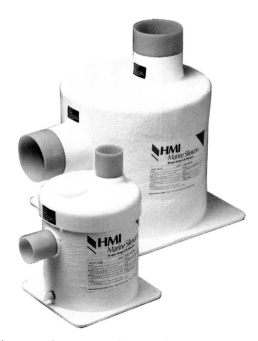

Above: Water lift silencers reduce noise and protect the engine against back flooding.

books have been written about marine exhaust systems, but the essential thing to grasp is that a boat's exhaust system is 'safety critical'. In other words, if it goes wrong you might sink!

The primary danger lies in one of the exhaust components springing a leak. If this happens, at least some of the raw cooling water from the engine will never make it back in to the ocean, but will gradually fill up the boat. By the time you notice that your boat is behaving a bit sluggishly and sitting lower in the water than usual, it can be too late.

The other danger posed by

Above: *Stainless steel exhaust riser. Raw water enters through the small tube and is sprayed into the exhaust pipe.*

exhaust leakage is carbon monoxide poisoning. This is particularly true of generators on bigger boats that run while people are asleep in the accommodation. CO poisoning is insidious and a number of people die each year because of it.

Wet exhausts are also potentially dangerous, because if water can get out, it can also – in certain conditions – get in. It is vitally important that the piping rises well above the waterline immediately after the engine. Often a component sensibly called a riser achieves this – and acts as the water injection point as well. The diagram below shows a boat with a low-set engine and badly designed exhaust in which the riser comes barely above the waterline. Water slopping up the exhaust pipe – perhaps when the boat is moored with its stern facing the waves – can run along the exhaust pipe, through the riser and

into the engine. That will mean replacing or rebuilding the engine. If it goes on for long enough the engine will overflow, and that will mean replacing the boat. The alternative to a solid riser is to loop the first part of the exhaust system upwards and fit the water injection elbow on the downward side.

STERNDRIVES

The first section of a sterndrive's exhaust is much like that on an inboard. Used cooling water is injected just after the exhaust manifold: inside the boat. The big rubber trunk that connects the engine's exhaust system to the transom shield (which then feeds it to the leg outside the boat) has a hard life and is prone to hardening and perishing. If it springs a leak, the water again ends up in the bilges, as with the inboard. This is one of the many good reasons why sterndrives and their associated

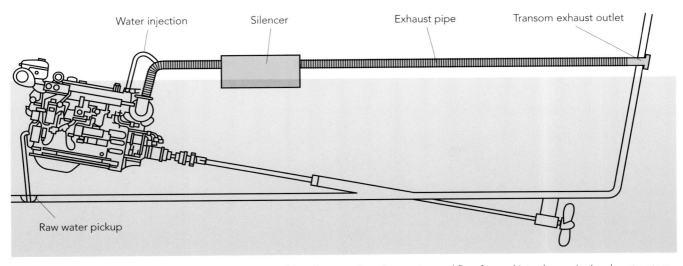

Water injection   Silencer   Exhaust pipe   Transom exhaust outlet

Raw water pickup

Above: *A poorly-designed wet exhaust system. Water could easily enter the exhaust pipe and flow forward into the engine's exhaust system.*

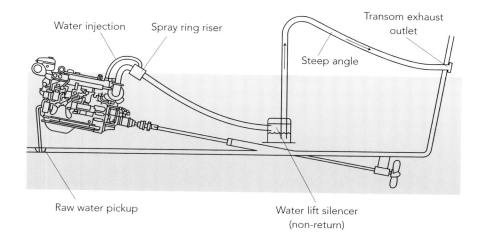

Water injection Spray ring riser

Transom exhaust outlet

Steep angle

Raw water pickup

Water lift silencer (non-return)

Left: A good exhaust installation with a 'non-return' waterlift muffler. Note the steep rise of the exhaust pipe from the transom forwards, making backflooding unlikely.

parts must be meticulously serviced in close accordance with the manufacturer's schedule.

Clearly, keeping your exhaust system in top condition is vitally important. Any suspicions that something might not be quite right should be investigated immediately, and a careful inspection should be part of your laying up schedule.

OUTBOARDS

Outboard exhaust systems are contained entirely within the leg and are very reliable. Lack of water due to a blockage of the cooling intake(s) will fry the powerhead long before the raised exhaust temperature causes problems lower down.

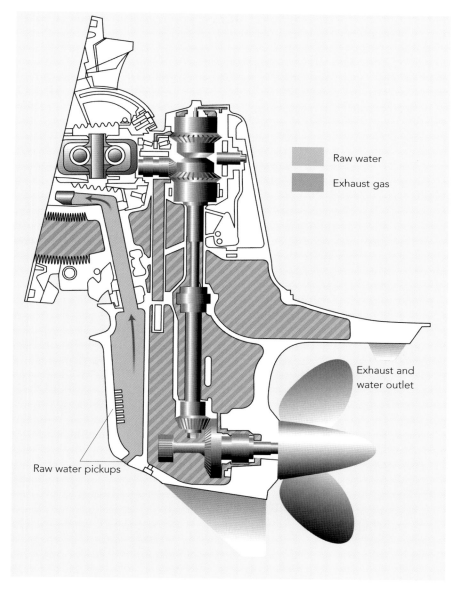

Raw water

Exhaust gas

Exhaust and water outlet

Raw water pickups

Left: A cutaway of a sterndrive leg, showing the internal workings, cooling water pickup and transfer pipe, along with the wet exhaust outlet above the propeller.

THE PROPELLER

The propeller is a key component on a powerboat, so it is important to know at least the basics regarding how it works and the best types available. Fortunately, however, you do not need exhaustive knowledge about propellers in order to enjoy your boating to the full. This is good news, as it would take a lifetime to read all the books written about propellers, how they work, and how best to optimize design and manufacture for a specific application.

When buying a new boat, you can be confident that the propeller is the right one for the boat – assuming you are going to use it in the way that the designer intended. For example, a high-powered sportsboat with an engine and prop optimized for 50 knots will not work as well on a slow speed fishing boat.

However, there are lots of boats running around with the wrong propeller – for a variety of reasons. The most common is that a previous owner has tried to second-guess the boat builder and fitted a different prop in search of increased performance, only to find himself going slower. In some cases, owners are blissfully unaware that their boat's performance and economy is below par, and there are an equal number who know it is but don't

realize that the propeller, not the engine, is the culprit.

This final component in the power train is almost as important as the engine itself for good performance, economy and long engine life. If the propeller is the wrong type, no amount of horsepower will help. That means that its diameter, pitch, number of blades and the size and shape of those blades must be correctly matched to the engine, the hull and what the boat is used for. Compare the shape of a tugboat propeller (below left), with that of an offshore raceboat prop (below right). Both are intended to handle the same horsepower. However, the former has a large diameter and fine pitch, being optimized for massive thrust at slow speed. The latter has a small diameter for minimum drag and a coarse pitch for high speed.

The theory

Essentially, a propeller pushes a boat forward because of the pressure differential between the front and rear faces of each blade. Surprisingly, it is the reduced pressure on the front that 'sucks' the propeller forward that does most of the work. This means that each blade is more like a rotating aeroplane wing than anything else, as aeroplanes are mostly held up by the reduction in pressure above their wings, not the slightly increased pressure beneath them.

A more scientific way of describing the process is that the pressure differential causes the water flowing through the prop to speed up, adding to its momentum. It is this increased momentum that results in a thrust force. If that concept tickles your fancy, your maths had better be up to scratch.

Above: *A five-bladed, high thrust propeller.*

Above: *A 'cleaver' type raceboat propeller.*

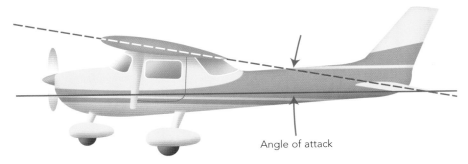

Above: *The angle of attack works in the same way for both boats and aeroplanes.*

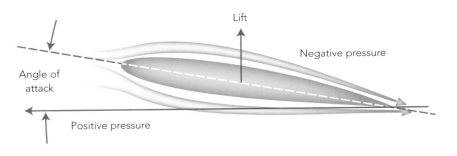

Above: *Propeller blades produce thrust in exactly the same way as an aircraft's wing produces lift.*

The angle at which an aeroplane wing meets the oncoming air, or a propeller blade meets the water, is called the angle of attack (see above). If an aeroplane is stationary the wing has no angle of attack and produces no lift. Theoretically, it could take off by going down the runway with its nose up at the desired angle of attack until sufficient speed is reached to produce the necessary lift. However, acceleration would be very slow due to excessive drag, and in any case, there is no way that the pilot can hold the nose up with the controls at low speed. So he keeps the plane level until enough speed has been gained for the airflow to produce enough lift. Then he raises the nose to increase the angle of attack – and

up he goes. You can watch this happen hundreds of times a day at any airport.

With a boat propeller, the process is slightly different. Because the blade angle is fixed, there is no way

of reducing the angle of attack at low speed. So acceleration is rather inefficient. The diagram below shows the instant of starting off. Power has been applied, the prop is rotating, but the boat has yet to move. The angle between the blade and the water (the angle of attack) is determined by the physical angle of the blade to its hub: in other words, its pitch.

As the boat picks up speed, the water comes more and more from ahead, reducing the angle of attack of the blades. This is partly offset by increased propeller rpm, but overall the angle of attack reduces during acceleration. If the throttles are left wide open, rpm and speed will obviously stabilize once full speed is reached.

At this point, our propeller blades should be operating at the angle of attack for which they were designed and transmitting the power from the engine(s) into the water as efficiently as possible.

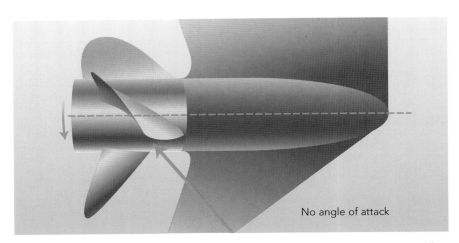

No angle of attack

Above: *At zero speed, angle of attack is determined by prop pitch, which is optimized for high speed. This means that acceleration is slow due to low efficiency.*

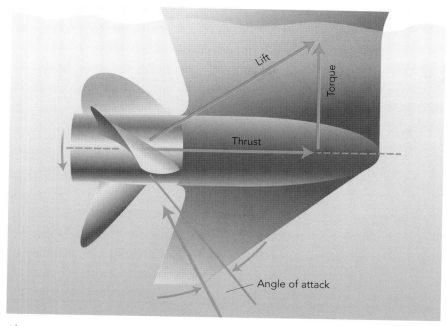

Above: At maximum speed, water inflow reduces the angle of attack to (hopefully) the design optimum. See also the relationship between blade force (lift), drag and forward thrust.

Prop, screw, or momentum modifier?

A slightly old-fashioned and salty word for propeller is 'screw' – and this is reasonably descriptive of how it works. The common wood or metal screw cuts its way through solid material without slipping – a boat propeller, like an aeroplane propeller, is working in a fluid. So a certain amount of slip is inevitable.

Actually, it is essential, but a subject beyond the scope of this book.

Before we consider how the blades act on the water to produce forward thrust, let's look at how props are measured and technically described.

The basic parameters are blade number and diameter – both self explanatory – plus pitch. You have probably guessed that pitch is

something to do with the angle of the blades to the hub and shaft, but may be surprised to find that it isn't measured in degrees but inches or millimetres. If we resurrect the wood screw analogy for a moment, the angle of the threads obviously dictate how quickly it will penetrate the material. So a wood screw that went in 5mm (⅕in) for every complete turn could be said to have a pitch of 5mm (⅕in). So, purely for measuring convenience, and so we can compare like with like, we assume that the water is solid and that there is no slip. So the basic measurements of a marine propeller are expressed as blade number, plus D inches x P inches. For example, 4-blade, 24in x 20in, or the metric equivalent, 610 mm x 508mm. The diagram below illustrates the principle.

The number and size of the blades depends very much on the size and shape of the boat, its maximum and cruising speeds, and its engine power. There are all sorts of computerized formulae available to help designers and

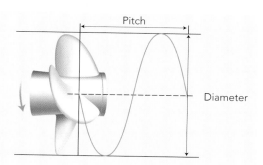

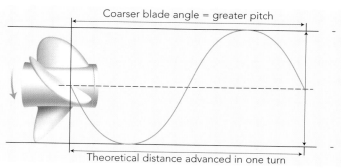

Above: The theoretical amount a propeller moves forward in one turn is called its 'advance' and is determined by blade pitch. The theoretical advance is never achieved in practice due to water slippage.

engineers, but getting it exactly right often requires an element of trial and error. Calculating the fluid flow around a propeller at any given time is enough to give even a powerful computer a headache.

Design and material

Most propellers fitted to inboard-powered craft are made of bronze – of which there are two basic types. Magnesium bronze is suitable for speeds up to 15 knots. Above that the added strength of nickel bronze is required. Nickel bronze is also more resistant to salt water corrosion, but is around 30 per cent more expensive. The image to the right shows a typical bronze propeller from a twin-engined motor cruiser.

Utility outboards often have cheap, plastic propellers, while bigger motors and all sterndrives

Left: A conventional, three-bladed bronze propeller.

use aluminium alloy or stainless steel. Aluminium propellers offer a good balance of performance and price but because the material is relatively soft, are easily damaged. Stainless steel propellers are

expensive but their thinner blades are more efficient, so are the norm in high performance boats. They are also less prone to damage. The photo below shows a standard aluminium propeller from a small outboard and a high performance stainless steel propeller. Note the large diameter hole in the centre of the latter, which is the 'through prop' exhaust outlet. See page 68 for more on outboards.

Propellers with individually replaceable blades are also available for outboards and sterndrives, as are special propellers in which the pitch can be altered by mechanical adjustment. This is useful if, for example, you want maximum speed one day and maximum thrust for heavy loads the next.

At the time of writing, carbon fibre composite propellers were just coming into the recreational

Above: Outboard or sterndrive propellers with 'thro-hub' exhausts.

Above: A stainless steel outboard or sterndrive propeller showing the exhaust passage between inner hub and outer ring.

Above: A multi-blade, high trust carbon fibre motor yacht propeller.

market. These are extremely efficient, totally resistant to corrosion, and it is reasonably easy to repair tip damage. They are also very expensive.

Twin counter-rotating props

Twin counter-rotating propellers are found only on sterndrives. They offer two basic advantages. Firstly, the counter-rotation eliminates torque steer on single-engined boats with manual (non-hydraulic) steering. Secondly, this is a way of increasing blade area without increasing diameter, and so is useful for powerful, high performance boats.

At the time of writing, only Volvo Penta's Duoprop, Mercury's Bravo III and Yamaha's TRP sterndrives used counter-rotating propellers. The word Duoprop is often used –

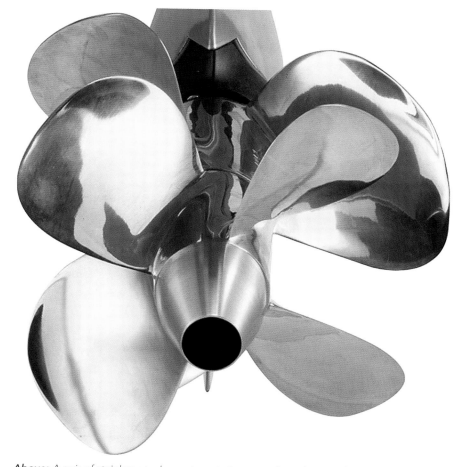

Above: A pair of stainless steel, counter-rotating propellers showing the exhaust outlet.

Above: Turning up the trailing edge of a propeller blade, as shown here, is known as 'cupping' and can improve high speed performance.

incorrectly – to describe all twin counter-rotating setups in the same way, much as ballpoint pens are called biros, when actually it is a registered product trademark.

High performance outboard propellers

Most outboard and sterndrive manufacturers offer a bewildering choice of expensive, high performance propeller options.

There are various modifications that can be made to the shape and profile of propeller blades to further tailor them for a specific job: for example, ultimate top speed at the expense of acceleration, or to correct some minor deficiency in hull design. Perhaps the most common is cupping, in which the trailing edge

of the blade is turned up slightly. This effectively increases the pitch at high rpm. At the other end of the spectrum are propellers designed to produce a much greater thrust when going backwards as they do when going forwards.

Blade design also affects bow-up trim on high performance boats, so the propeller must be carefully matched to the hull design and the boat's centre of gravity if maximum efficiency is to be realized. To fully describe such variations and their specific characteristics would fill the rest of this book. Reams of information are available from outboard manufacturers and 'third party' propeller specialists, and your friendly local dealer will be delighted to oblige with more help.

Propeller problems in practice

DAMAGE

If you experience poor performance and the engine is known to be in good health, the propeller is the prime suspect. The first thing to check for is physical damage. Even slightly bent or broken tips caused by grounding can have a drastic effect. If all is well, then it is likely that the boat, engine and propeller are not correctly matched.

INCORRECT PITCH OR DIAMETER

You can check for this quite simply. You only need to look in the engine handbook and find out how many revolutions per minute your engine should achieve at full power. (Technically, this is called 'maximum rated rpm'). Load the boat as you would on a normal day and do some high speed runs using full throttle. Watch the tachometers (rev counters) closely. Unless you have a very light, high performance boat, rpm will increase fairly slowly to start with, then come on with a rush until they approach the maximum. The last hundred or so revolutions will come up quite gradually, but in less than 30 seconds should settle down at that max rpm 'book' figure. In this case, your engine and prop are perfectly matched to your boat. Strictly speaking that sentence should include the caveat 'at that weight'. Running more heavily will pull the rpm and speed down; running more lightly will result in max rpm being reached earlier. However, unless you do either on a regular basis, you can relax.

It therefore follows that if max rated rpm is not reached even with the throttles wide open (WOT) you are either too heavy for the prop or the prop has too much pitch – known as being too coarse. So you need a 'finer' prop. And if max rpm comes up early and swings past the max before stabilizing a little over the book limit, you are either running lighter than the boat designer expected or your prop has insufficient pitch. In this case, a coarser prop would see you going a bit faster.

It is a good idea to carry out the above procedure during the sea

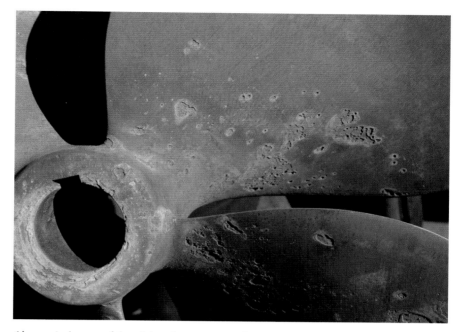

Above: A closeup of the pitting that can occur due to cavitation.

Above: Seven hundred and fifty horsepower on the back of an American 'muscle boat', courtesy of three Yamaha Vx250 2-stroke outboards.

trial of any boat you are considering buying. It only takes a few minutes and could save a lot of subsequent expense.

Bronze and aluminium propellers can be slightly altered by a specialist, but if the disparity is very great, then a new one is the only option. However, bear in mind that propellers are expensive.

If you own a fast outboard or a sterndrive powered craft and are tempted by the advertisements for 'souped up' props, consult your dealer or an acknowledged expert before buying. You don't want to be one of those people with a slow boat and an empty wallet.

Apart from incorrect pitch – or a combination of incorrect pitch and diameter – the most common propeller problems experienced in practice are ventilation and cavitation.

VENTILATION

Ventilation occurs when a propeller gets too close to the surface and starts to suck air into the low pressure area on the front of its blades. This most frequently occurs in twin outboard or sterndrive boats during sharp turns, especially when accelerating hard. (Inboard powered craft are not subject to ventilation for, I hope, obvious reasons).

The symptoms of ventilation are a decrease in thrust and an audible increase in rpm of the affected engine. The temporary solution is to either get the prop deeper down in the water by slackening the turn, or reducing power. If the problem is encountered frequently, the only choices are to drive the boat more gently or, in the case of outboard motors, fit a version with a longer leg. Although it is possible to extend sterndrive legs with special parts, the cost involved is rarely worthwhile.

CAVITATION

Cavitation is caused by the low pressure area on the front of the propeller blades falling to a level where the water actually boils. (The boiling point of water falls as pressure decreases. On top of Mount Everest it is 87°C /189°F, not the usual 100°C/212°F at sea level).

This boiling causes bubbles to form in the water which are very

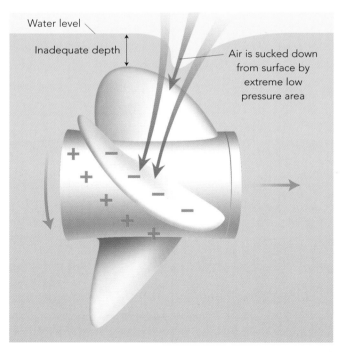

Above: *Ventilation occurs when a prop working hard at inadequate depth draws air down from the surface.*

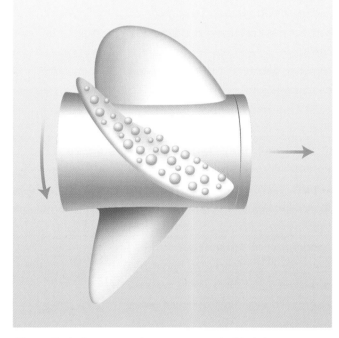

Above: *Cavitation occurs when pressure on the blade becomes so low that water boils in tiny bubbles that collapse with amazing force.*

Above: A tugboat propeller such as this has a large diameter and fine pitch, and is optimized for massive thrust at slow speed.

Above: Always keep your propeller protected with its cover when it is out of the water.

similar to those you see in a saucepan. As these move to higher pressure areas near the trailing edge and tip of the blade, they collapse with extraordinary force. Bronze and aluminium propellers can be eroded with thousands of tiny pits which eventually weaken the blades.

Cavitation does not hurt performance anything like as much as ventilation and can sometimes go completely unnoticed. The symptoms of cavitation are similar to medium frequency vibration from the rear of the boat under conditions of harsh acceleration. There are a number of possible cures, including fitting a prop with less pitch, more blades (to spread the load), or altering the blade shape. This is definitely a job for a propeller specialist.

The importance of the propeller

Your propeller is where the horsepower of your engine meets the water. It is a component often taken for granted and frequently abused. The right propeller – in good condition – is essential

regardless of whether performance, handling or economy is your priority. Unfortunately, there is a good deal of misinformation about propellers doing the rounds in the boating world. If you need advice, get it from an accredited and reputable expert, not a self-appointed one.

Above: A beautiful inboard-powered wooden motor launch.

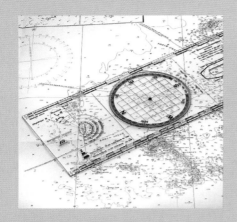

NAVIGATION AND PILOTAGE

Even in a world in which electronic chart plotters, radar and satellite navigation have become ordinary, so-called 'traditional' navigation has its place.

Navigation is not difficult. Many of the concepts and techniques are familiar to anyone who has walked, ridden or driven on land, and whilst few people nowadays rely exclusively on traditional methods, there are still plenty of situations in which 'trad-nav' is actually quicker and easier than doing the same job electronically. If nothing else, a basic knowledge of trad-nav helps make sense of navigators' jargon (explaining, for instance, the difference between course and track) and provides a useful back-up and cross-check for the electronics.

Direction

Direction is so important in navigation that we have several different words for it, each one referring to a different kind of direction:

- **Bearing** is the direction of one object from another.
- **Course** is the direction in which the vessel is being steered.
- **Heading** is the direction the vessel happens to be pointing in at any given moment.
- **Track angle** is the direction in which the vessel is actually moving: it is often abbreviated to **track**, and can also be known as **ground track**, **course made good**, or **course over ground**.
- **Water track** means the direction in which the vessel is moving through the water, and is sometimes called the **wake course**.

Most people are familiar with the concept of compass points, at least so far as the four cardinal points (north, south, east and west) are concerned. These, and the four 'half cardinal' and eight 'quarter cardinal' points are still widely used for giving approximate directions.

For most navigational purposes, however, they have been replaced by the three figure notation, in which directions are referred to as angles, measured clockwise from north.

COMPASSES

The instrument used to measure direction is called a compass. Although there are several technologies available, almost all the compasses used in small craft use the Earth's magnetic field as a reference. Some use a magnetized needle, bar or ring as a sensor, while others do the job electronically.

All magnetic compasses, however, are subject to two main errors:

- **Variation** is caused by the fact that the Earth's magnetic field is not perfectly lined up with its axis of spin. The effect varies from place to place and from time to time, but it is shown on navigational charts and reference books. At present around the UK it is generally less than five, and is slowly reducing.

- **Deviation** is caused by magnetic material on board the boat distorting the effect of the Earth's magnetic field, so it is different for every boat, and changes depending on the boat's heading. Deviation can usually be reduced to just a degree or so by a skilled compass adjuster, but it is still up to the skipper or navigator of the boat to ensure that it is kept to a minimum by keeping magnetic material (especially magnets) well away from the compass.

Both types of error can be allowed for by simple arithmetic, using the 'CadET Rule'. This is a reminder that to get from C (Compass) to T (True) you have to 'ad' (add) E (Easterly) errors.

So if your compass heading is 135, the deviation is 4 west and the variation is 3 west, then:

Above: *A typical ship's compass.*

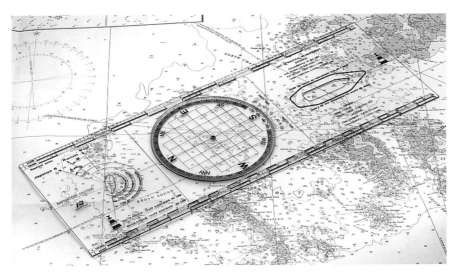

Above: A Breton-type plotter.

135	Compass heading (shown by the compass)
− 4	Westerly deviation subtracted
131	Magnetic heading
− 3	Westerly variation subtracted
128	True heading (needed for most navigation calculations)

If you have calculated that the course to steer is 257, with variation 3 west and deviation 6 east, then:

257	True course required
− 6	Easterly variation subtracted (because you are converting from true to compass)
251	Magnetic heading
+ 3	Westerly deviation added
254	Compass heading

No helmsman can steer a small boat accurate to one degree: it is better to round off the answer to the nearest five or even ten degrees.

DIRECTION ON A CHART

A marine chart is much more than just a map: it is also a worksheet and record of events, on which various navigation calculations are made, and the boat's position and movement are recorded. There are many different chartwork instruments available, but the most popular is commonly known as a 'Breton-type plotter'.

It consists of a transparent rectangular base, on which is mounted a circular protractor, graduated in degrees.

To measure the direction of a line:
Lay one edge of the plotter (or its centreline) along the line to be measured, and rotate the protractor until the grid on its face is lined up with the parallels and meridians on the chart.

Read off the direction from where the centreline of the plotter meets the edges of the protractor.

Over a period of about twenty years, the US government caused a revolution in navigation that was as important as anything since the invention of the compass – maybe more so.

The Global Positioning System (GPS) was originally intended, in 1973, to be a military navigation system, but it was so expensive that by the time it was declared fully operational in 1995, it had been decided that civilians could use it, too. And by that time, we

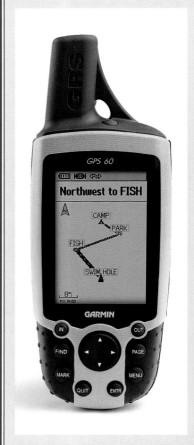

Above: A hand-held GPS.

GPS

already were. Thousands of small craft were using basic GPS receivers that cost only a few hundred pounds. Since then, the system has been made even more accurate, receivers have become much more sophisticated and prices have continued to fall.

GPS uses a constellation of a couple of dozen satellites, all orbiting about 20,000km (12,427 miles) above the Earth's surface, and all transmitting coded messages that say, in effect 'I am here' and 'the time is now'. A receiver can find out how far it is from each satellite by comparing the time at which the message was sent with the time at which it was received… and if it knows its distance from each of four satellites, and where those four satellites were at the time, it can work out where it is. Of course it is not quite that simple: there are all sorts of problems to be overcome, ranging from the mundane fact that no practical receiver can contain a clock that is perfectly accurate to the bizarre reality that the satellites are moving so fast that time itself is distorted.

However, the problems have been overcome, and GPS can now tell you where you are, at any time of the night or day and practically anywhere in the world, to an accuracy of about 5m (16ft).

To a receiver capable of performing the complex calculations required to calculate where it is from the GPS satellite signals, most navigational calculations are childishly simple, so even a cheap, hand-held receiver will tell you where you are, where you are going and how quickly, and where you are in relation to any of a number of stored positions (waypoints).

More sophisticated devices, usually called 'chart plotters' can do all that, but display your position and planned route on an electronic map.

Marine chart plotters were, in some ways, the fore-runners of in-car navigation systems, but they almost invariably have much bigger screens in order to display the much more sophisticated maps (charts) required for navigation at sea.

If you are planning on buying a GPS

Above: GPS systems make use of a network of satellites orbiting the Earth.

system, the range now available is quite staggering. As always, consult your local dealer for the best advice.

Above: A more sophisticated chart plotter can display your position on a map.

To draw a line in a particular direction:

Rotate the protractor so that the required direction is lined up with the centreline marked on the base plate.

Place the whole thing on the chart, with one of its edges touching the starting point of the line, and adjust its position until the protractor grid lines are parallel with the parallels and meridians on the chart.

It is easier to keep the baseplate in the right place if you stick the point of a pencil or dividers into the starting point and rest the baseplate against it.

Distance

Distance, at sea, is usually measured in **sea miles**. A sea mile is defined as a minute of latitude (a sixtieth of a degree) measured at the Earth's surface. This is very convenient in

some respects: in particular, it means that the latitude scale on the side of a navigational chart serves as a scale of distances.

Unfortunately, the Earth is not a perfect sphere, so a sea mile varies slightly in length, from place to place. A **nautical mile** is a standard measurement of 1,872m (6,141ft), approximately equal to the average length of a sea mile. For most practical purposes, a nautical mile and a sea mile can be treated as equal.

LOGS AND SPEEDOS

The device used to measure the distance a boat has travelled is known as a log. Most logs work by counting the revolutions of a paddlewheel or spinner which protrudes through the boat's hull, though some older versions count the revolutions of a spinner towed astern. In either case, it is important

to appreciate that they are really measuring the water flow past the boat, rather than the boat's movement over the ground.

Through-hull logs, in particular, are subject to a variety of errors, and should be calibrated according to the manufacturer's instructions before they are relied upon. They may also become fouled by weed or debris: again, the manufacturer's instructions should be consulted.

DISTANCE ON A CHART

Navigation dividers are similar to those used in technical drawing, but they are generally more robust, and have blunt points to reduce the damage to the chart. 'Single-handed dividers' have a distinct, semicircular bend in each leg that allows them to be opened and closed with one hand. Squeezing the two semicircles together between your thumb and first and

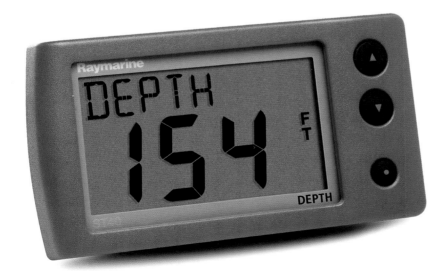

Above: A log measures the distance a boat has travelled and can also gauge depth.

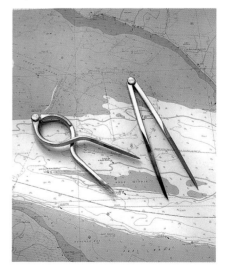

Above: Single-handed dividers (left) and standard navigation dividers (right).

second fingers makes the legs cross, and moves the points further apart, while squeezing the straight part of the legs moves them closer together.

Position

On land, you could describe the position of something by referring to a fixed landmark, as in 'Buxton is about twenty miles southeast of Manchester'.

At sea, you could say 'Seven Stones light vessel is fourteen miles west of Lands End'. For greater precision, of course, you can give direction in terms of degrees and use fractions of a mile: 'The fairway buoy is 236 degrees, 2.7 miles from the lighthouse.'

LATITUDE AND LONGITUDE

Alternatively, on land, you could describe the position of something by referring to its 'grid reference' on a map or road atlas: 'Buxton is on page 52, C6'. Of course, this only works if the person you are talking to is using the same map, so for marine navigation we use an international reference system known as latitude and longitude, based on natural reference points rather than on an arbitrary grid.

Our world is a ball of rock, spinning through space. The ends of its axis of spin are called the north and south poles. Midway between them, around the fattest part of the Earth, is an imaginary line called the equator.

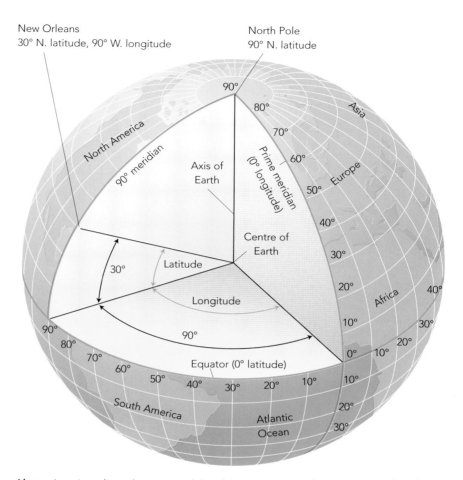

Above: *Imaginary lines drawn around the globe give us the reference points referred to as latitude (horizontal lines) and longitude (vertical lines).*

The **latitude** of a place is its distance from the equator, expressed as an angle measured in degrees at the centre of the Earth. Falmouth, for instance, is fifty degrees north of the equator.

There is no obvious starting point from which to base our east–west measurement, but by international agreement the reference line is one that passes through Greenwich, in southeast London. It is called the 'prime meridian'

The **longitude** of a place is the angle between the prime meridian and the meridian passing through the place.

Position is given by combining latitude and longitude: Falmouth, for instance, is fifty degrees north of the equator and five degrees west of the prime meridian: 50N 005W.

For greater precision, degrees can be subdivided into sixtieths, called minutes. Each minute can be further subdivided into sixtieths, called seconds or (more often) into tenths, hundredths, and thousandths. Black Rock Beacon, for instance, is at 50 08.'71N 00501.'99W.

When specifying a position, latitude and longitude must always be used together, with latitude

Above: *Coastal navigation charts are based on Mercator projection, which distorts areas and distances, to some extent, but not directions.*

given first. Their directions (north or south, and east or west, must always be included.)

Charts (marine maps) usually have a grid of horizontal and vertical lines. The vertical lines represent meridians, stretching from pole to pole. The horizontal lines represent parallels of latitude, parallel to the equator.

Charts

Charts are marine maps. Like land maps, they appear to be a 'bird's eye view' or 'satellite picture' of the Earth's surface. It is better, though, to visualize them

as diagrams of how the Earth would look if it were possible to flatten it out.

Flattening a spherical shape such as the Earth inevitably involves some element of distortion. Which types of distortion are acceptable and which are not depends on the use for which the map or chart is intended. Charts used for coastal navigation are almost always based on Mercator projection, in which areas are distorted, but directions are not. Distances are distorted to some extent, but over the area covered by most charts, the distortion is minimal.

SCALE

The scale of a chart refers to the relationship between a distance in the real world and the corresponding distance on the chart, and is usually expressed as a ratio. For instance, if a distance of one mile (1,852m) is represented by 25mm on the chart, the chart scale is 0.025/1852, or approximately 1:75,000.

1:75,000 is a fairly typical scale for coastal navigation. For greater detail of small areas, a larger scale may be used: harbour plans, for instance, may be at a scale of 1:6250 scale (1 mile = 296mm), while for a broad overview of a large area, a smaller scale such as 1:500,000 may be used.

Few charts have a separate 'scale' for measuring distance, but remember that on any normal navigational chart, the latitude markings on the side of a chart are its scale of distance.

SYMBOLS AND ABBREVIATIONS

Landmarks such as chimneys, churches and lighthouses are often far more important than their scaled-down size on a chart would suggest, while most buoys and beacons would disappear altogether if they were reduced to suit the scale of a chart. To overcome this problem, important features are represented by symbols. Different publishers use different symbols, but as a general rule, most important landmarks are represented by a diagrammatic drawing of the object, with a circle representing its precise position. Two notable exceptions are churches (often represented by Maltese crosses) and lighthouses (often represented as stars).

UPDATING CHARTS

Sandbanks shift, buildings are built and demolished, and buoys are added, moved, or taken away, so charts can go out of date even before they are published. To give them a reasonable working life, chart publishers produce corrections that detail such changes at regular intervals. In the UK, the definitive source for these updates are Admiralty Notices to Mariners, published every week by the UK Hydrographic Office, and most readily available from the UKHO website (www.ukho.gov.uk). Each notice gives simple instructions about how to update a chart.

Where am I?

Although navigation is mainly concerned with knowing where you are going, knowing where you **are** is known as fixing your position or 'getting a fix' and is an important first step. Although most navigators nowadays rely on GPS (the Global Positioning System) for this, traditional navigation offers several good alternatives.

A SINGLE POINT FIX

The simplest technique is known as the **single point fix** or **landmark fix**. It involves passing close to a fixed

and clearly identifiable object, such as a buoy or beacon, so it is particularly useful at the very start of a passage, when you are likely to be passing close to a harbour wall, or to a pile or beacon marking a channel. Buoys are not quite as good, because they move around, though not, usually, by enough to make a significant difference.

A single-point fix is good so long as it meets three conditions:

- You must be able to positively identify the object;
- The object must be clearly shown on the chart;
- You must pass close enough to it for the difference between the boat's position and the object's position to be of no practical significance.

The conventional chartwork symbol for a fix is a spot representing the boat's position, surrounded by a circle, and labelled with the time.

POSITION LINES

A more sophisticated but rather more useful kind of fix depends on a concept known as 'position lines'. The idea is simple enough. Suppose, for instance, that you see a fort directly south of you. You could represent your line of sight as a pencil line on the chart, drawn in a north–south direction, and passing through the symbol that represents the lighthouse. Your position, of course, must be somewhere along your line of sight.

If, at the same time, you looked west and saw a church, you would

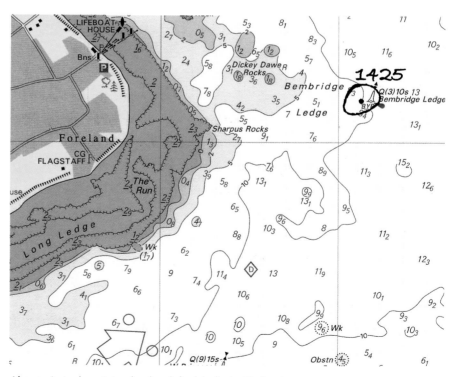

Above: A single point or landmark fix, labelled with the time.

be able to draw an east–west line representing your line of sight to the church. The only place that is on both lines at once is where they cross, so that must be your position.

Of course, your lines of sight, or position lines, do not have to lie exactly east–west or north–south: we can measure any direction, reasonably accurately, with a hand bearing compass. In practice, though, it is normal to take three position lines, rather than just two, because then each position line serves as a check on the other two, and the size of the triangle they form where they meet gives a good idea of the accuracy of the final fix.

Nor do position lines have to be found by measuring direction: you can get a very good position line by noticing that two objects are in line with each other, and drawing a single line that passes through both of them – called a transit.

You can also get a position line by using radar to measure a distance. Suppose, for instance, that you are three miles from a headland. Your position line, in this case, is a circle, with a radius of three miles, with the headland at its centre.

Tides

All this business of position fixing would be almost irrelevant if only boats moved in the direction they were pointing. If only that were true, you could set off from Poole, for instance, and steer 190 for 72 miles, and expect to arrive at Cherbourg. Unfortunately it doesn't work that way! All sorts of things conspire against you: very few helmsmen can steer more accurately than give or take five degrees, and the wind may push the boat sideways.

However, by far the biggest factor is that the water itself is seldom still. All around the Earth, huge volumes

of water are sloshing around the oceans, pulled this way and that by the gravitational effects of the sun and moon. In some places, the effects are barely noticeable: in the Virgin Isles, for instance, sea level rises and falls by only about 0.5m (19 in). But around the Atlantic coast of Europe, much bigger tides are common, and around parts of the Channel Islands the tidal rise and fall can be as much as 12m (39ft).

As navigators, we are concerned with both the horizontal and vertical effects of tide. The horizontal effects because they have to be allowed for if we are going to find our intended destination, and the vertical effects because they will determine what we find when we get there, and what hazards we need to avoid along the way. A rock that is plainly visible at low tide may become a dangerous hazard when it is

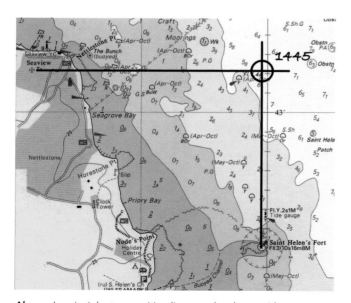

Above: In principle, two position lines can be drawn with a compass.

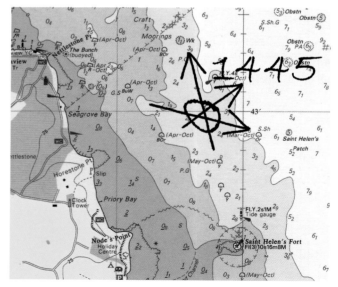

Above: In practice, three position lines give a better fix.

covered by the rising tide, for instance, only to become perfectly innocuous again if the water level rises so far that we can safely pass straight over it.

TIDE TABLES

The times and heights of high and low water vary from place to place and from day to day, but as they are caused by the gravity of the sun and moon, they are quite predictable. This means that details can be published months or even years in advance in the form of tide tables, and on websites, or they can be calculated by economical computer programmes.

In principle, a tide table is rather like a bus timetable: it shows you when each high water and low water is going to arrive at the place concerned. Unlike a bus timetable, it also tells you the height of tide – meaning the height of the sea surface above a level known as **chart datum**.

Depths shown on charts are measured below chart datum, which is meant to be the lowest level to which the tide will ever fall. So the charts and tide tables complement each other very well:

- You will always have more water than is shown on the chart.
- Working out the actual depth at any spot is a simple matter of adding the height of tide to the charted depth.

The only time you should have to deal with subtracting is when you are looking at an area which dries out at low tide, but is covered at high tide, in which case you can think of it as having 'negative depth'.

Things are a little more complicated when it comes to working out the height of tide for times in between high and low water, or for minor ports for which you do not have tide tables.

TIDE CURVES

The tide does not rise or fall at a constant rate. In general, at low water, it starts rising quite slowly for the first hour, then speeds up over the next couple of hours to reach a maximum rate of change at about three hours after low water. Then it starts slowing down again, until it

---

TIME ZONE (UT) — For Summer Time add ONE hour in **non-shaded** areas

PLYMOUTH   LAT 50°22'N   LONG 4°11'W — TIMES AND HEIGHTS OF HIGH AND LOW WATERS

Dates in red are SPRINGS · Dates in Blue are NEAPS

YEAR 2008

MAY

Day	Time m	Time m	Time m	Time m
1 TH	0122 4.5	0757 1.7	1418 4.5	2027 1.8
2 F	0236 4.8	0900 1.4	1515 4.8	2127 1.4
3 SA	0334 5.0	0955 1.0	1604 5.0	2220 1.0
4 SU	0425 5.3	1046 0.8	1653 5.3	2310 0.7
5 M	0515 5.0	1134 1.7	1739 5.5	●2356 0.6
6 TU	0604 5.5	1219 0.5	1825 5.6	
7 W	0041 0.5	0651 5.5	1304 0.6	1909 5.6
8 TH	0126 0.6	0739 5.4	1347 0.8	1953 5.5
9 F	0210 0.8	0827 5.1	1431 1.1	2038 5.3
10 SA	0257 1.1	0918 4.9	1518 1.4	2126 5.0
11 SU	0349 1.4	1016 4.6	1612 1.9	2224 4.8
12 M	0450 1.8	1125 4.4	1715 2.0	◐2339 4.6
13 TU	0603 1.9	1237 4.3	1831 2.1	
14 W	0055 4.5	0720 1.8	1320 4.4	1945 1.9
15 TH	0159 4.6	0825 1.6	1437 4.6	2047 1.7
16 F	0245 4.8	0918 1.4	1525 4.7	2139 1.5
17 SA	0341 4.9	1005 1.3	1607 4.9	2224 1.3
18 SU	0424 5.0	1046 1.2	1645 5.0	2304 1.2
19 M	0502 5.0	1124 1.1	1720 5.1	2341 1.1
20 TU	0539 5.0	1158 1.7	1418 1.7 ○	
21 W	0015 1.1	0613 5.0	1230 1.2	1827 5.2
22 TH	0046 1.2	0648 5.0	1259 1.3	1900 5.1
23 F	0115 1.3	0722 5.0	1327 1.4	1932 5.1
24 SA	0145 1.4	0756 4.7	1356 1.6	2004 4.9
25 SU	0217 1.5	0832 4.6	1429 1.7	2039 4.8
26 M	0255 1.7	0912 4.5	1510 1.9	2121 4.7
27 TU	0344 1.8	1001 4.4	1603 2.0	2214 4.6
28 W	0447 1.9	1100 4.3	1713 2.0	◑2316 4.6
29 TH	0600 1.8	1208 4.4	1830 2.0	
30 F	0027 4.6	0710 1.7	1319 4.5	1941 1.7
31 SA	0142 4.5	0817 1.5	1427 4.7	2048 1.5

JUNE

Day	Time m	Time m	Time m	Time m
1 SU	0252 4.9	0919 1.2	1527 5.0	2148 1.2
2 M	0354 5.1	1016 1.0	1623 5.2	2244 1.0
3 TU	0451 5.2	1110 0.9	1716 5.4	●2337 0.8
4 W	0456 5.3	1201 0.8	1807 5.5	
5 TH	0028 0.7	0638 5.3	1251 0.8	1856 5.5
6 F	0118 0.7	0731 5.3	1339 0.8	1945 5.5
7 SA	0206 0.7	0823 5.1	1426 1.0	2033 5.4
8 SU	0254 0.9	0914 5.0	1513 1.2	2121 5.1
9 M	0342 1.1	1005 4.8	1600 1.4	2210 5.0
10 TU	0431 1.4	1057 4.6	1649 1.7	◑2303 4.8
11 W	0542 1.6	1152 4.5	1743 1.9	
12 TH	0002 4.6	0620 1.8	1248 4.4	1843 2.0
13 F	0103 4.5	0722 1.9	1343 4.4	1948 2.0
14 SA	0202 4.5	0824 1.8	1435 4.5	2049 1.9
15 SU	0257 4.6	0919 1.7	1525 4.7	2143 1.7
16 M	0347 4.7	1008 1.6	1610 4.9	2231 1.6
17 TU	0433 4.8	1051 1.5	1653 5.0	2313 1.4
18 W	0515 4.8	1130 1.4	1732 5.1	○2352 1.4
19 TH	0556 4.9	1207 1.4	1811 5.1	
20 F	0028 1.3	0635 4.9	1242 1.4	1847 5.1
21 SA	0103 1.3	0713 4.8	1317 1.4	1923 5.1
22 SU	0138 1.3	0750 4.8	1350 1.4	1956 5.0
23 M	0213 1.3	0826 4.7	1425 1.5	2031 5.0
24 TU	0249 1.4	0902 4.7	1502 1.5	2108 4.9
25 W	0329 1.5	0943 4.6	1544 1.6	2152 4.9
26 TH	0415 1.5	1031 4.5	1635 1.7	◑2244 4.8
27 F	0511 1.6	1128 4.5	1738 1.8	2344 4.7
28 SA	0620 1.7	1234 4.5	1855 1.8	
29 SU	0100 4.6	0735 1.7	1348 4.6	2012 1.7
30 M	0220 4.7	0848 1.5	1459 4.8	2124 1.5

JULY

Day	Time m	Time m	Time m	Time m
1 TU	0333 4.9	0955 1.3	1603 5.1	2228 1.2
2 W	0437 5.0	1056 1.1	1701 5.3	2326 0.9
3 TH	0535 5.1	1151 0.9	1755 5.5	●
4 F	0020 0.7	0630 5.2	1243 0.8	1846 5.5
5 SA	0111 0.6	0723 5.2	1331 0.7	1935 5.6
6 SU	0158 0.6	0812 5.2	1415 0.8	2021 5.5
7 M	0241 0.7	0857 5.1	1457 0.9	2102 5.3
8 TU	0322 0.9	0937 4.9	1536 1.1	2140 5.1
9 W	0401 1.2	1014 4.8	1614 1.4	2214 4.9
10 TH	0446 1.5	1050 4.6	1655 1.7	◑2251 4.6
11 F	0522 1.8	1152 4.5	1743 2.0	2339 4.4
12 SA	0613 2.0	1230 4.3	1842 2.2	
13 SU	0048 4.5	0715 2.2	1340 4.3	1950 2.2
14 M	0209 4.5	0824 2.1	1446 4.4	2100 2.1
15 TU	0304 4.6	0929 1.8	1542 4.7	2200 1.8
16 W	0410 4.6	1023 1.7	1630 4.9	2250 1.6
17 TH	0457 4.7	1109 1.5	1714 5.0	2334 1.4
18 F	0540 4.9	1150 1.4	1755 5.1	○
19 SA	0014 1.2	0621 4.9	1229 1.3	1834 5.2
20 SU	0051 1.1	0701 4.9	1306 1.2	1911 5.2
21 M	0127 1.1	0738 4.9	1340 1.2	1946 5.2
22 TU	0201 1.0	0813 4.9	1413 1.2	2019 5.2
23 W	0234 1.1	0846 4.9	1446 1.2	2053 5.1
24 TH	0308 1.2	0922 4.8	1522 1.3	2131 5.0
25 F	0346 1.3	1002 4.7	1604 1.5	◑2216 4.8
26 SA	0433 1.6	1054 4.6	1658 1.8	2314 4.6
27 SU	0535 1.8	1200 4.5	1814 2.0	
28 M	0032 4.5	0701 2.0	1323 4.5	1950 2.0
29 TU	0204 4.5	0832 1.9	1445 4.7	2114 1.7
30 W	0326 4.6	0947 1.6	1554 5.0	2223 1.3
31 TH	0432 4.9	1050 1.2	1653 5.3	2320 0.9

AUGUST

Day	Time m	Time m	Time m	Time m
1 F	0529 5.1	1143 0.9	1745 5.5	
2 SA	0011 0.6	0620 5.2	1232 0.6	1832 5.6
3 SU	0058 0.4	0707 5.3	1315 0.5	1917 5.6
4 M	0140 0.5	0749 5.3	1355 0.6	1957 5.6
5 TU	0218 0.5	0826 5.2	1431 0.7	2030 5.4
6 W	0252 0.8	0856 5.1	1503 1.0	2058 5.2
7 TH	0323 1.1	0922 4.9	1537 1.3	2125 4.9
8 F	0352 1.5	0950 4.7	1605 1.7	◐2155 4.7
9 SA	0423 1.9	1025 4.5	1644 2.1	2236 4.4
10 SU	0508 2.2	1116 4.3	1744 2.4	2334 4.1
11 M	0617 2.4	1234 4.2	1901 2.5	
12 TU	0116 4.0	0736 2.4	1413 4.3	2022 2.3
13 W	0252 4.2	0855 2.2	1519 4.6	2135 2.0
14 TH	0350 4.5	0959 1.9	1610 4.8	2229 1.6
15 F	0437 4.7	1048 1.5	1653 5.1	2313 1.3
16 SA	0520 4.9	1131 1.3	1735 5.2	○2354 1.1
17 SU	0601 5.0	1210 1.1	1814 5.3	
18 M	0031 0.9	0640 5.1	1247 0.9	1851 5.4
19 TU	0107 0.8	0717 5.2	1321 0.9	1927 5.4
20 W	0141 0.8	0751 5.2	1354 0.9	2001 5.4
21 TH	0213 0.9	0824 5.1	1426 1.0	2035 5.3
22 F	0245 1.0	0858 5.0	1500 1.2	2111 5.1
23 SA	0321 1.3	0937 4.9	1539 1.5	◑2154 4.8
24 SU	0404 1.7	1027 4.6	1632 1.9	2253 4.5
25 M	0505 2.0	1137 4.4	1753 2.2	
26 TU	0021 4.3	0645 2.3	1313 4.4	1949 2.2
27 W	0207 4.3	0833 2.1	1443 4.6	2116 1.8
28 TH	0330 4.6	0946 1.6	1551 5.0	2218 1.3
29 F	0430 4.9	1041 1.2	1644 5.3	2309 0.8
30 SA	0518 5.2	1129 0.8	1730 5.5	2354 0.5
31 SU	0602 5.3	1212 0.5	1812 5.6	

Above: Tide tables show the times and heights of high and low water and can be published months or even years in advance.

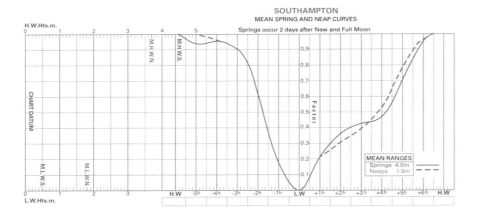

Above: Tidal curve predictions.

9.1.7 ST MARY'S
Isles of Scilly 49°55'·14N 06°18'·71W ✹✹✹✷✷✷
CHARTS AC *34, 883, 5603.10-11*; Imray C7; Stanfords 2; OS 203
TIDES –0630 Dover; ML 3·2; Duration 0600
Standard Port PLYMOUTH (→)

Times				Height (metres)			
High Water		Low Water		MHWS	MHWN	MLWN	MLWS
0000	0600	0000	0600	5·5	4·4	2·2	0·8
1200	1800	1200	1800				
Differences ST MARY'S							
–0035	–0100	–0040	–0025	+0·2	–0·1	–0·2	–0·1

Above: A tidal difference table.

9.1.8 NEWLYN
Cornwall 50°06'·19N 05°32'·58W ✹✹✷✷✷
CHARTS AC *777, 2345, 5603.7*; Imray C7, 2400.10; Stan 2; OS 203
TIDES –0635 Dover; ML 3·2; Duration 0555
Standard Port PLYMOUTH (→)

Times				Height (metres)			
High Water		Low Water		MHWS	MHWN	MLWN	MLWS
0000	0600	0000	0600	5·5	4·4	2·2	0·8
1200	1800	1200	1800				
Differences NEWLYN							
–0040	–0110	–0035	–0025	+0·1	0·0	–0·2	0·0

stops rising altogether at high water, before following a similar slow–fast–slow pattern as it falls.

As a rule of thumb, you can say that the tide:

- rises **one** twelfth of its range in the **first** hour after low water;
- rises **two** twelfths of its range in the **second** hour after low water;
- rises **three** twelfths of its range in the **third** hour after low water;
- rises **three** twelfths of its range in the **fourth** hour after low water;
- rises **two** twelfths of its range in the **fifth** hour after low water;
- rises **one** twelfth of its range in the **sixth** hour after low water.

Then it reaches high water, and follows the same 1–2–3–3–2–1 pattern as it falls.

In some places, though, particularly where islands or narrow entrances obstruct the free flow of the tide, the pattern is distorted, so the tide tables include graphs to show the water level changes, hour by hour.

TIDAL DIFFERENCE TABLES
Full tide tables are not published for ever single port and harbour. For many minor ports, we have to use difference tables. Again, these are very much like bus timetables where instead of listing the time for every stop along the route, it lists only the most important ones, with a note to the effect that the bus arrives at Little Hamden seven minutes after leaving Great Hamden.

TIDAL STREAMS
Whether the tide rising and falling causes tidal streams or whether tidal streams make the water level rise and fall is a bit of an academic question: the simple fact is that they go together. So if the tide outside a harbour was flowing eastwards an hour after high water today, you would expect it to be flowing eastwards an hour after high water tomorrow, and the day after, and so on. But you would also expect that it would flow faster when there was a low low water and a high high water, and less quickly when the range is less, and you would be right – that is exactly the principle on which tidal stream predictions are based.

Published either as tables or as chartlets, tidal stream predictions show the direction and speed of the tidal stream at each hour of the tidal cycle, referred to the time of high water at a major port nearby.

ALLOWING FOR TIDAL STREAMS
There are two ways you can allow for tidal streams – either before they have affected you, or afterwards.

The 'afterwards' method is a classic navigation technique known as 'estimated position.'

You start from your last known position (a fix, see page 107), and from that draw a line representing

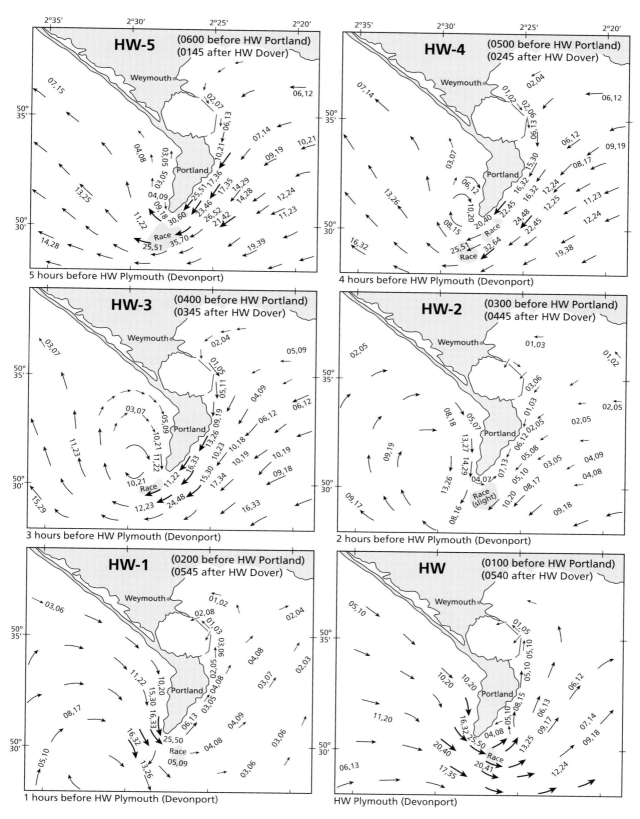

Above: *Tidal stream predictions.*

the direction the boat has moved through the water. Then, you measure the distance you have travelled from the fix, and mark that. It's called your DR or 'ded reckoning'. Nowadays, it's almost always mis-spelled as 'dead reckoning' – but it comes from the word 'deduced' rather than having anything to do with being dead accurate!

Now imagine that you are cruising in company with a boat that is capable of infinite speed, that covers exactly the same distance instantaneously, but then has to stop to wait for you to catch up. They would have arrived at the spot marked as a DR position, but then drifted with the tide. You could draw their movement in as a line from your DR, in the direction of the tide, and with a length corresponding to the distance they have drifted in the time you have been travelling. The end of that line represents where they should have got to.

And as you have travelled in the same direction as they have, for the same distance, and been subject to the same tidal stream, you should both have ended up in the same place. This is called your estimated position (EP).

The EP is all very well, but it is a bit silly to allow tidal streams to push us in a direction we don't necessarily want to go. So there is a better way. It's quicker and easier, and it doesn't involve trying to draw on charts while the boat is bouncing about. It does involve a bit of arithmetic, however, and it's not easy to see why it works, although work it does.

Start by drawing a line on the chart from where you are to where you want to go, and write down the direction.

Then, work out the average of the tidal streams that are going to affect you – so if you think you will be going for three hours, add up the total tidal stream and divide by three to find the average rate.

If the tidal stream is behind you or in front of you, you don't need to allow anything: just steer the boat in the direction of the line.

If the tidal stream is across you, then multiply the speed of the average tidal stream by sixty, and divide by your boat speed. The answer is the number of degrees you should steer up tide to counteract its effect.

If the tide will be pushing you to starboard, then you should subtract the offset from your planned track. If the tide will be pushing you to port, you should add it. This basic equation is easy to remember if you use alliteration and think 'pushed to port means plus'.

Suppose, for instance, that our intended track (the direction we want to go) is 190, and we expect to be under way for three hours at about 25 knots. The tidal stream will be pushing us westwards (to starboard), gently at first but increasing from 1.5 knots in the first hour to 4.5 knots in the third hour. The average tidal stream is three knots.

Multiplied by 60 and divided by the boat speed, that is 3 x 60 / 25 = 36 / 5 or about 7

As it is pushing to starboard, it must be subtracted, so we need to steer 183.

Above: Pilotage is a skill that takes many years to perfect.

Pilotage

GPS and chart plotters are excellent for showing where you are and where you are going. In every passage, though, there comes a moment at which the priorities change, when getting from A to B is suddenly less important than getting out of A or into B without hitting anything.

In some cases, it is very easy. Finding your way into an artificial harbour seldom involves much more than aiming at the gap between the harbour walls. In daylight, at least, it's a piece of cake.

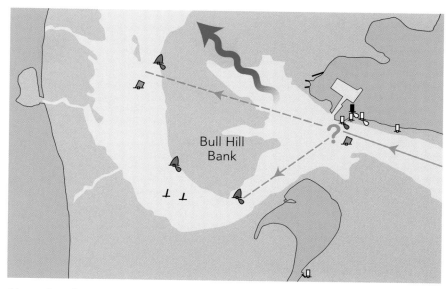

Above: Buoy hopping in the River Exe. Instead of going between the red and green buoys beyond Bull Hill Bank, aim for the solitary green buoy off to port.

BUOY HOPPING

Natural rivers can be a bit more tricky, with bends and banks getting in the way. In crowded areas, it is not much of a problem: in a river that is lined with moorings, following the channel is just a matter of picking the line of clear water between the rows.

Even in the busiest rivers, however, the moorings stop short of the river mouth, and more widely spaced navigation marks take over.

If the buoys or marks were arranged in pairs, with each red matched by a green, following the channel would be a simple matter of steering between each pair of buoys in turn. It is sometimes like that in real life, but not always.

The River Exe in England is a good example. Coming into the river, heading northwestwards, there is a red buoy just off the entrance to the marina in what used to be

Exmouth docks. The chart clearly shows that to carry on up the river, you need to swing to port at this point, towards the green buoys that mark the edge of Bull Hill Bank.

It is much less obvious in real life, however. As you pass the red buoy off the docks, you see another red buoy, almost dead ahead, and there, just to the right of it, is a green. It seems obvious that you are meant to go between them. What is not so obvious is that this will take you straight across the shallow sand of the Bull Hill Bank, and that the buoy you should be aiming for is the solitary green, just off the beach on your port beam.

Having avoided that trap, the Exe has another one ready to catch anyone who is feeling a bit too smug. At low water, what there is of the current follows the curve of the main channel around Bull Hill Bank. As the tide rises, however, it covers

the bank, and by half tide there can be three or four knots of tide flowing in through the entrance and straight across the bank. So, as you make the turn around the red buoy, the tide that was pushing you in is now pushing you sideways. As you aim for the green buoy, it still pushes you sideways. At harbour speeds, its effect is pretty significant: if you simply aim for the green buoy, it will push you in a graceful curve onto the sandbank.

The solution is to line up the target buoy with something on the shoreline beyond. It does not have to be marked on the chart, so long as you can see it, and it doesn't move – even a parked car or sleeping cow will do, so long as they stay parked or sleeping. Then steer to keep the buoy and the landmark lined up with each other. You may not seem to be aiming at the buoy, but you can be sure that you are

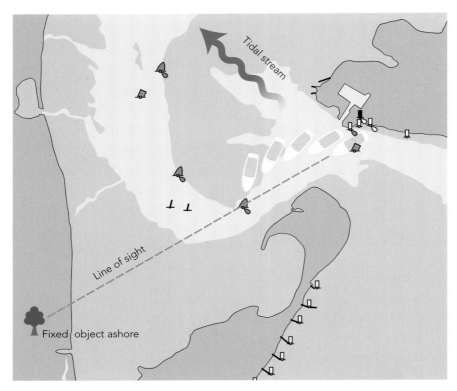

Above: *When buoy hopping, line up the target buoy with a fixed object on the shoreline beyond. Keep the buoy and target lined up and you will counteract the effects of the tide.*

sliding crab-wise along the straight line represented by your original line of sight.

Make sure that you know the bearing and distance of each buoy from the previous one.

Leave the driving to someone else, if possible, so that you can pick out the next-but-one buoy; this way, you are always working one step ahead of the helmsman.

Avoid just 'aiming at' a buoy: try to line it up with something beyond, and keep it in line.

TRANSITS
Keeping two objects lined up with each other is such a great way of following a very precise straight-line track that a lot of harbours use

special transit marks called leading marks instead of buoys.

The principle is simple: a pair of distinctive marks are set up so that they appear to be in line with each other when seen from a vessel which is following the channel. When you are heading towards the marks, the secret is to follow the front mark. In other words, if the mark nearest you appears to slide to the left of the one further away, steer to port, and vice versa. If you are out-bound, and looking backwards to see the marks, follow the back mark.

Always remember, however, that the existence of a transit does not necessarily mean that there is enough water to pass safely through.

CLEARING LINES
One of the most powerful pilotage tools of all is a trick known as clearing lines. We probably use it, unwittingly, every day of our lives, and on foot as well as in cars or boats. It just means drawing a line around a hazard, and making sure that we do not cross it.

This translates most easily into boats in the context of radar. Suppose, for instance, that we are heading for the River Yealm, in the northeastern corner of a bay that is fringed by rocky outcrops. We can see, from the chart, that all the rocks on one side of the bay are within 0.5km (0.3 miles) of the shore, so as long as we stay more than 1.5km (0.3 miles) from the shore, we can't possibly hit them. The rocks on the other side of the bay are all more than 1.5km (0.9 miles) from the shore, so as long as we are closer than 1.5km (0.9 miles) to the shore, we can't possibly hit them, either.

An important point to remember is not to rely on radar ranges from sloping shorelines: you can never tell which bit of the beach you are looking at. You don't have to use radar to use clearing lines, though: clearing bearings work just as well as clearing ranges. In this particular example, there is a very convenient church at the head of the bay, which would be on a bearing of 003 if we were as close to the eastern rocks as we dare go, and on a bearing of 042 if we were as far to the west as we dare. The traditional tool for measuring bearings is a hand bearing compass, but for many purposes it is quicker and easier to use the steering compass: just point the boat at the church, and see what the steering compass says: if it is between 003 and 042, we must be between the two clearing lines.

PLANNING PILOTAGE

This handful of pretty simple pilotage techniques will get you into almost anywhere that you can fit a boat. It is no good getting to the harbour entrance, though, before you start trying to decide which technique to use. Pilotage is usually simple, and that is really the whole point of it: it is the purest, simplest kind of navigation there is, but it only works if you have done all the reading, chartwork, calculations, and measurements in advance.

- Calculate the height of tide, so

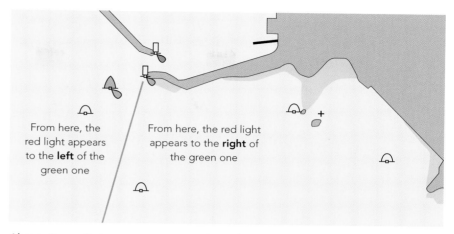

Above: You can't always trust your eyes when piloting.

that you know what is really a hazard and what you can go straight over.
- Use charts and pilot books, to get a 'feel' for the place.
- Make notes in a form you can understand: 'Green buoy half mile to port' means more than 'Number fifteen buoy'.

- Have a back-up plan if possible, in case you can't identify a transit or a buoy is out of position.
- Don't be afraid to get in close: use clearing lines to tell you how close you can afford to go while you are looking for the marks that will guide you in.

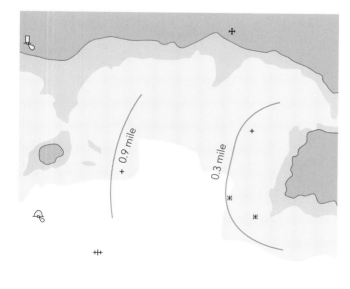

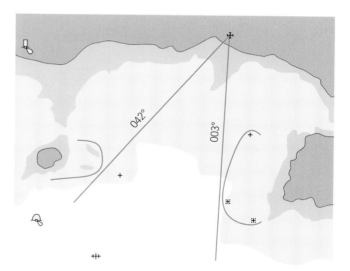

1 mile

Above: Clearing ranges.

BUOYS

Lighthouses have been in use for thousands of years, but they are vastly outnumbered by much smaller, and much more recent, buoys and beacons. At first, each country had its own system of buoyage, using different shapes and colours to signify different things. Gradually, however, they adopted the best features of each other's systems, until, in the early 1970s there were just two systems left. Essentially, these boil down to the European system, used around most of the world and known as IALA A, and the American system, used around the USA and the ports of the Pacific rim.

Within the IALA A system, there are two sub-systems: lateral marks are used to mark the port and starboard sides of channels, while cardinal marks are used to mark the northern, eastern, southern or western sides of specific hazards. Other marks are included in the system, to mark the beginning of harbour approach channels, or isolated dangers, or for 'special purposes', such as marking the edges of waterskiing areas. The US system comprises different marks.

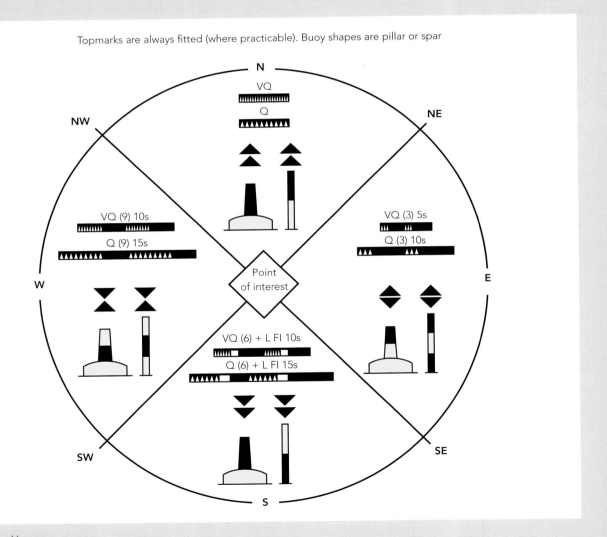

Topmarks are always fitted (where practicable). Buoy shapes are pillar or spar

Left: Cardinal buoyage.

Port hand

Can — Pillar — Spar

Topmark (if any): single can

Buoyage direction

Starboard hand

Conical — Pillar — Spar

Topmark (if any): single cone, point upward

Lights, when fitted, may have any phase characteristic other than that used for preferred channels

Examples:

Quick flashing
Flashing
Long flashing
Group flashing

Preferred channel to starboard

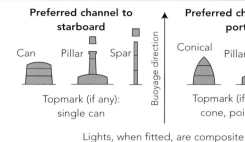

Can — Pillar — Spar

Topmark (if any): single can

Buoyage direction

Preferred channel to port

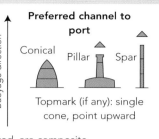

Conical — Pillar — Spar

Topmark (if any): single cone, point upward

Lights, when fitted, are composite group flashing Fl (2 + 1)

Above: *Lateral buoyage.*

Isolated danger marks

Topmarks are always fitted (where practicable)

Shape: optional, but not conflicting with lateral marks; pillar or spar preferred

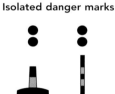

Light, when fitted, is **white**. Group flashing (2)

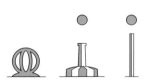 Fl (2)

Safe water marks

Topmark (if any): single sphere

Shape: spherical or pillar or spar

Light, when fitted, is **white**. Isophase or Occulting or one Long Flash every 10 seconds or Morse 'A'

Isophase
Occulting
LF 10s
Morse 'A'

Special marks

Topmark (if any): single X shape

Shape: optional, but not conflicting with navigational marks

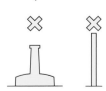

Light, when fitted, is **yellow** and may have any phase characteristic not used for white lights

Examples
 Fl Y
Fl(4) Y

Above: *Miscellaneous buoyage.*

REGULATIONS

One of the wonders of recreational boating is that, even in these modern times, it exists with the minimum of regulation. We don't (yet) have obligatory licensing or registration, and we can cruise almost wherever we choose. Yet wherever we go, we are governed by an internationally recognized code, in order to avoid collisions.

The rules by which we abide on the water are known, variously, as the International Regulations for Preventing Collisions at Sea, the collision regulations, COLREGs or, most simply, the rules of the road. They are presided over by the International Maritime Organization (IMO), a body whose roots can be traced back to the sinking of the *Titanic*, and the need for international rules governing various aspects of boat building and conduct on the water.

The COLREGs are there, essentially, to stop us bumping into one another. The modern COLREGs were formulated in 1972, although they are amended and brought up to date from time to time. In this chapter we will take you through the main points that relate to powerboaters on the water, including safe speeds, right of way, handling in a narrow channel, light and sound signals and your responsibilities in fog or at night. We will try not to get too bogged down in legalspeak, but please remember, that it is your responsibility to have read the COLREGs at some point, and to keep up to date with developments or amendments. They don't change very often, but if you haven't looked at the regulations for a few years, it is always good to refresh your memory. You can find the COLREGs in almanacs, or you can obtain copies from chandlers, general reference works or the internet.

Let's start with some of the basic rules, then move on to other important ones. We don't have the space to cover every regulation here, but we will give you an overview, at least.

Who do the rules apply to?

In a word, everyone. They apply to 'all vessels upon the high seas and in all waters connected therewith navigable by seagoing vessels'. That means everyone from RIBs to supertankers, and from sailing dinghys to tall ships. It certainly includes you! And because the COLREGs are overseen by the IMO, they cover everywhere you are ever likely to end up. The IMO is an agency of the United Nations, and that means that 170 countries are signed up to its conventions.

It is worth mentioning a couple of other points here. Firstly, the fact that international regulations exist does not mean that local ones don't, too. Harbour authorities will usually have their own regulations, which is why you should always have an almanac that covers the areas you are travelling through.

Secondly, though the rules tell you what to do in many circumstances, they do not override common sense. We will keep coming back to this point, but the sea is still an old-fashioned place where skippers think for themselves and are trusted to do so. In the words of the COLREGs, following the rules does not exonerate you if you have failed to take heed of the 'ordinary practice of seamen', and you are likewise authorized to depart from the rules 'to avoid immediate danger'.

Speed

The COLREGs do not set out a speed limit as such, but they do specify that a boat should 'proceed at a safe speed so that she can... avoid collision and be stopped

Above: *On today's busy waters, knowledge of the COLREGS is essential.*

with a distance appropriate to the prevailing circumstance and conditions'.

You should take into consideration such things as the visibility, the amount of traffic around you, the state of the wind, sea and current, your draught and any navigational hazards nearby.

This is one of the areas where, although the COLREGs lay out guidelines rather than specific speeds, local harbour authorities will in many cases enforce a specific speed limit in certain areas. An almanac will inform you of the rules by which you must abide.

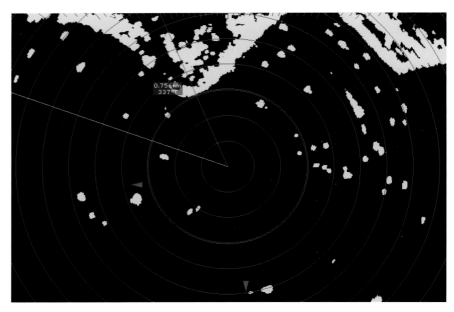

Above: Your radar can help you to avoid collisions.

Keeping a lookout

There are lots of distractions on a boat, whether it is watching the scenery or talking to your friends. Nevertheless, every vessel needs to have a lookout at all times – either the skipper or one of the crew.

The point of a lookout is to check the likelihood of a collision, and the easiest way to work this out is to hold your course and take bearings between your boat and the vessel that you are concerned about.

The key here is to hold your heading and speed constant. This is easiest if you have an autopilot fitted; if not, the helmsman should watch the compass carefully. Now, using a hand compass, take a series of bearings between yourself and the other boat. If the bearings are changing significantly then you are not on a collision course, but if they stay roughly the same then you may be at risk of a crash.

In reality, it can be hard to take accurate bearings when your boat

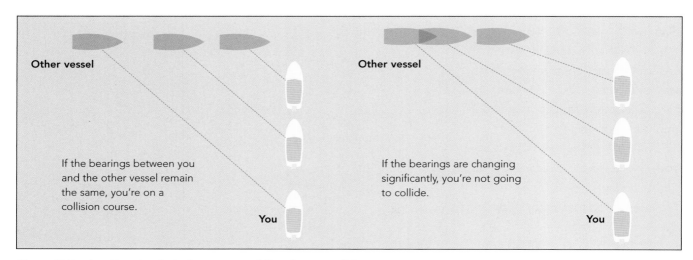

Other vessel

If the bearings between you and the other vessel remain the same, you're on a collision course.

You

Other vessel

If the bearings are changing significantly, you're not going to collide.

You

Above: Taking hand bearings is the best way to tell if you're on a collision course.

is rolling around. If you prefer, you can also 'take a bearing' by noting a position on your boat in the line of sight between you and the target. For example, the target boat could in line with a vertical stanchion pole on your vessel. Now hold your course and speed; if the target remains and continues to line up with the same position on your boat, then you are on a collision course. If it moves one way or the other, then you should be fine.

Does your boat have radar fitted? If it does, the COLREGs demand that you make 'proper use' of it to determine the risk of collision. One way you can do this is by using the electronic bearing line (EBL) function. Once again, you need to keep your speed and heading constant, then line up the EBL between yourself and the target boat on your radar screen. If the target boat is moving to one side of the EBL then you should be fine; if it approaches along the EBL, then you are on a collision course.

Avoiding collisions

One of the purposes of the COLREGs is to describe 'rights of way' and who should give way in various circumstances that you might encounter.

Reading the regulations, though, you will soon notice that the term 'right of way' is never used – and there is a good reason for that. On the water, there are 'stand-to' vessels and 'give-way' vessels. The 'give-way' vessel is instructed to

'take early and substantial action to keep well clear'.

The point here is that it is not clever to make a tiny alteration to your course or speed to narrowly miss another boat. If you do, it is unlikely that the other boat will

notice that you have acted at all – and that means its skipper may feel that he or she has to act as well. It is not hard to imagine that as you are making small alterations, the other skipper might be doing the same – so that you actually remain

---

THE CONVENTION

When vessels are approaching each other head on, there is a convention that says that any movement to avoid collision should be to starboard, so that the boats will pass port side to port side.

It is easy to see why there has to be a convention here, otherwise when two vessels attempt to avoid each other, one might move to starboard and the other to port – resulting in a collision.

This convention also applies – in

general – to other collision avoidance manoeuvres. Your preference should always be to move to starboard, if possible. Of course, situations vary and you should judge each one as it appears to you. However, if you are thinking of moving to port instead of starboard, consider what might happen if the other boat obeyed the convention and moved to starboard. Might you be putting both boats in danger?

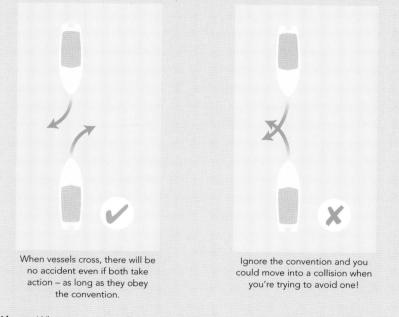

When vessels cross, there will be no accident even if both take action – as long as they obey the convention.

Ignore the convention and you could move into a collision when you're trying to avoid one!

Above: *When power vessels cross, they should move to starboard if at all possible.*

THE RULES FOR SAILORS

Although they do not apply to powerboaters, it is worth knowing the rules that apply when sailing boats have a risk of collision.

If the boats have the wind on different sides, then the vessel with the wind on its port side should keep out of the way of the other. If they both have the wind on the same side, then the vessel to windward should keep out of the way of the other.

On a more general note, many powerboaters have never been sailing, and so yachts' behaviour can appear somewhat bizarre. If a yacht needs to travel directly into the wind then it cannot just point and go. Instead, it has to take a zig-zag course, called 'tacking'. A powerboater should be aware that tacking boats change direction very suddenly. It isn't their fault, and if you are keeping your distance and a proper lookout then it won't be a problem.

---

on a collision course rather than getting out of each other's way.

The best action to take is to change your course, and to do so early and decisively, such that you leave other boats in no doubt that you are acting to avoid collision. If for some reason you decide to alter your speed rather than your course, remember that this may not be obvious to other skippers, so make sure that you change your speed decisively and significantly.

So far, so simple. But if you are the 'stand-on' vessel then you are not totally in the clear – you have responsibilities, as well.

To begin with, you should hold your course and speed, which makes it easiest for the give-way vessel to avoid you. However, if it becomes apparent that the give-way vessel is not taking action, then the stand-on vessel may take action

as well. And if the vessels come so close together that a collision can only be avoided by both of them taking action, then they *both* must do so.

This is another example of the COLREGs accommodating common sense as well as just rules. If you are the skipper of a stand-to vessel then your boat is still your responsibility. You should stay aware

and act as appropriate, rather than continue blithely on, and this is the reason that the regulations refer to 'give-way' and 'stand-to' vessels rather than the simpler idea of having 'right of way'.

The 'pecking order'

There are many different types of vessel at sea, and the COLREGs take this into account. In particular, it is easier for some boats to manoeuvre than others, and the regulations make sure that manoeuvrable vessels stay out of the way of less manoeuvrable ones.

For us powerboaters, this is bad news! Our engines mean that we can move pretty much as we please, so we're at the bottom of the 'pecking order', below vessels not under command, vessels restricted in their ability to manoeuvre, vessels engaged in fishing, and sailing vessels.

To expand on those definitions, a vessel not under command is one that, through some kind of mechanical failure or other problem,

Above: A vessel not under command is the 'stand-on' vessel at all times.

cannot manoeuvre properly. It should show this by displaying two balls in a vertical line (see below left).

A vessel restricted in its ability to manoeuvre is one that, because of its employment, may be unable to keep out of the way of other vessels. This could be for any number of reasons, from laying navigation marks or cables to clearing mines. The boat itself may be quite manoeuvrable, but if you are trying to dredge a channel then you cannot very well divert every time a sailing boat is heading for you. So these restricted vessels are granted a special status in the COLREGs; look out for their identifying marks of three shapes in a vertical line – a ball, a diamond and another ball (see above right).

Vessels engaged in fishing also have other things to think about than avoiding traffic. They should

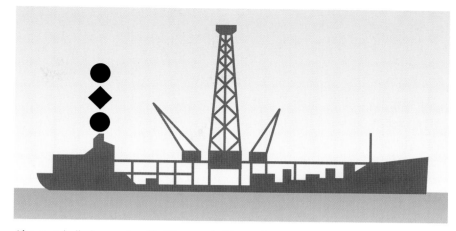

Above: A ball, diamond and ball in a vertical line indicates a vessel restricted in its ability to manoeuvre.

always be given a wide berth because (a) they are trying to work, and (b) they may have nets or lines extending for some distance, which you would be well advised to stay clear of. Fishing vessels' identifying marks consist of two cones in a vertical line, with the apex together, like an hourglass (see below).

Another type of boat that cannot

manoeuvre easily is the sailing yacht. Unlike us, sailors cannot just 'point and go' – they are constrained by the wind. As a result, power almost always gives way to sail.

The relationship between sailors and powerboaters is often a strained one. They call us 'stinkpots', and in return they are often dubbed 'rag and stick men' or 'raggies'. Powerboaters don't do our sport any favours by acting thoughtlessly. The average yachtsman is looking for a bit of a peace and quiet; they don't take kindly to being 'buzzed' by motorboats roaring past at close quarters, and why should they? It's not much fun to bob up and down uncontrollably for five minutes because a motorboat has just steamed past at full chat. Take a look behind you and watch your wake – a little courtesy on the water costs nothing.

Having said that, sailors are not saints, either. Problems commonly arise because sailors often stick

Above: The 'hourglass' indicates a vessel engaged in fishing.

slavishly to the 'power gives way to sail' mantra, even though there are exceptions to the rule.

If a yacht is using its engines – even if the sails are up, too – it's technically a motorsailor, which means it fits into the 'pecking order' like any other powerboat would do. Any yacht with its engines on should display a cone forwards, with the point facing downwards (see below).

The other exceptions to the 'power gives way to sail' rule are when you are in a narrow channel, a traffic separation scheme or a when the sailing boat is overtaking. We'll come back to all these later in this chapter.

Overtaking

There are two sets of regulations for avoiding collisions – one set for when the vessels are in sight of one

Above: *Keep your wash to a minimum when passing sailing boats.*

another, and one set for vessels in restricted visibility, such as heavy rain or fog. Let's start by looking at the regulations applying to boats who can see each other.

If you are overtaking, then it is up to you to stay out of the way of the

vessel you are overtaking. You are defined as overtaking another vessel if you are 'coming from a direction more than 22.5° abaft her beam' (see below).

As a point of courtesy you should, of course, leave plenty of space

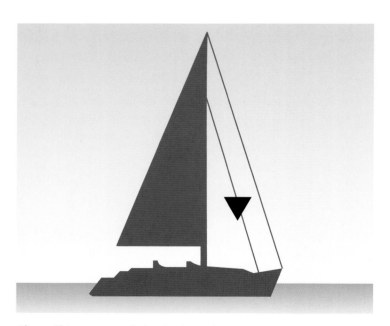

Above: *This means a yacht is using its engines.*

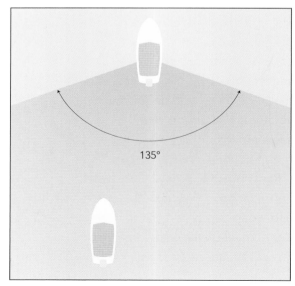

Above: *A vessel is overtaking if it is within the arc 135° behind another vessel.*

between yourself and the boat you are overtaking.

Overtaking is one of the exceptions to the 'power gives way to sail' rule, so if you are being overtaken by a sailing boat, you are the 'stand-to' vessel.

Head-on

When two powerboats are approaching each other head-on, or almost head-on, both should alter their course to starboard, passing port side to port side.

For the reasoning behind this, see 'The Convention', on page 121.

Crossing

When boats are crossing, the one that has the other boat to its starboard side is the give-way vessel. An easy way of remembering this is that it is like a UK road roundabout – see right.

Alternatively, you can use the navigation lights as traffic lights to help you remember who should give way (we will come back to nav lights later in this chapter). If you can see the other boat's green nav light, that's 'green to go', and it means you are the stand-on vessel. If you see a red light, that means you are the give-way vessel.

Remember, the rules for boats approaching each other head-on and boats crossing only apply to boats that are at the same level in the 'pecking order'. As a powerboater, you are the give-way vessel whenever a sailing boat is crossing you or approaching head-on.

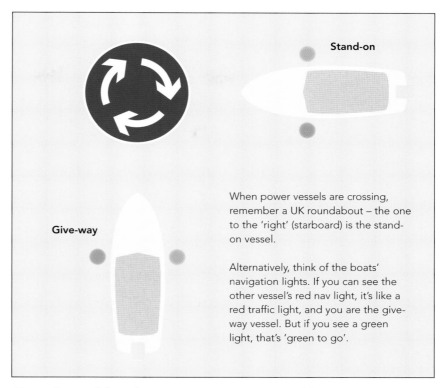

When power vessels are crossing, remember a UK roundabout – the one to the 'right' (starboard) is the stand-on vessel.

Alternatively, think of the boats' navigation lights. If you can see the other vessel's red nav light, it's like a red traffic light, and you are the give-way vessel. But if you see a green light, that's 'green to go'.

Above: *Crossing follows the same conventions as a UK roundabout.*

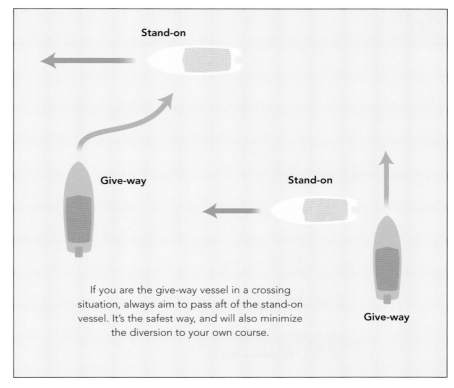

If you are the give-way vessel in a crossing situation, always aim to pass aft of the stand-on vessel. It's the safest way, and will also minimize the diversion to your own course.

Above: *Giving way.*

Above: Proceed at a safe speed when in a narrow channel or approaching harbour.

Narrow channels

There are a couple of circumstances that over-ride some other COLREGs, and one of these is the case of a vessel or vessels in narrow channels.

What do we mean by a 'narrow channel'? That is not a straightforward question, because the COLREGs are not specific. However, the principle is pretty clear. For a large tanker or commercial vessel approaching a harbour, it is unlikely to be able to stray outside of the dredged channel without running aground. The same channel may very well not count as 'narrow' for powerboaters like us, partly because there is so much room to manoeuvre and partly because we can probably stray a little outside it without running aground. Heading up a small creek at low tide, however, we may well be as constrained to the channel as a supertanker approaching port.

THE IMPORTANCE OF COMMON SENSE

The COLREGs covering head-on and crossing situations tell you what to do when there is a risk of collision between yourself and another power vessel. In these circumstances, the COLREGs don't distinguish between supertankers (as long as they are not restricted to a channel, for example) and RIBs, which means that a RIB skipper may consider himself to be the stand-on vessel, and a tanker to be the give-way vessel.

However, use your common sense. A tanker has an immense turning circle that will dwarf yours. Because of its large draught, the waters it can enter are much more restricted than yours. The skipper is trying to work, and may have many more things to think about than you do, as may the designated lookout. The tanker is considerably more visible than you are, often all the way to the horizon.

Take all these factors into account, and stay out of merchant ships' way. See them early and take clear, decisive action. By the time they notice you there won't be a risk of collision and they will give you no more than a moment's thought, which makes you a far better skipper than if you plough on regardless, relying on the letter of the law to prevent a collision that will be far worse for you than it will be for them.

The point is that where a vessel is unable to leave the channel it is in, it needs special protection. For this reason, the COLREGs stipulate that 'a vessel of less than 20m (66ft) in length or a sailing vessel shall not impede the passage of a vessel which can safely navigate only within a narrow channel or fairway.' In other words, no matter how you are crossing or what is happening, you don't get in the way of those boats restricted to a channel. This rule over-rides 'power give way to sail'.

That is the most important rule concerning channels, but there are a couple of others, too. Where possible, you should keep to the edge of the channel, on your starboard side – so essentially, boats drive on the right-hand side of the 'road'.

To keep the channel clear, boats engaged in fishing should not impede any other vessel proceeding along the channel. And if at all possible, you should avoid anchoring in a channel.

If the channel is very narrow, then overtaking may also be difficult, and special instructions apply.

Sometimes you may find that it is only possible to overtake the boat in front of you if that boat moves out of the way for you. In this case, you must employ sound signals (see overleaf) if you wish to come past. Two prolonged blasts followed by one short blast means 'I intend to overtake on your starboard side'; two prolonged blasts followed by two short blasts means 'I intend to overtake on your port side'. If the vessel being overtaken agrees to co-operate, it should reply with one prolonged, one short, one prolonged and one short blast, then move as appropriate. Even if this happens, it is still the responsibility of the overtaking vessel to keep out of the way of the boat it is overtaking.

In reality, although sound signals are prescribed by the COLREGs, your first response to an overtaking situation like this would usually be to hail the other vessel on your VHF and explain what you would like to do. It is only if this course of action fails for some reason that you would generally start using sound signals.

Finally, it may also be necessary to use sound signals if you are approaching a bend or an obstruction where you cannot see what is ahead. As well as generally proceeding with caution in this circumstance, you should sound one prolonged blast. Any other vessel on the other side of the bend or obstruction should reply with a prolonged blast.

This last case will not arise very often for a typical powerboat. It is far more likely that you will be the recipient of a sound signal from another, considerably larger, vessel, and you should remember to reply and then proceed with caution.

Above: *Watch out for sailing boats 'tacking' in a narrow channel.*

SOUND SIGNALS

There are two types of sound signals: those for manoeuvring/giving warnings to other boats, and those for use in restricted visibility. The former are generally only required for unusual situations in which other vessels really need to know what you are doing; the latter may be required if visibility is really bad.

A vessel of 12m (39ft) or more must carry a whistle and bell for making sound signals; smaller vessels must carry 'some means of making an efficient sound signal'.

Sound signals take the form of 'short blasts' (about one second long) and 'prolonged blasts' (four to six seconds long). In the following table, short blasts are represented as '-', prolonged blasts as '—'.

Restricted visibility

—	Power vessel making way
— —	Power vessel under way, but stopped
— — -	Sailing vessel, vessel not under command, vessel restricted in its ability to manoeuvre, vessel constrained by its draught, vessel towing

Manouevring

-	I am altering course to starboard
- -	I am altering course to port

Manouevring *continued*

- - -	My engines are operating astern (though I may not necessarily be actually moving astern)
— — -	I intend to overtake on your starboard side
— — - -	I intend to overtake on your port side
— - — -	I accept your wish to overtake
- - - - -	Please make your intentions clear / I doubt you are taking sufficient action to avoid a collision
—	Signal made when nearing a bend or area of channel where other vessels may be obscured. The same signal is used as a response for vessels that are approaching from the other direction

Traffic separation schemes

Traffic separation schemes (TSSs) are the motorways of the marine world, and they exist to allow commercial vessels to make quick and safe passage along major routes. They consist of two lanes, accommodating ships travelling in opposite directions – much like a dual carriageway road – and a 'separation zone' to keep the lanes apart.

Where possible, you should keep out of TSSs. The COLREGs permit boats of under 20m (66ft), and all sailing boats, to use inshore traffic zones instead, and doing so will keep you out of the way of commercial traffic. If you are not using a TSS you should avoid it by as wide a margin as possible, so as not to confuse anyone. All vessels under 20m (66ft) (and all sailing vessels) are prevented in the COLREGs from impeding power vessels following a lane.

If for some reason you do wish to travel along a TSS, then a couple of rules are pretty obvious: stay out of the separation zone except in an emergency (it is there to *separate*!) and, just as on the motorway, do not travel the wrong way down a lane. When you enter the TSS, you should

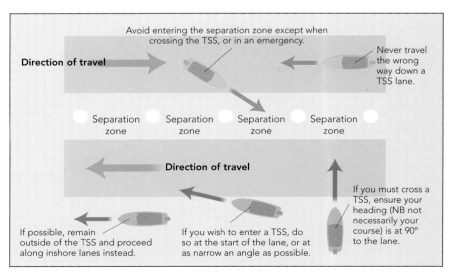

Above: A few basic rules of traffic separation schemes.

THE RULES OF INLAND WATERWAYS

There are numerous conventions that apply on rivers and canals, some based on the COLREGs, some unique to inland waterways in general, and some specific to the waterway you are travelling on. As usual, it is up to you to find the regulations specific to the area you are in, which will also cover such things as speed limits, where you can moor and areas you must avoid.

Generally speaking, the main principle of boating inland is to stay to the right and overtake to port. Watch your wash at all times in order to avoid bank erosion or disruption to other users of the waterway, and stay out of the way of commercial traffic.

Use your common sense when it comes to mooring – don't tie up too near to tunnels, narrow bridges, locks or other bottlenecks.

Above: Try to stay to starboard and overtake to port.

Above: Watch out for speed limits.

Above: Be aware of any by-laws covering access or mooring.

Above: Make sure that you are clear on the rules before venturing out.

ideally do so at the start of a lane but, failing that, enter at the narrowest angle you can.

Some circumstances may require you to cross a TSS. If you need to, you should bear in mind first that you may not impede any vessels proceeding along a lane – be watchful and treat TSSs with the caution they deserve. When you do so, you should cross, as near as possible, at a heading at right-angles to the lane. Just to reiterate, that is a *heading* at right-angles – the wind may affect your course, but it is the heading that is important.

As you are crossing the TSS, you are permitted to continue through the separation zone; then, again, you must cross the other lane of the TSS at right-angles to the direction of the traffic.

Restricted visibility

Some of the sections in this chapter (eg those referring to the pecking order, overtaking, head-on and crossing) only apply when vessels have sight of one another. In restricted visibility, different rules are required because it may be difficult to tell, for example, whether a blob on your radar screen is a sailing boat or a powerboat. Not only that, but if you have a radar and another vessel does not, how can they be expected to give way to you? They don't even know you are there!

This is why, when visibility is reduced, there are no give-way and stand-to vessels. The following rules apply equally to all vessels.

Firstly, you should move at a speed that takes into account the visibility so that, if a boat suddenly looms out of the fog, you will have enough time to manoeuvre out of the way.

If you have radar and believe that there is a risk of collision with another vessel, the COLREGs remind you that there are two types of action you should avoid. If the vessel is forward of your beam, then you should avoid changing your

Above: Always show consideration to 'working' vessels.

course to port. See 'The Convention' on page 121 to remind yourself why. If the vessel is level with your beam, or aft of it, do not steer towards it. See the illustration to the right to understand why.

There are no special overtaking rules in reduced visibility. You may know that a vessel is passing you (if you have radar) but do they know you are there? Don't assume anything – just stay out of their way as much as possible.

In reduced visibility, listen out for fog signals. Unless you are sure no risk of collision exists (for example, if you are using radar), then if you hear a fog signal apparently forward of your beam, you should reduce your speed immediately. If necessary you may have to stop altogether until you are sure no further risk of collision exists.

The special rules already covered for narrow channels and TSSs still apply, even in reduced visibility. As should have been made clear, both of these areas require the utmost caution, even at the best of times. In reduced visibility, always navigate with the greatest of care.

Lights and shapes

The COLREGs only really work if you can identify the other boats and obstacles around you. It is all very well knowing that 'power gives way to sail', but that is only useful if you can distinguish one from another, even at a distance, in poor visibility or at night.

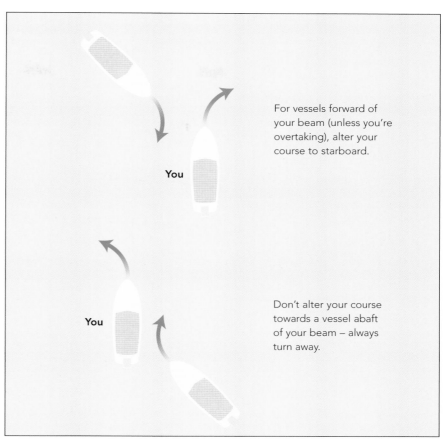

For vessels forward of your beam (unless you're overtaking), alter your course to starboard.

Don't alter your course towards a vessel abaft of your beam – always turn away.

Above: These conventions will keep you safe.

Above: Take extra care in reduced visibility.

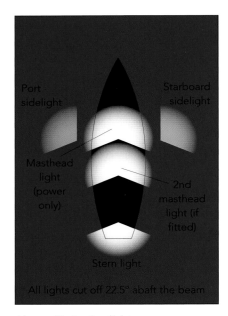

Above: Navigation lights.

The COLREGs specify that lights must be turned on between 'sunset and sunrise', but also in restricted visibility or 'any other circumstances when deemed necessary'. When the lights are in operation, it is important not only that you show the right ones, but also that you don't show additional lights, including cabin lights, bright torches and so on. In the daytime, vessels identify themselves by means of shapes, not lights.

Let's begin by defining some of the more common lights, and then we will examine how these are used to identify vessels at night or in poor visibility.

Sidelights are the red and green lights that are used to identify the orientation of another vessel, with a red light for port side and green light for starboard. They are designed such that they can be seen only in a restricted arc, from the bow of the boat up to 22.5° abaft of the beam. We covered earlier how the sidelights can be used to determine give-way and stand-on vessels when powerboats cross each other's path.

A **sternlight** is a white light that shines from 22.5° degrees abaft of each beam, through the stern. If you can see another vessel's sternlight, that means you are the overtaking vessel, according to the COLREGs.

Sidelights and sternlights are displayed by pretty much all vessels under way (that is, moving through the water).

Steaming lights are white lights that are displayed at, or close to, the masthead of the vessel. They are visible from the bow to 22.5° abaft of each beam or, in other words, through the coverage of the sidelights combined.

In some cases, it is acceptable to replace these navigation lights with a bow or mast lantern, which produce two or more lights from one bulb. A bow lantern contains both sidelights (so it looks red in the port sidelight sector and green in the starboard sector). A mast lantern contains both sidelights and the sternlight, as well. In either case, these lanterns replace the traditional side and sternlights – they should never be used in addition to them.

Let's now take a look at some of the more common light combinations you might see on the water, and also the shapes that are used by the same vessels in the day. Remember that this is only a small selection of the possible lights you might see at night – read up on the subject further before attempting a night passage.

Above: Navigation lights can be seen here on the radar mast and the side of the cabin.

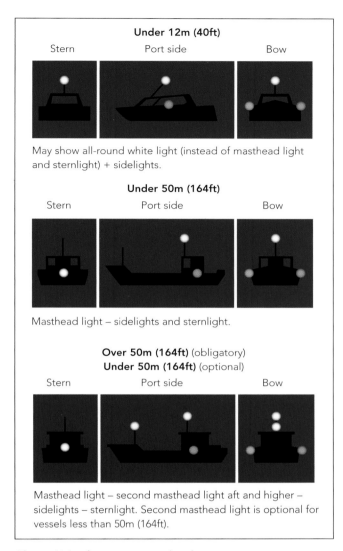

Above: *Lights for a power vessel under way.*

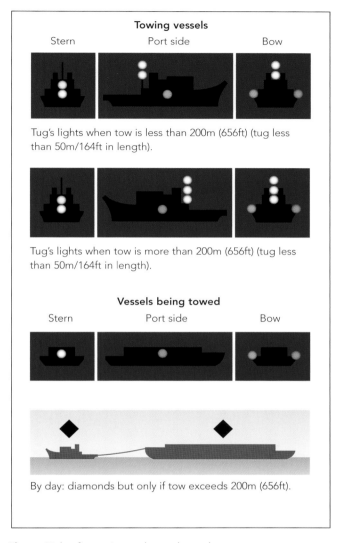

Above: *Lights for towing and towed vessels.*

POWER VESSEL UNDER WAY

In theory, these vessels show sidelights, sternlight and two steaming lights, with the aft light higher than the forward one.

In practice, vessels under 50m (164ft) long may choose to display only one steaming light; vessels under 12m (39ft) may use an all-round white light instead of a steaming light and sternlight.

Shapes: none

TOWING VESSELS

If the tow is less than 200m (656ft) long (measured from the stern of the towed vessel to the stern of the towing vessel), then the towing vessel shows sidelights, sternlights, an additional yellow light with the same arc as the sternlight, and two steaming lights, one above the other.

If the tow is longer than 200m (656ft), the towing vessel should show a third steaming light below the other two.

Shapes: if the tow is longer than 200m (656ft), then a diamond shape is displayed wherever it can be seen clearly.

TOWED VESSELS

The towed vessel displays sidelights and sternlight, but no steaming light (because it is not under power).

Shapes: If the tow is longer than

200m (656ft), then a diamond shape should be shown, as with the towing vessel.

SAILING VESSELS UNDERWAY

A sailboat can either show sidelights and a sternlight or, if under 20m (66ft) long, a masthead lantern, with no other lights. If a skipper opts for the former, he may also display an all-round red light over an all-round green light, but this is rarely seen.

If a sailboat has its engine on then it uses the same lights as a powerboat – that is, sidelights,

sternlight and white steaming light.

Shapes: none when engine is off. When the engine is on, a cone should be shown forward, with the apex pointing down.

VESSEL FISHING (OTHER THAN TRAWLING)

These vessels should show a red all-round light over a white all-round light. It should show sidelights and sternlight if making way, and if the gear extends more than 150m (492ft) there should be an all-round white light in the direction of the gear.

Shapes: two cones, one above the other, apexes pointing towards each other. For a vessel under 20m (66ft) long, a basket can be used instead.

VESSEL TRAWLING

Vessels trawling show an all-round green light over an all-round white light, plus sidelights and sternlights if making way. If the vessel is over 50m (164ft) then it must show a white steaming light when underway, aft and above the white and green lights. If under 50m (164ft), this steaming light is optional.

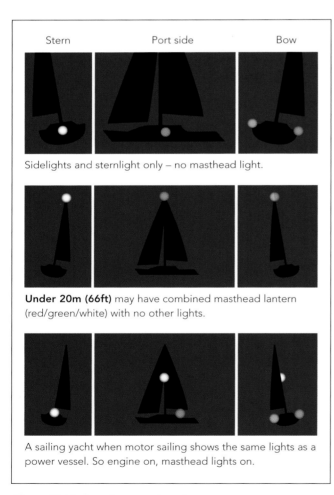

Sidelights and sternlight only – no masthead light.

Under 20m (66ft) may have combined masthead lantern (red/green/white) with no other lights.

A sailing yacht when motor sailing shows the same lights as a power vessel. So engine on, masthead lights on.

Above: *Lights for sailing vessels underway.*

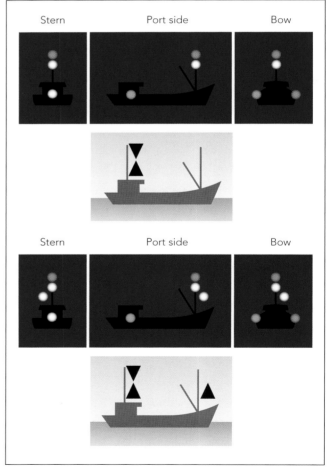

Above: *Lights for a vessel fishing (other than trawling).*

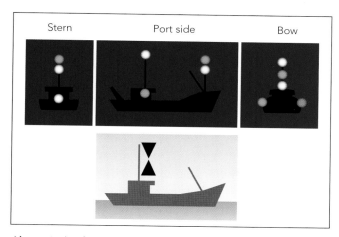

Above: Lights for a vessel trawling.

Under 50m (164ft)

Over 50m (164ft) (obligatory)
Under 50m (164ft) (optional)

All round white light forward.

A second white light aft (lower than forward light).

Larger vessels will usually also show deck working lights.

Above: Lights for vessels at anchor.

Shapes: two cones, one above, apexes pointing towards each other.

VESSELS AT ANCHOR

When at anchor, a vessel displays no sidelights, sternlights or steaming lights. Instead, it shows a white all-round light in its forward area, and another lower white all-round light towards the stern. Vessels under 50m (164ft) only need show one all-round light.

Shapes: Anchored vessels show a black ball in a visible area at their forward area.

LIGHTS: THEORY VS PRACTICE

Identifying vessels by their lights is easy isn't it? Those big coloured blobs are pretty unambiguous, aren't they?

In a book, yes. In reality, no. Lights in the distance twinkle as if they are flashing, even when they are not. Lights bob out of sight behind waves and then bob back into sight again. Lights are displayed wrongly, and can easily be confused with extraneous cabin or reading lights, not to mention the lights of towns or marinas in the background.

Taking a boat out at night is a remarkable, moving experience that gives a real sense of the connection between even modern powerboaters and those who, for generations, have lived and worked on the waves. The complex but logical patterns of twinkling lights and the melancholic toll of buoys' bells are things that every serious boater should allow him or herself to experience – but the conditions should always be treated with the utmost respect. Fail to concentrate and you can lose your bearings in an instant; the chances of a collision increase dramatically. Interpreting lights and sounds in reality is a far from straightforward task, and so night passages are only for the knowledgeable, the wary and the experienced.

Above: The lights of towns or marinas can make identifying vessel lights tricky.

COMMUNICATIONS

Mobile phones mean that we now take instant long-range communication very much for granted. But mobile phones are really quite short-range radios: if it were not for the network of closely spaced phone masts they would hardly work at all, and would be useless for distances greater than a few miles.

   At sea, where there are no phone masts, their capability is very limited: there is some coverage offshore, but it is patchy and unreliable. It is good enough for chatting to friends, but less than ideal for important messages, and particularly not for safety purposes. For that, we need to turn to one of several different kinds of radio.

Waves – and big numbers

'Radio' consists of ripples of electrical and magnetic energy that spread out from a transmitting aerial rather like ripples on the surface of a pond, but in three dimensions. If the ripples are close together, they are known, logically enough as 'short wave', and if they are far apart, they are known as 'long wave'. However, although some radios do still refer to wavelength (in metres), it is more common to refer to radio 'frequencies' in hertz – the number of waves that arrive at a given place in one second.

Frequency and wavelength are completely interconnected: if you know the frequency of a radio transmission, you can find its wavelength, and vice versa.

We are talking here about huge numbers: radio transmissions with a wavelength of 1,500 metres, for instance, have a frequency of 200,000 Hz. To save writing all those noughts, we usually use kilohertz (thousands of hertz) or megahertz (millions of hertz) .

We are quite used to the idea that in order to communicate with someone, you have to be 'on the same wavelength', but wavelength and frequency have another effect that in some ways is even more important, because they affect the way the radio waves are bent as they pass through the atmosphere. In general terms, the lower the frequency or the longer the

Above: Modern communication equipment is well worth investing in.

wavelength, the more the radio waves bend.

So medium frequencies are good for medium ranges – a few hundred miles – because they bend over the horizon. Low frequencies are even better at bending, but unfortunately they cannot carry voice messages, so their use is limited to things like long-range radio navigation aids and low-speed data services.

The snag with medium frequencies is that they are easily absorbed by the Earth's surface, so they run out of power after a few hundred miles. For worldwide radio communication, we need to go up a step, to the high frequency range. HF radio does not bend around the horizon, but it can be bent by a layer of electrically charged particles, high in the Earth's atmosphere. So

Above: A very high frequency marine transceiver.

Above: A typical fixed radio consists of a compact box with a display and control panel on the front.

HF communication can cover vast distances by using the outer layers of the atmosphere as a kind of mirror, bouncing messages to parts of the earth that would be way beyond the horizon of the transmitting antenna. That is why HF (or short wave) is used for international broadcasts such as the BBC World Service.

The next step up takes us into a range known as very high frequency.

This is so high that it hardly bends at all, neither over the horizon nor in the ionosphere, so VHF transmissions are limited to a few tens of miles – depending very much on the height of the aerial. Now, this may sound pretty limited, especially compared with the world-wide ranges achieved by HF. But in practice, it is just what we need.

We seldom need to contact a harbourmaster, a coastguard or even another boat that is more than about 48km (30 miles) away, which is well within the range of a decent VHF radio. More often, we are concerned with ranges of less than 8km (5 miles) – which can be achieved even by a low-powered hand-held VHF.

We use even higher frequencies, too. Little 'PMR' (personal mobile radios) use ultra high frequencies for voice communication over ranges of

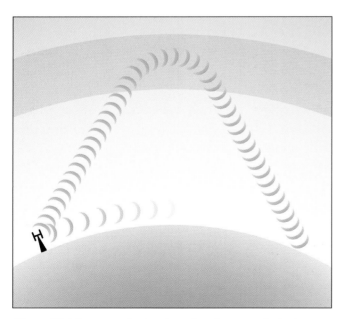

Above: High frequency (top) and medium frequency (below) waves.

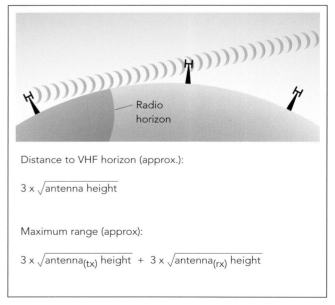

Radio horizon

Distance to VHF horizon (approx.):

$$3 \times \sqrt{\text{antenna height}}$$

Maximum range (approx):

$$3 \times \sqrt{\text{antenna}_{(tx)} \text{ height}} \; + \; 3 \times \sqrt{\text{antenna}_{(rx)} \text{ height}}$$

Above: Very high frequency waves.

up to about 5km (3 miles). PMR radios are cheap and easy to use, and – in countries which allow them to be used at all – they suffer few of the rules and regulations that affect the more heavy-duty radio-communications systems. So they are great for boat-to-boat communication when you are out with friends, or for keeping in touch with family members who have gone ashore.

At the very top of the frequency tree, so far as radiocomms are concerned, are microwaves. They are even shorter and faster than UHF waves, with wavelengths measured in centimetres and frequencies in gigahertz (thousands of megahertz). In a way, they are a step back to the HF principle, except that instead of relying on the atmosphere to reflect signals back to the Earth's surface, microwaves are used in satellite communications systems.

GMDSS

When the heroic radio operator on board the sinking *Titanic* tapped out a distress message in morse code, he was relying almost entirely on luck. In those days, there was no guarantee that anyone within range would be listening. Gradually, as radios became more capable and more commonplace, rules and regulations followed – but until the tail end of the 20th century, a cargo ship could quite legitimately set out across the Pacific with nothing more than an MF radio good for a couple of hundred miles. A cross-channel

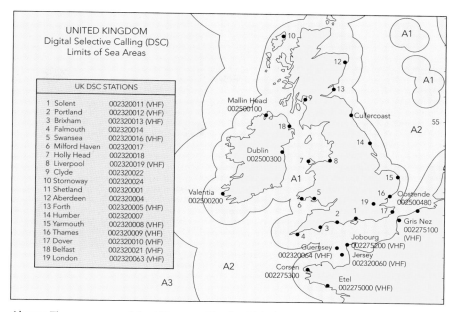

Above: The areas around the UK covered by the Global Maritime Distress and Safety System (GMDSS).

ferry, by contrast, had to have a worldwide communications system, even though it was never out of sight of land, because the rules were based on the size of ship and the number of passengers, rather than the area in which it was operating.

Clearly, this was silly, so eventually the rules were changed. Now, the world is divided into areas, roughly corresponding to the coverage available from VHF, MF, HF and satellite communications systems, and all based on the assumption that a ship must be able to make direct radio contact with the coastguard ashore.

This is called the Global Maritime Distress and Safety System (GMDSS) – and although it is not compulsory for small pleasure craft, we can still be a part of it, so long as we obey the basic rules.

VHF radio

This goes some way towards explaining the apparent irony that although, in most countries, you can drive a powerboat without a licence or any formal training, those freedoms don't extend to using the radio that is screwed to it or tucked in your pocket.

For that – in the UK and in most other countries – you need two licences.

The first is called a Ship Radio Licence. Until recently, the UK version looked like a car tax disk, and served much the same purpose: it ensured that money flowed from our bank accounts to those of the government. Fortunately, the government realized that this particular tax cost more to administer than it produced, so they scrapped it. Unfortunately, they have not scrapped the licence – just the fee. You now have to download a licence from the Ofcom website (www.ofcom.org.uk/licensing/olc).

Just like a car's tax disk, a Ship Radio Licence relates to the boat. An alternative, called a Ship Portable Radio Licence, relates to a particular radio and is the one to get for a hand-held radio that is likely to be moved from boat to boat.

The second kind of licence is called an Authority to Operate. It is the radio equivalent of a driving licence and – like a driving licence – it relates to an individual and can only be obtained after taking a test. There are several possible ways to qualify for an AtO, but in the UK the most common is a one-day Short Range Certificate (SRC) course.

Above: Fixed radios are mounted either in a bracket or recessed into a bulkhead, and have a separate antenna mounted on a mast.

SETTING UP THE RADIO

Panel layouts vary between different makes and models, but the general principles apply across the whole range, from a £50 hand-held to a £500 fixed set.

Above: Radios such as this are powered by the vessel's electrical system.

Switch the radio on, and turn the squelch control right down. This increases the sensitivity of the receiver so much that you will hear a background hissing or crackling noise.

Adjust the volume so that the hissing or crackling sound is loud enough to be distinctly audible over any background noise, without being deafening.

Adjust the squelch, this time turning it up until the noise just stops – but no more. Turning the squelch control up makes the radio less sensitive, so the aim is to set the squelch at the lowest level that will block the unwanted noise without losing incoming calls.

Choose a channel.

Choose an appropriate transmitter power. Most radios offer a choice of high or low power, but some have other options. Whichever you choose, it only affects the radio's transmitter: it has nothing to do with its ability to receive. This means that it is often forgotten, so a lot of radios are probably never switched down to low power. However, that is a shame, because using high power when you don't need it is down-right antisocial.

Listen! Never try to talk over someone else's conversation. One of the quirks of VHF radio is that a receiver can only receive one transmission at a time, so if you try to talk over someone else, either your call will go unheard – which is confusing and a waste of time – or you will obliterate their call. They will then repeat their message, so you will have to wait longer before the channel becomes vacant.

If you hear nothing, press the switch on the side of the microphone and speak clearly into the microphone, holding it a couple of inches from the side of your mouth. The microphone switch is often called the PTT switch (for 'press to talk'), but it could just as well be called the 'RTL switch'. No-one ever does call it the RTL switch, which is rather a shame because it makes the point that you have to release it to listen, as soon as you have finished talking.

Over. Before releasing the PTT (or RTL) switch, use the word 'over' to indicate that you will be waiting for a reply, or 'out' to indicate that the conversation has ended.

CHOOSING A CHANNEL
In order to communicate with

Channel Designators	Notes	Transmitting frequency (MHz)		Inter-ship	Port operations		Public Corresp.
		Ship stations	Coast stations		Single frequency	Two frequency	
60		156.025	160.625			✔	✔
01		156.050	160.650			✔	✔
61		156.075	160.675			✔	✔
02		156.100	160.700			✔	✔
62		156.125	160.725			✔	✔
03		156.150	160.750			✔	✔
63		156.175	160.775			✔	✔
04		156.200	160.800			✔	✔
64		156.225	160.825			✔	✔
05		156.250	160.850			✔	✔
65		156.275	160.875			✔	✔
06		156.300		✔			
66		156.325	160.925			✔	✔
07		156.350	160.950			✔	✔
67		156.375	156.375	✔	✔	HMCG SAR	
08		156.400		✔			
68		156.425	156.425		✔		
09		156.450	156.450	✔	✔		
69		156.475	156.475	✔	✔		
10		156.500	156.500	✔	✔	Oil Pollution	
70		156.525	156.525	Digital selective calling for distress safety and calling			
11		156.550	156.550		✔		
71		156.575	156.575		✔		
12		156.600	156.600		✔		
72		156.625		✔			
13		156.650	156.650	✔	✔		
73		156.675	156.675	✔	✔	HMCG SAR	
14		156.700	156.700		✔		
74		156.725	156.725		✔		

Channel Designators	Notes	Transmitting frequency (MHz)		Inter-ship	Port operations		Public Corresp.
		Ship stations	Coast stations		Single frequency	Two frequency	
15	2	156.750	156.750	✔	✔	Also on-board coms	
75	4	156.775					
16		156.800	156.800	DISTRESS, SAFETY AND CALLING			
76	4	156.825			✔		
17	2	156.850	156.850	✔	✔	Also on-board coms	
77		156.875		✔			
18		156.900	161.500		✔	✔	✔
78		156.925	161.525			✔	✔
19		156.950	161.550			✔	✔
79		156.975	161.575			✔	✔
20		157.000	161.600	Also Marinas etc UK only	✔	✔	✔
80		157.025	161.625			✔	✔
21		157.050	161.650			✔	✔
81		157.075	161.675			✔	✔
22		157.100	161.700			✔	✔
82		157.125	161.725		✔	✔	✔
23		157.150	161.750			✔	✔
83		157.175	161.775		✔	✔	✔
24		157.200	161.800			✔	✔
84		157.225	161.825		✔	✔	✔
25		157.250	161.850			✔	✔
85		157.275	161.875		✔	✔	✔
26		157.300	161.900			✔	✔
86		157.325	161.925		✔	✔	✔
27		157.350	161.950			✔	✔
87		157.375			✔		
28		157.400	162.000			✔	✔
88		157.425			✔		
AIS1	3	161.975	161.975				
AIS2	3	162.025	162.025				

Above: A channel chart, detailing which channels have which designated use.

someone, you have to be 'on the same wavelength'. In practice, the wavelengths and frequencies involved in VHF communication are so spectacularly unmemorable that we invariably refer to them by 'channel numbers' instead, which makes life considerably easier for everyone.

Almost all radios nowadays offer a choice of 55 'international' channels, plus a couple of 'private' channels (They are not really 'private': it just means that they are allocated by an individual government, rather than

Speaker	What to say	Notes
Tornado:	Whirlwind, Whirlwind, Whirlwind, **this is** Tornado, Tornado. **Over.**	Give the name of the vessel you are calling, up to three times, followed by the words 'this is', and your own boat name. The word 'over' indicates that you are about to stop transmitting to wait for a reply.
Whirlwind:	Tornado, Tornado, **this is** Whirlwind. **Over.**	Tornado is obviously expecting a reply, so there is no point repeating the name more than once or twice.
Tornado:	Whirlwind, **this is** Tornado. Channel seventy-two, please, seven two. **Over.**	The vessel that received the call is officially 'in control' of the communication, but it makes sense for the vessel that made the call to choose the working channel.
Whirlwind:	Tornado, **this is** Whirlwind. Channel seventy-two. **Over.**	It is easy to lose each other while changing channels. Confirming the channel reduces the risk of confusion.

Both operators now have to switch to the agreed working channel, ready to start the main business of their call.

Speaker	What to say	Notes
Tornado:	Whirlwind, Whirlwind, **this is** Tornado, Tornado. **Over.**	Whoever said 'over' last is the one who is waiting for a reply. Whirlwind said 'over', so it is up to Tornado to respond.
Whirlwind:	Tornado, **this is** Whirlwind. **Over.**	Now that communication has been established, the exchange of names can be reduced, but it must continue.
Tornado:	Whirlwind, **this is** Tornado. We're heading for Helford this evening, and wondered if you'd like to meet up with us there. **Over.**	Keep it short and simple, and use everyday language.

Speaker	What to say	Notes
Whirlwind:	Tornado, **this is** Whirlwind. That sounds good to me. Shall we see you in the pub at about eight, then? **Over**.	There is nothing wrong with arranging a rendezvous like this, but do not let the conversation degenerate into chit-chat or gossip.
Tornado:	Whirlwind, **this is** Tornado. Yes, see you there at eight. **Out**.	The conversation is over: Tornado is not requesting a reply, so she uses the procedure word 'out' to say so.
Whirlwind:	Tornado, **this is** Whirlwind. **Out**.	Although not strictly necessary, it is common and acceptable for Whirlwind to confirm that she has also finished the conversation.

Left and above: *Calling another boat. Remember that you must give the name of the vessel you are calling and your own boat name every time you press the PTT switch.*

by international agreement). However, you can't use any channel you like. For technical reasons, some of them can't be used for boat-to-boat traffic, and in any case the purpose of each channel is laid down by law.

Don't bother with the channel usage charts published in the instruction book that came with your radio, because for some reason most of them are wrong. Refer to the official channel chart in the illustration below.

You will see that channel 16 is the distress, safety, and calling channel, and that there are several other 'working' channels such as 06, 08, 72, and 77 that are approved for boat-to-boat calls. Other channels are reserved for other purposes, such as communicating with harbour masters (known as 'port operations'). Channel 80 is particularly significant, because it is the channel that is used by most marinas in the UK.

CALLING ANOTHER BOAT

The fact that there are so many channels to choose from means that unless you have agreed beforehand that you are going to call someone on a specific channel, you are extremely unlikely to be able to find them if you rely on chance alone. So most people keep their radios switched to channel 16. However, you cannot have a conversation on channel 16: it is both antisocial and illegal. So you have to make contact on channel 16, and then switch to another channel.

CALLING A HARBOUR MASTER OR MARINA

A British ship radio licence costs nothing and allows you to use any of 57 channels, but the licence for a UK harbour or marina operator costs £100 per channel. Not surprisingly, most harbourmasters and marinas go for just one channel, and have all the other channels on their radios disabled, saving themselves a great deal of unnecessary expenditure.

Consequently, there is absolutely no point in calling a harbour on channel 16 and expecting to choose a working channel: they probably won't be listening, won't be able to reply, and more often than not will not have a choice of channels. Find out the appropriate channel in advance, from a yachtsmen's

Speaker	What to say	Notes
Cyclone:	Weymouth Harbour Radio, Weymouth Harbour Radio, **this is** motor yacht Cyclone, Cyclone, on channel 74. **Over.**	The call is similar to an intership call, except that the shore side operator may be monitoring several different channels. It will help him to help you if you tell him which you are using. It may also be a good idea to include a very brief description of your own vessel.
Weymouth Harbour Radio:	Cyclone, Weymouth Harbour Radio. **Over.**	Busy radio operators often omit the 'this is'.
Cyclone:	Weymouth Harbour Radio, **this is** Cyclone. I'm a ten metre sports cruiser about half an hour out of the harbour, and would like a berth for the night. **Over.**	You are already on the right channel, so you can go straight ahead with your message.
Weymouth Harbour Radio:	Cyclone, Weymouth Harbour Radio. Yes, come right on up to the marina, and we will find you a berth. Stand by on this channel. **Out.**	
Cyclone:	Weymouth Harbour Radio, **this is** Cyclone. Standing by. **Out.**	The conversation is over: Cyclone is not requesting a reply, so she uses the procedure word 'out' to say so.

Above: Calling a harbour master or marina.

almanac, pilot book or chart, and call directly on that channel. Remember that with 57 to choose from, the only sure way to find out the correct one is to ask the harbourmaster or marine operator.

CALLING THE COASTGUARD

The coastguard has access to every channel that's available to us, plus a few extras. But a coastguard station may be dealing with several calls at once, so it is no good calling up and expecting to be asked which channel you would like. Call on channel 16, just as though you were calling another boat, but be ready for the coastguard to specify the working channel. In UK waters it will usually be channel 67, but not always.

DISTRESS CALLS

The law says that a distress call may only be made if a vessel, vehicle, aircraft or person is in grave and imminent danger. So if you have got a rope around your prop or have run out of fuel, it probably does not warrant a distress call, because you are unlikely to be in 'grave and imminent danger'. However, a man overboard situation almost certainly *does* qualify.

It is a good idea to think of the distress call in two parts: the **call** itself, followed by the distress **message**.

The **call** is the initial shout for help. It is sent on channel 16, on high power, and goes as follows:

Mayday, Mayday, Mayday
this is
*Rubber Duck, Rubber Duck,
Rubber Duck.*

Don't wait for a reply, Just pause briefly, and carry straight on with the **distress message**. Some people like to think of the distress message as 'most important bits first', while others prefer the mnemonic 'MIPDANIO'. It does not matter how you remember it, but it does help others to help you if you get the various bits of information in the right order:

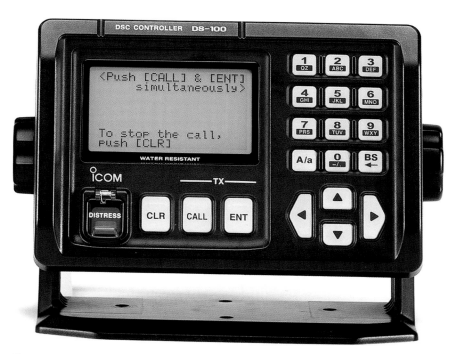

Above: *A digital selective calling controller encodes and interprets DSC messages and has the facility to alert another vessel or rescue centre directly.*

M Mayday (yes, you've just said it, but say it again!).

I Identity: your boat name (yes, you've just said it, but say it again!).

P Position: either a latitude and longitude, or the direction and distance from a charted landmark, or even the name of the nearest buoy.

D Distress: what's wrong.

A Assistance required: in most cases this will be 'request immediate assistance', because if you're inclined to be picky about whether you get rescued by helicopter or lifeboat, perhaps you should be asking yourself whether you really are in 'grave and imminent danger'.

N Number of people on board.

I Information that might

help rescuers.

O Over (because if ever there was a time when you wanted a reply, this is it!).

DIGITAL SELECTIVE CALLING

Digital selective calling (DSC) is a facility that automates many of the procedures that would otherwise be carried out by voice on channel 16. The part that gets people excited is that it can send the electronic equivalent of a distress call, complete with the boat's position, but it can also speed up and simplify ordinary boat-to-boat calls, so long as both vessels have a DSC controller built into their radios or connected to them.

Like the controls of radios themselves, the controls, displays, and menu systems of DSC

controllers vary, but the general principle is that every radio has a unique nine-digit maritime mobile service identity (MMSI) number. To call another vessel, you tell your DSC controller that you want to make a routine call; the MMSI of the vessel you want to contact; and the working channel you would like to use. It then uses channel 70 to transmit that information in the form of a very short burst of digital code. The DSC controller onboard your target receives the message, recognizes that it is being called, and sounds an alarm. Assuming that the recipient is prepared to take your call, he acknowledges it by pressing the appropriate button on his DSC controller, and both radios switch automatically to the working channel you selected. All

Above: Even small boats are well-advised to carry a small satellite communicator such as an EPIRB for use in emergencies.

the business of calling on channel 16 and changing channels is removed: you just have to pick up the microphone and get on with your call.

The distress button provides a short cut into a special section of the DSC controller's menu, in which, instead of selecting who you want to call, you specify the nature of the distress situation. Assuming your DSC controller is connected to a GPS set, it then broadcasts a distress message, complete with your position and a one-word description of what is wrong, that will appear on the screen of every other DSC controller within range.

EPIRBs

VHF suits most small craft very well, and few motor boats carry enough fuel to go far enough offshore to warrant getting involved with the much more expensive equipment and more complicated operating and licencing procedures

associated with MF and HF. Satellite communications, however, are a different matter.

We are not talking, here, of satellite telephones – though they are fast becoming a practical, but still expensive proposition for even small and mid-range motor boats. Instead there is a special type of satellite communicator that is designed exclusively for use in distress situations. Of course you hope that you are never going to need it, but the prices of these devices have fallen to such an extent that it is getting increasingly difficult to think of a good reason not to carry one.

The initials EPIRB stand for emergency position indicating radio beacon, and can refer to any compact, self-contained radio that transmits an automated distress signal.

Unfortunately, the term is now used to refer to any of several different things. They all fit that

general description, but while some of them can summon help from anywhere in the world and at any time of the day or night, there are others that operate only over a range of a few hundred metres, and some that are simply obsolete.

To further confuse the issue, there are other things called ELTs (emergency location transmitters) and PLBs (personal locator beacons), which – at least in principle – are much the same as EPIRBs. In practice, though, there are significant differences.

An ELT is a beacon intended for use in aircraft, with a shock-sensitive trigger to set it off automatically if the aircraft crashes.

PLB officially refers to a device intended for use ashore, that is manually operated and does not

Above: An emergency position indicating radio beacon (EPIRB).

necessarily float. Even if it does float, it probably doesn't float upright! But there's no law that says you can't have one on a boat, and they are becoming increasingly popular as marine equipment.

COSPAS–SARSAT

Emergency radio beacons were first developed for aircraft, back in the 1940s and '50s. The idea, then, was that the signals from the emergency beacon on a crashed aircraft might be detected by other aircraft that happened to be passing, and that potential rescuers could then use radio direction finding to home in on the crash site.

As those first beacons were intended for aircraft, it made sense to use the aviation distress frequencies: 121.5MHz and 243MHz.

However, in 1979 something quite remarkable happened. The USA, France, the Soviet Union, and Canada got together in what was surely the world's most unlikely alliance, to set up a satellite system – called Cospas–Sarsat – that would listen out for EPIRB signals, instead of relying on the off-chance that they might be picked up by passing aircraft.

Of course, with thousands of 121.5 and 243MHz EPIRBs already in use, it made sense for Cospas–Sarsat to operate on those frequencies. But the system was also designed to work on a new, dedicated frequency of 406MHz.

As it was originally conceived, the Cospas–Sarsat used four satellites in

Above: *Personal locator beacons are becoming increasingly popular.*

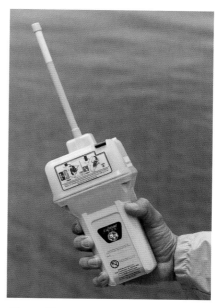

Above: *This EPIRB is designed to withstand exposure to UV rays, oil and seawater.*

low earth orbits: two Russian ones (Cospas), 1,000km (621 miles) above the Earth's surface, and two American ones (Sarsat) at 850km (528 miles), all carrying equipment supplied by France and Canada.

It is relatively easy to get a satellite to fly around the equator. The clever bit about the Cospas–Sarsat satellites is that they go around the poles, and at such low altitudes that each satellite has to whizz around the Earth in just over an hour and a half – travelling at over 25,000 kph (15,500 mph) – if it is to avoid dropping out of orbit. With the Earth revolving inside the satellite orbits, this means that at some stage, every bit of the Earth's surface will pass through the field of view of at least one satellite – though if you miss one satellite, you may have to wait

an hour or so for the next.

DOPPLER POSITIONING

A big advantage of the fast-moving, low-flying satellites of the Cospas–Sarsat system is that the satellites can work out the position of the EPIRB, using a technique known as Doppler positioning.

There can't be many people who have gone through life without noticing that if you stand by the side of a busy road, the road and engine noise produced by each car seems to drop in pitch at the moment it passes you. This is called the Doppler effect.

The same thing happens to EPIRB transmissions as they are received by a satellite. When the satellite is flying towards the EPIRB, it receives a slightly higher frequency than when it is flying away. By analyzing how quickly the frequency changes, the satellite can work out how far away it was from the EPIRB: if the satellite passes directly over the EPIRB, the frequency changes more abruptly than if it passes some distance away.

Simply knowing how far away the EPIRB was would be ambiguous, because it could be either east or west of the satellite's track. But of course, the EPIRB isn't really stationary. The Earth's rotation means that so far as the satellite is concerned, an EPIRB drifting in the English Channel is really moving eastwards at about 600 knots. This, in turn, means that if the EPIRB is west of the satellite's path, the signal received by the satellite will be at a higher frequency than if it is east of the satellite.

GEOSAR

A relatively recent refinement of the system is that Cospas–Sarsat equipment has now been built into some more conventional communications satellites, to form a supplementary system called Geosar.

Unlike the original Leosar (low Earth orbit) system, the Geosar satellites fly around the equator in such high orbits that it takes 24 hours to complete each round trip, so each satellite effectively 'hovers' over a particular spot on the Earth. (That's why you don't have to keep moving your satellite TV dish.) Another advantage of the geostationary orbit is that it is so high that each satellite can 'see' almost a third of the Earth's surface at once, so the five geosar satellites, between them, provide continuous and overlapping coverage of almost the whole globe. Only the areas within about 20 degrees of the north and south poles are left out.

One big snag with the Geosar satellites is that although they can receive an EPIRB transmission as soon as it is sent, and download it almost instantaneously to a search and rescue organization ashore, they can't use Doppler positioning to work out where the signal is coming from. In other words they can relay a distress alert immediately, but they can't locate where it is coming from.

So a new breed of EPIRBs has built-in GPS receivers, and includes the position from the GPS in the distress message.

121.5MHZ EPIRBS

A 121.5MHz EPIRB is a relatively small, cheap and simple device that starts transmitting a continuous high-pitched warbling tone when it is switched on, and goes on doing so until it is switched off or runs out of batteries. Its power output is less than a tenth of a watt, and its signal conveys no information except that someone, somewhere, is in distress.

The main drawbacks of a 121.5MHz EPIRB are that it may have to transmit for an hour or more before a satellite passes close enough to receive a signal. Even then, it can't pass the information on unless it can 'see' an earth terminal at the same time. This means that roughly a third of the Earth's surface – mostly the mid-ocean areas – isn't covered. And when the message finally does get out, the position of the anonymous casualty is so vague that the initial search area will probably extend to something like 965 sq km (600 sq miles).

For the authorities, all these drawbacks are compounded by a terrible record of false alarms. The VHF band in which 121.5MHz

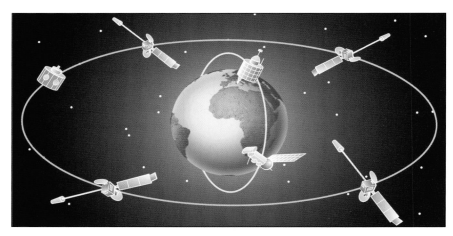

Above: *The Leosar and Geosar satellite systems.*

beacons operate is particularly busy, and the signal is so weak and so simple that it is easily confused with all sorts of other radio transmissions, with the result that less than a quarter of one per cent of 121.5MHz alerts are genuine.

In addition, the warbling tone of a 121.5MHz is completely anonymous, so there is no way of confirming whether any particular alert is one of the two in a thousand that are genuine.

As a result of these concerns, the 121.5MHz facility is being closed down. The Russian Cospas satellites are no longer capable of receiving and processing 121.5MHz signals, and the American Sarsat satellites will follow suit in February 2009.

So if you are thinking of buying an EPIRB now, it makes sense to forget the 121.5MHz versions.

406MHZ EPIRBS

406MHz EPIRBs are bigger than 121.5MHz versions, and are roughly three times the price, but they are much more sophisticated.

Instead of the anonymous warbling of a 121.5MHz beacon, a 406MHz EPIRB transmits short bursts of digital data on a frequency reserved specifically for EPIRBs.

Transmitting a half-second burst every fifty seconds means that a 406MHz EPIRB can transmit fifty times as much power as a 121.5MHz version, while sending digital data means that it can identify itself. The higher power, reduced interference, and more stable frequency mean

Above: Polica vessels require excellent communications systems, as suggested by the radio masts visible here.

that the satellites' Doppler positioning is much more accurate than when they are dealing with a 121.5MHz EPIRB, so the position is likely to be accurate to within a couple of miles – and it gets better with each satellite that passes. However, an increasing proportion of 406MHz EPIRBs go a step further by including GPS, and including position in their messages. The advantages are obvious.

The main drawback of sending such short bursts of data is that it is impossible for ships, lifeboats or aircraft to 'home in' on the signal. But there's an easy solution: all 406MHz EPIRBs include a low-powered 121.5MHz transmitter as well. EPIRBs (and some PLBs) also have a flashing light, to guide rescuers to the exact spot.

EPIRB CATEGORIES

EPIRBs are available in several different categories.

A 'Cat 1 EPIRB' is a 406MHz EPIRB stowed in an automatic bracket from which it will float free and be switched on automatically if the vessel sinks far enough for the bracket to be immersed to a depth of about 2–4m (6–12 ft). This is the only type that meets the full requirements of GMDSS for commercial shipping, but they are not necessarily ideal for recreational craft.

A 'Cat 2 EPIRB' has to be manually removed from its bracket (or may not have a bracket at all). Depending on the make and model, the action of removing it from its bracket may be enough to activate it, or it may have to be

EPIRB CATEGORIES

	121.5MHz	406MHz	406MHz +
GPS coverage	65% of global	Global	Global
False alerts	> 98% false	Approximately 92% false	Approximately 92% false
Sources of alerts	80% not from beacons	All from beacons	All from beacons
Time to first alert	Average 45 min	Instantaneous	Instantaneous
Location time	Average 60 min	Average 60 min	Instantaneous
Position accuracy	15–25km (9–16 miles)	2–5km (1–3 miles)	20m (66ft)
Search area	1,295 sq km(500 sq miles)	65 sq km (25 sq miles)	Negligible

121.5MHz beacons are not recognized under GMDSS and will not be received by Cospas Sarsat after 2009.

turned the right way up, or placed in seawater. It doesn't really matter which, as the point is that by the time it is floating upright in seawater, it will have switched itself on.

PLBs are smaller and less capable than proper EPIRBs, with smaller batteries, no flashing light, and much less buoyancy. Most will still float if you drop them, but they need to be held upright to work. The big virtue is that without the bulk that an EPIRB requires in order to float upright, they can easily fit in a pocket or clip to a lifejacket, making them ideal for very small boats or short-handed sailors.

Navtex

Down at the unfashionable end of the radio spectrum, where frequencies are still measured in kilohertz and wavelengths run to several hundred metres, there is a broadcast service called Navtex.

As the first half of the name suggests, this is a system

for broadcasting navigational information, including weather forecasts, search and rescue information, and warnings about things such as the movement of oil rigs, the demise of light buoys, or the presence of semi-submerged containers.

As the second syllable suggests, it's a text-based system, broadcast in the form of a stream of rapid pulses that can be interpreted by a

dedicated Navtex receiver and reassembled into a printed message that can either be printed onto paper or displayed on a screen.

There is a lot to be said for having a written weather forecast waiting for when you are ready to look at it, but you could still be forgiven for thinking that the need for such specialized equipment might limit the appeal of Navtex to

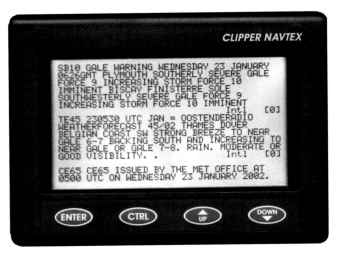

Above: A relatively affordable Navtex system.

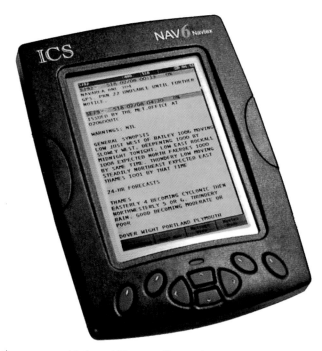

Above: A rather more sophisticated Navtex, offering dual channel reception as standard.

recreational boat-owners.

However, once you have bought a receiver, for about the price of a decent mobile phone, the service itself is free, and the process of actually receiving messages is almost entirely automatic – you just switch the receiver on and it will soon start displaying navigational warnings, weather forecasts, and such like. You don't even have to tune it in.

Nor does it matter if you have missed a message, because each one is regularly repeated until it becomes out of date.

HOW IT WORKS

There are well over a hundred Navtex transmitting stations dotted around the world, each with a range of several hundreds of miles.

They all operate on one of two frequencies (518kHz or 490kHz), so they have to take it in turns to transmit, to avoid interfering with each other.

When its time slot comes around, each station transmits a string of messages. Some will be brand new, while others may already have been broadcast many times over the preceding days or weeks. These may be 'old news' but they are repeated for the benefit of ships that are only just arriving in the area or for those that have only just switched on.

For the user, all these messages, repeated every four hours and arriving from each of perhaps half a dozen different transmitters within range, could quickly become a deluge of irrelevant information.

Yet the receiver allows you to select which stations you want to receive and to reject certain types of messages, and it will automatically reject messages that it has already received.

Above: Both recreational boats and working vessels can benefit from Navtex systems.

DESIGN AND CONSTRUCTION

Boats are lovely things to look at. From the sweeping curves of the superstructure to the glint of a stainless stanchion in the sunshine, there is something about a well-designed boat that makes the spirit soar. For most of us, though, boats are more than just something to look at. When you are on the water, the well-designed powerboat positively fizzes along, gripping aggressively through turns and capably handling waves, chop and spray. The secret to all this lies in the hull.

The dark arts of hydrodynamics these days rival Formula One in their complexity. A modern hull may rely on a combination of angles, chines, steps, tunnels, twists and turns to seek out the perfect compromise for a particular boat design.

There is no doubt that hull design is a compromise. The naval architect will want to produce a dart that flies over most of the waves and cuts through the rest with ease; the marketing man, meanwhile, wants the boat to spread out like a whale so that it can accommodate the generous cabin(s) that buyers hanker for.

Meanwhile, the hull design itself needs to find a compromise between the conditions that the boat is likely to encounter. A boat that flies over flat water might be great fun but if it can't handle any chop then it won't go into production. Similarly, manoeuvra-

Above: To choose your boat, picture how you will use it.

bility at high speed will need to be matched by some degree of capability in the marina, too.

Your requirements

The boat you need will be defined by several things. First of all, where will you take it? Will you be mainly inland or close to shore, or are you planning on leaving the coast,

maybe crossing the English Channel or heading even further afield? It makes a big difference to the capabilities (and probably the price!) of the boat you will end up with.

Although this kind of reckoning is useful, it does have its limitations. One of the most common questions newcomers ask is, 'What size/type

Above: There is a style of boat for practically every use you can think of.

Above: Slow-speed manoeuvring relies on hull shape and style.

your accommodation needs to fit inside your chosen hull – and it is amazing how much compromise (or expense) might be required to include all the cabins and facilities that you might be dreaming of.

Take all these factors into consideration, add more practical matters such as your budget and the space in your chosen marina (or on your driveway), and you now know what you are up against in the search for the perfect hull.

Displacement hulls

In the crudest terms, there are two types of hull: displacement and planing. The former rides deep in the water and pushes it out of the way as it moves; the latter rises up in the water and skims along the top.

Let's begin by looking at displacement hulls. Traditionally these are either 'round-bilge' – shaped somewhat like a wine-glass – or 'hard chine', with straighter sides.

There are numerous benefits of

of boat do I need to cross the Channel?' And the problem with answering that question is that you can row across the Channel in a bathtub – if the conditions are right – and if the conditions are against you, then you might not get across in a commercial ferry.

Secondly, what kind of boating do you want to do? Are you happy to plod along, with excellent fuel economy and great seakeeping, because you want to be able to cover long distances? Or are you more interested in the white-knuckle ride of a fast boat, in which you can have more thrills during a quick blast around the bay than in a slow cruise to Cherbourg? Alternatively, perhaps you are more

interested in a niche interest such as waterskiing, wakeboarding or deep-sea fishing.

Finally, who will be on board, and what will they be doing? It's a pretty obvious point to say that all

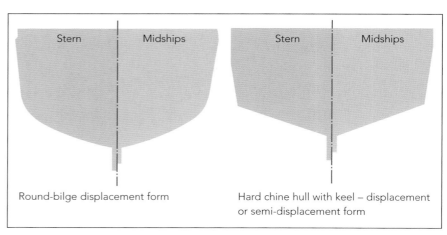

Stern	Midships

Round-bilge displacement form

Stern	Midships

Hard chine hull with keel – displacement or semi-displacement form

Above: Cross-sections, at the stern and midships, of displacement hulls.

Above: *Displacement hulls ride deep in the water, pushing it out of the way as they move.*

a displacement hull, but we will begin by looking at the design's big drawback: lack of speed. As already mentioned, a displacement hull works by pushing water out of the way, and there is a limit to how quickly it can do this. The boat creates two big waves, one at the bow and one at the stern, and the quicker the boat goes, the further these waves move apart. If the distance becomes too far, the stern wave no longer supports the hull, so the boat will ride 'bow up', struggling to get over the bow wave that it is itself creating. From here you can make the engine work harder, but the only significant result will be that the ride becomes more uncomfortable, without much of an increase in speed. This maximum rate of knots is known as the hull speed, and it effectively limits the maximum speed of a

displacement hull. If you are not into figures, all you need to know is that the longer the waterline of the boat, the higher the hull speed. Mathematicians should refer to the hull speed box on page 156 to see how this maximum speed is calculated.

That's the bad news, but it isn't all doom and gloom for the displacement hull. With the top speed limited, there is no point fitting multiple fuel-hungry engines, so displacement boats tend to be fitted with one engine, which reduces the initial cost. The engine

Above: *Boats with displacement hulls lack speed, but they are good in rough weather.*

CALCULATING HULL SPEED

When a boat is moving through – rather than over – the water, the hull's maximum speed is dependent on the length of the waterline (not the length overall). As a general rule of thumb, the hull speed (in knots) will be approximately the square root of the waterline length (in feet) multiplied by 1.5. So a 5m (16ft) boat will be limited to around six knots; an 8m (25ft) boat might reach up to 7.5 knots.

As an aside, you won't hear naval architects talk much about hull speed, because it is really only a theoretical maximum, governed by that factor of 1.5 which has been largely picked at random. In reality, boat builders are interested in the real 'length to speed' ratio that relates the square root of the waterline with the boat's maximum speed in real life. Anything over 1 is good; more than 1.3 is exceptional.

The upshot of all this – if you'd rather not get too mired in the figures – is that the longer the waterline length, the higher the maximum speed of a displacement vessel.

---

is unlikely to be worked particularly hard, so fuel economy should be very good. As we have seen, it is the length of the waterline that limits the speed, not the weight, so these are good load-carrying vessels. For the leisure boater that means the weight of the fitout is not important, so the interior can be really solid, and made of traditional rather than modern weight-saving materials. The only restriction is that the weight needs to be low down, as anything high up could accentuate the boat's roll at sea. A further cost saving is made from the engine specification, because whereas a sportsboat engine will be made of expensive, light components, the displacement engine can be a cheaper, more traditional block.

On the water, displacement hulls generally make very seaworthy vessels, because they are able to plod their way through even quite fierce seas. And because these vessels are made for handling at low speeds, they are fairly easy to control at 'marina speed' – unlike some planing boats which struggle to respond when not moving at a decent rate of knots.

Planing hulls

If boats that sit in the water are restricted to quite slow speeds, how will we get the adrenaline rush that the average powerboater craves? The answer is to get the boat up and out of the drink!

The principle of the planing hull is simple. Instead of being trapped behind the bow wave, the planing hull will rise up and 'surf' along it instead. To achieve this, boat designers create hulls that minimize hydrodynamic drag, which increases

Above: A flat bottom is only really suitable for very calm waters.

by the cube of the speed of the boat. In comparison, the aero-dynamic drag of cars and aeroplanes increases by the square of the speed, which explains why smooth, almost featureless surfaces are the hallmarks of the underside of the typical boat. And whereas a Formula One designer will be looking to produce downforce to hold the car to the track, a naval architect may look for some 'lift', in order to help the boat rise up on the plane quickly. Get it wrong, though, and the boat will be losing contact with the water or even, in the case of offshore powerboat races, somersaulting in the air.

In fact, a good hull shape for getting up on the plane is a flat bottom, which reduces drag to a bare minimum. Unfortunately, life is not that simple. Put a flat-bottomed boat in anything other than mirror-smooth waters and every change in the water surface will be transmitted through the hull to you and your passengers. As the waves start to

build, the hull will 'slam' from one wave to the next, making the flat-bottomed boat uncomfortable in even the kind of mildly choppy sea that is more the norm than the exception.

Moreover, flat-bottomed boats do not have a pivot point about which to turn, so you will find yourself sliding across the water more like a hovercraft than a powerboat. Boat builders may fit skegs (like upside-down shark fins) to the hull to try and generate some grip, but you will never be able to pull much of a turn without sliding.

Despite all this, there is a role for flat-bottomed boats, though obviously the water will have to be flat calm all the time. One example would be the airboat of the swamps and bayous of Florida. These aluminium boats do slide rather than turn, but they have the advantage that they can pass over waterways clogged with plant life that would stop an ordinary vessel in its tracks. In addition, the minimal

Above: Reducing 'slamming' is important for a planing hull.

wash created by a shallow-draught boat skimming over the water has environmental benefits for plant life along the banks.

But for those of us not lucky enough to be cruising the Floridean waterways, we need a compromise. We need a boat with minimal drag that can get up on the plane easily, but that can grip the water to turn sharply. We need a sharp hull shape

Above: For designers of racing powerboats, the key is to get 'lift' without the boat taking off.

that can cut through waves, but we don't want our interior space to be overly cramped by steep sides.

The answer lies in the world of the V-shaped hull.

V-shaped hulls

If a boat has a V-shaped cross-section – which, let's face it, is how we instinctively think of a boat's shape – then it provides a couple of benefits immediately. The dart-like shape will cut through waves rather than slam into them and, when turning, the V-shape allows the boat to heel into the turn, dig in and grip.

V-shaped hulls are normally divided into 'medium-V' and 'deep-V' categories, with the crucial distinction being what is known as the deadrise. This is the angle

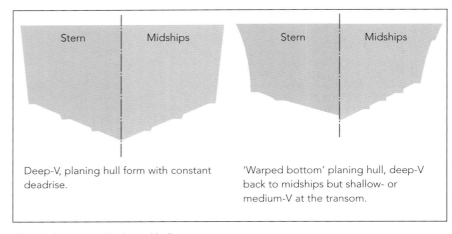

Deep-V, planing hull form with constant deadrise.

'Warped bottom' planing hull, deep-V back to midships but shallow- or medium-V at the transom.

Above: *Two typical V-shaped hulls.*

between the bottom of the hull and the horizontal, so that a flat-bottomed boat would have a deadrise of 0 degrees.

The traditional deep-V hull, which is used for high-performance or race boats, might have a deadrise of upwards of 20 degrees or even 30 degrees, forming a sharp dart. Because of all that surface area in the water, there is lots of drag, and so you will need vast amounts of horsepower to get up on the plane. Once you are there, you will cut through the waves easily, so you should not need to slow up in medium-sized waves. When you turn, the boat will heel all the way over onto the angle of the hull sides, which will give you an exhilarating, grippy ride. However, the boat may also be quite unstable and difficult to control, not least because the tendency will always be for the boat to tip one way or the other.

Reduce the angle of the deadrise, perhaps to 11–20 degrees, and you will get the compromise of the 'medium-V' hull. You will still cut through waves, but the boat will be easier to get on the plane. Just as importantly for the modern leisure boat designer, the flatter the hull, the more space there is inside for accommodation, whether it be

Above: *Note how modern hulls tend to 'flatten out' towards the stern.*

Above: V-shaped hulls can deal with a certain amount of chop.

space for a Porta Potti or a full-width master stateroom. If you ever get onboard a pure performance craft – the waterborne equivalent of a Ferrari – you will be amazed at how the steep sides of the hull mean that there is barely room to sit down below, even on a 30 or 35ft craft.

THE IMPORTANCE OF TRIM

The deep-V's ability to heel helps it to grip the water and turn sharply, but it can also cause difficulties in a crosswind.

When you steer against the wind to prevent the nose being blown off course, this causes the boat to bank and run on the flat side of the angled hull, which gives the crew a rough ride. This can be corrected on twin-engine outboard or twin sterndrive rigs by trimming the engine/drive on the windward side further 'up' and the leeward drive 'down'. Alternatively, if your boat is fitted with trim tabs (hydroelectric plates that are used to change the angle of the boat's ride), then you

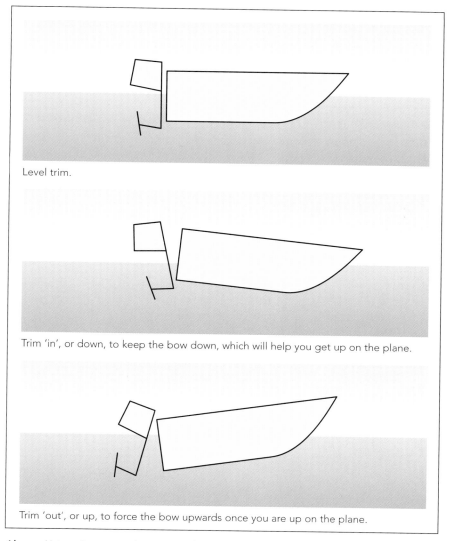

Level trim.

Trim 'in', or down, to keep the bow down, which will help you get up on the plane.

Trim 'out', or up, to force the bow upwards once you are up on the plane.

Above: Using trim to set a boat up on the plane.

can use them in a similar way to counter the banking tendency and keep the boat on an even keel.

Trim is also used – in fact, more commonly – to help a boat get up on the plane in the first place. At low speed, ensure the engine is 'trimmed in' (that is, pushed against the stern of the boat). This will keep the boat relatively flat in the water, and means that as the bow rises over the bow wave, the rest of the boat will start to rise, too.

Once you are up on the plane and the speed of the boat is increasing, you can start to trim out, which will push the bow up and out of the water altogether. At optimum trim, the amount of boat in the water is reduced, which in turn cuts hydrodynamic drag and increases your speed.

If you trim out too far, you may hear the engine pitch change as the propeller starts to take in air as well as water. This 'cavitation' should be avoided. You may also find that as you trim out too far, the boat starts to slam in any waves. When you are learning how to trim, watch your log or GPS. With the throttle held in the same place, the boat will get quicker as you trim out; once you see the speed drop, trim back in slightly and you should be at optimum trim (for that speed and the prevailing conditions).

When you want to turn, trim back down to get the bow into the water; this will help the boat to dig in rather than slide.

The modern reality

As attractive as it might be to see hull design in these simple terms, modern hulls bear only a passing resemblance to these stereotypes, and it is easy to see why.

With computer simulations and more powerful engines, we know more and more about hydrodynamic drag and turbulence at high speeds, which has in turn led to innovations in hull design.

As we have seen, standard deep-V hulls suffer from their large surface area. Those steep sides in contact with the water cause drag, which increases the power needed to get up on the plane. And that is where strakes come in.

A strake is the name for any ridge or line that runs along a boat. Most boats have a rubbing strake, which is the ridge on the side of the hull that is designed to take the brunt of the impact if you scrape along the side of a pontoon. However, in the context of hull design, a strake is a longitudinal ridge, with a roughly triangular cross-section, along the underside of the hull. As speed starts to increase, the boat lifts very slightly on its strakes, which then help the boat as a whole to rise up on the plane. Strakes also cut up waves into bubbly, aerated water, which causes less drag than more 'solid' water.

It is increasingly common for sportsboat manufacturers to talked about 'stepped' hulls.

Above: The right hull and the right boat for your purposes makes for a great day out.

STEPS, TUNNELS AND STRAKES

What this means is that, midships or towards the aft of the hull, there are one or more additional, flattened planing surfaces (steps). This means that this portion of the hull is running on a cushion of air rather than being in direct contact with the water, which in turn means less drag and also a more comfortable ride, thanks to the air pocket acting as a shock absorber, pulling the hull down towards the water to stop it flying upwards, but insulating it from the majority of turbulence.

It could be argued that stepped hulls should be viewed a little like spoilers on cars. Sometimes they are necessary for proper handling; sometimes they have a small but beneficial effect; sometimes they are purely cosmetic. In some cases, riding on a cushion of air can make turning difficult, but, with increasingly sophisticated steps, this need not happen.

Finally, you may also see boats with tunnels in the hulls, though these are generally found only on very high-performance race boats. It was mentioned earlier that strakes on a hull aim to aerate the water to minimize drag. Unfortunately, while hulls like bubbly water, propellers don't. Propellers like to grip on calm, undisturbed water for maximum effect. The solution? Build a tunnel into your hull leading up to the prop(s), so that the water the prop

Above: Raceboats will use strakes, tunnels and steps for top performance.

grips on has not been in contact with much hull. Again, tunnels vary in their effectiveness – don't think that just because a boat has one, it is better than one that does not.

Above: Tunnels in the hull protect 'clean' water for the props.

Above: A cruiser such as this has maximum interior space at the expense of a fast hull.

We saw earlier that the ideal planing surface is the flat bottom, but that the action of the waves makes the ride uncomfortable. However, if we look at how a V-shaped hull interacts with the water, the vast majority of the waves will be hitting the bow of the boat. Here, the V-shape, coupled with the momentum of the boat, will cause the waves to break up and splash out of the way.

What this means is that boat designers can reduce the deadrise at the stern to create a flatter area, without compromising ride quality. This flatter section will increase lift, making it easier for the boat to get up on the plane and to stay there, and it will also add stability to the hull, as it will reduce the tendency for the boat to tip one way or the other.

Any boat designer building a cuddy or a cabin cruiser will want to maximize interior space, and so the pressure is on to reduce the length of the deep- or medium-V section, flatten the deadrise early and thus gain more interior space towards the stern. The effect will be less grip when turning, and potentially some slamming in heavy weather – and we are back once again to the point about knowing how you plan to use your boat. Is the ability to withstand a chop important, or would you rather have more interior space? There is no right or wrong answer – it is all down to your preference.

The reality is that 'monohedral' hulls (those that keep a constant deadrise from bow to stern) are very rarely found these days, and so most boats – although they may be called 'medium-V' or 'deep-V' – are actually a 'variable-V' or 'warped bottom' design.

As a result, beware of manufacturers quoting deadrises, because this figure will tend to change along the length of the boat. It is generally the deadrise at the transom (the very aft of the boat) that is considered the most useful

Above: A compromise between speed and comfort must be reached for luxury yachts.

figure. A boat might have a deadrise of 30 or 40 degrees at the bow, but if this quickly flattens out to 10 degrees, you will certainly slam in rough weather.

Semi-displacement hulls

This talk of compromise brings us neatly onto the semi-displacement hull, which combines some of the virtues of planing and displacement craft. As with a variable-V, the aft section of a displacement boat can flatten off without adversely affecting the handling or ride. And with this in place, the boat will begin to lift as it increases in speed, thus gaining some of the benefits of a planing hull.

Semi-displacement boats won't raise up on the plane as well or as efficiently as a planing craft, and nor will they match the economy of a genuine displacement hull. However, as a compromise, they will be easier to control at low speeds and yet capable of eating up the miles in open water, which makes them ideal for many uses. If you want a boat that will cross the Channel relatively swiftly and take you through European waterways for a month or two, a semi-displacement hull cannot be bettered.

Semi-displacement hulls also prove their worth in rough conditions. The general rule (and only experience will teach you when this isn't the case) is that the rougher the sea, the slower you must go. For the out-and-out planing craft, the problem comes when the speed

Above: *Semi-displacement hulls are less efficient, but make the boat easier to handle.*

drops so much that you fall off the plane. Suddenly the boat is not only in rough seas, but riding at an attitude that it is not really designed for. Steering becomes difficult, the boat will rock and roll, and the kids will probably start crying.

In a semi-displacement craft, falling off the plane is not an issue, and you just plod your way to your destination. On the negative side,

in flat conditions your kids will point to Sunseekers as they roar past and moan, 'Why can't we have one of those?'.

In truth, as with the monohedral hull, the true displacement boat is a dying breed. You will still find them on the genuine little ship, take-me-across-the-Atlantic motor-yachts, but in the vast majority of other cases, most hulls will generate

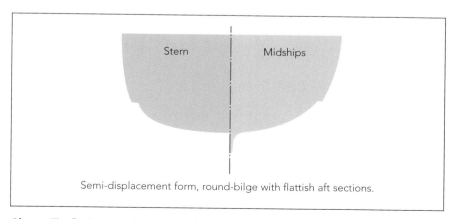

Semi-displacement form, round-bilge with flattish aft sections.

Above: *The flat bottom of a semi-displacement hull generates lift to get on the plane.*

HANDLING PROBLEMS

Two of the more common handling problems for planing boats are 'chine-walking' and 'porpoising'.

The chine is the point where the bottom of the hull meets the sides. When a deep-V hull picks up speed and rises on the plane, it rests on an increasingly small, essentially triangular, area. In some cases, the boat will lose its balance and fall one way or the other onto its chine. When this is corrected, the boat falls the other way – and this rhythmical falling one way and the other is known as 'chine walking'.

Some boats are more susceptible to chine walking than others. At very high speeds or in rough seas it could become dangerous, and at any speed it is an inefficient and uncomfortable way to travel.

If you feel your boat start to chine walk, the simplest way to stop it is to reduce your speed or trim in slightly, to increase the amount of deep-V in the water. As you gain experience, you will learn to counter chine walking by very small touches of helm. If you regularly experience the same problem, you

should talk to your dealer or boatyard.

'Porpoising' is when your boat rocks fore-and-aft, like a rocking horse, even in fairly settled conditions. Again, unless the problem is so pronounced that you cannot control the boat or you are going to get thrown overboard, it is more of an annoyance than a danger. The solution is normally to trim in a little to flatten the attitude of the boat. If your boat porpoises regularly, it could be because there is too much weight aft, which is causing the bow to ride at a height that is not stable.

enough lift to make a difference to top-end cruising speeds.

Furthermore, it is getting harder and harder to distinguish between semi-displacement and planing hulls. Semi-displacement boats are getting better on the plane and reaching higher speeds; planing hulls are building outwards to gain more accommodation, and getting better at low-speed handling, too.

Catamarans

Catamarans are the Marmite of powerboating – you either love them or you hate them. Unlike Marmite, they are not a common sight, so we won't dwell on them for too long here.

Like monohulls, cats are available in displacement or planing forms, but powercats are more usually displacement.

The advantage of two hulls over one is a smoother, more stable ride and, in some cases, increased interior space (though this is more of a factor the bigger the cat).

Critics of powercats usually begin by saying they are ugly, then move

Above: The catamaran is a common shape for ferries.

on to say that they are expensive for what you get and – in most but not all cases – the increased beam can lead to higher marina fees than monohulls of a similar length.

If you think you are interested in a powercat, take a seatrial, remembering to compare the accommodation to a similarly priced (not necessarily the same size) monohull. Traditionally, powercats did not turn as well as monohulls but, as with everything else, advances in naval architecture have reduced this drawback on some well-designed examples.

How boats are made

The material of choice for modern boat manufacture is glass-reinforced plastic, which is also known as GRP or 'fibreglass', though this last term is really a brand name rather than the name of the material in general.

The advantage of GRP for the boat builder is that it is perfectly suited to mass manufacture.

Above: Powercats have displacement hulls and provide a smooth ride.

Producing the mould is a very high-cost, precision job, but once that is done, identical hulls can be produced at minimal cost.

For the boat buyer, the main advantage of GRP over traditional materials such as wood or steel is that it requires relatively little maintenance. However, don't believe anyone who tells you that it is maintenance free – it isn't.

To build a boat, manufacturers begin by creating the mould, which is itself a two-part process. Firstly, they build an exact replica of the hull. This can be made of anything at all,

Above: GRP boats are produced from a mould...

Above: ...making it easy to produce many identical GRP hulls.

Above: Producing a hull can still appear quite agricultural.

and it doesn't need to float. What it does need to be is perfect, because every boat created from the mould will look exactly like this one. The dimensions will be identical, and every crack, flourish and blemish will be reproduced like-for-like. There is no margin for error – if there is a problem with the mould, a new one will need to be created from scratch.

From this replica boat can be made a mould, which is itself made of GRP. This is a negative image of the hull, known as a 'female' mould. GRP will be layered into the mould to produce a hull; the first layer that goes into the mould will be the exterior of the hull, and each successive layer will be closer to the interior of the finished boat.

WHAT IS GRP?

Glass-reinforced plastic consists of fine strands of glass-fibre, which is impregnated with resin. The composite material that is produced is exceptionally rigid, which is just what a boat manufacturer needs.

The glass fibres themselves are around a tenth of the thickness of human hair (about 0.005–0.01mm). The strands, being glass, are actually clear, but they appear white because of the way light refracts through the mass of fibres.

For boat manufacture, the glass fibres are typically provided in 'mats' of fibres meshed together. These are laid in the mould and coated with polyester resin, which is also mixed with a catalyst to make it harden. The resin causes the binding material in the mats to dissolve, creating a hard plastic that is reinforced throughout with the strong glass-fibre. Generally speaking, the more strands there are, the stronger the structure, with a typical proportion being 20 per cent glass-fibre to 80 per cent resin.

When you look at a hull, however, you don't see GRP. The first layer that goes into the mould is gelcoat, which is essentially coloured, unreinforced resin. It is smooth, highly polished (assuming that the mould is similarly polished) and has all that shininess that you would expect from the exterior of your brand new pride and joy.

Following the layer of gelcoat, the hull is built up of layer upon layer of GRP. GRP is translucent, and usually contains some visible traces of the

Gelcoat (outer side is made smooth by mould)

Resin

Glass-reinforced plastic

Resin

Glass-reinforced plastic

Resin

Inner side, not controlled by mould, is uneven

Above: Hulls are made from layers of GRP, resin and gelcoat.

glass-fibre matting. If you open a locker or look into your bilges or engine bay, you may find uncovered GRP, though in many cases even this will have received a layer of gelcoat to hide its rather workman-like appearance.

Each layer of GRP is bonded to the next with resin, building up a sufficiently thick hull. One of the beauties of GRP is that extra thickness can easily be added wherever it is needed, which is often achieved by spraying strands of glass-fibre mixed with resin onto the required area. The compromise for the boat builder is to produce a hull with sufficient strength where it is needed, without carrying excessive weight.

IS IT STRONG ENOUGH?

GRP may be a wondrous material, but the idea of a boat built entirely of plastic can be quite a scary one. Will it really be strong enough?

On smaller boats, it is possible to add all the strength you need through the use of curvature. Those strakes, grooves, ridges and flourishes on your sportsboat are not just there to look nice – they add strength, because GRP is far more rigid when it is curved than when it is straight.

Additional strength in the hull is provided through stringers and sandwich layers. Where the hull will be put under most strain – such as around the engine – the structure can be strengthened

Above: Wooden 'stringers' are used to reinforce the hull.

with layers of balsa wood or PVC sandwiched between the coats of GRP. This will also be used on the boat's 'stringers', which are the beams, either transverse or longitudinal, that are used to support the hull.

Above: GRP is strong enough to withstand considerable forces.

MAINTENANCE

Boating is not just a hobby – it is a way of life. That is partly because, for the die-hard boater, you will never stop daydreaming of being out on the water. It's partly because, when you meet another boater, you will quickly get onto the subject of boats, and that's that for the evening. It is also because owning a boat is not just about turning the key and heading into the deep blue yonder. Boats need maintenance, and the true boater will grow to love their boat, and love caring for her.

In fact, that's a bit of a lie. No, not the part about loving caring for your boat – there really is something therapeutic about going through the proper processes – but because, these days, many boaters don't do much maintenance at all. We live in a time-poor age (or so they say), and so it can make sense to pay for the work to be done for you rather than doing it yourself.

Pretty much everything you do on a boat, even cleaning, you can pay someone else to do. And while there is nothing wrong with that *per se*, if you don't know anything about the job that you are paying for, then you are liable to be taken for a ride in terms of cost, and the quality of the job that is being done.

In this chapter we will examine the basic principles of powerboat maintenance: cleaning, antifouling, winterization and preventing corrosion. Each boat is different, and you will need to refer to your owner's manual, or even a workshop manual, in order to take on some tasks. However, whether you are a DIYer or not, this chapter will give you a good overview of why we do what we do, and how we go about it.

Corrosion

We will keep coming back to this, but boats live in a hostile environment. If a boat spends its time in saltwater, then all you can do is put off the inevitable – brine is horrible stuff that will eat away at virtually anything it spends time in contact with. Add algae and

Above: *Look after your boat, and it will last a lifetime.*

barnacles into the equation and you can see why a neglected boat looks very nasty, very quickly!

Corrosion is a real danger for any bits of metal that spend time in the water, and particularly your outdrive, shaft, prop and so on. The damage corrosion can cause to your engine is greater than thousands of hours of regular use. If you have a steel hull, then your whole boat is at risk.

For boaters, there are essentially two types of corrosion. What is known as electrolytic corrosion occurs because of the presence of a current, for example from a poorly installed electrical system. It should not happen, and it can be prevented.

Far more worrying for the boater is 'galvanic corrosion'. Without wanting to go too far into the science of the matter, when two metals are in an electrolyte (such as water, and particularly saltwater), it

is possible that there will be a flow of ions from one to the other, and this causes corrosion.

The way that the ions flow is always the same, because metals exist in a simple hierarchy that defines how susceptible to

Above: *Corrosion is always a danger, particularly in saltwater.*

Above: *Electrolytic corrosion has damaged this light.*

Above: *Anodes, such as this one on a rudder, are designed to corrode ahead of more expensive components.*

corrosion they are (called a metal's 'galvanic potential'). If a metal is not very susceptible, it is called noble; more vulnerable metals are called base. The table below shows how the noble/base hierarchy works, with graphite, platinum and titanium being some of the substances least likely to corrode, while magnesium, zinc and aluminium are some of the most likely.

When metals are in an electrolyte together, the ions flow from the base metal to the noble, and the result is that the base metal (the 'anode') corrodes. However, in order to do this, the metals also need to be 'connected electrically', which means that an electrical current could pass from one to another. Therefore, it is possible to prevent corrosion by electrically insulating one metal from another. However, that is difficult to do effectively in practice and, besides, corrosion can still occur because of small differences in potential between two parts of the same metal, for example caused by inconsistencies in the manufacture.

Generally speaking, boats counter galvanic corrosion by means of 'sacrificial anodes'. The idea is that if very base metals are electrically connected to metals elsewhere on

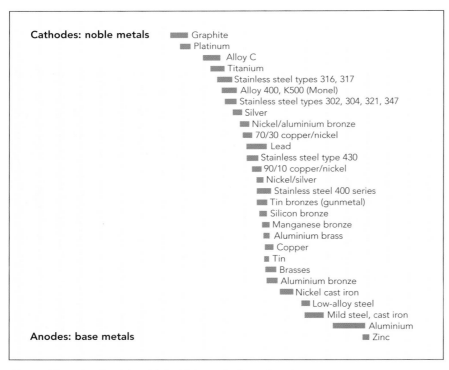

Cathodes: noble metals
- Graphite
- Platinum
- Alloy C
- Titanium
- Stainless steel types 316, 317
- Alloy 400, K500 (Monel)
- Stainless steel types 302, 304, 321, 347
- Silver
- Nickel/aluminium bronze
- 70/30 copper/nickel
- Lead
- Stainless steel type 430
- 90/10 copper/nickel
- Nickel/silver
- Stainless steel 400 series
- Tin bronzes (gunmetal)
- Silicon bronze
- Manganese bronze
- Aluminium brass
- Copper
- Tin
- Brasses
- Aluminium bronze
- Nickel cast iron
- Low-alloy steel
- Mild steel, cast iron
- Aluminium
- Zinc

Anodes: base metals

Above: *The galvanic table, with 'noble' metals above 'base' ones.*

the boat, then the base metals will corrode in preference to all the more noble ones. So if you deliberately place some very base metals around your boat, then these will corrode instead of the more expensive equipment on your vessel. When the anodes become very corroded, they can be thrown away and replaced with more.

MINIMIZING CORROSION

So that is the theory of galvanic corrosion. But how does it relate to maintenance?

Firstly, if any areas of your boat are relying on paint to keep them out of the electrolyte, then that paint must be 100 per cent unbroken. Even a tiny area of bare metal – whether on an aluminium outdrive or a steel hull – will corrode rapidly.

As for your anodes, they should be replaced when they are 50–75 per cent wasted. They are usually made from zinc (for saltwater), magnesium (for freshwater) or aluminium (for brackish water), and should be replaced like-for-like. Don't save money by buying cheap ones, as impurities in the metal can render the anode useless or, worse still, damaging to other (more expensive) areas of your boat.

Anodes will be spread all over your boat, so you should know where they all are. Some will be specifically bonded to the area they are protecting, in order to ensure that they are 'electrically connected' at all times. This bonding should be done with good

Above: *Propellers are highly vulnerable to corrosion.*

quality, heavy gauge wire, which should be tested periodically to ensure that there is a strong, low-resistance connection.

If you keep your boat out of the water, then that is it – and you should not need to replace your anodes more than once a season. However, if you keep your boat in the water, you could be susceptible to corrosion courtesy of other boats, as well.

If your boat is connected to shorepower, and another boat

Above: *Properly placed anodes would restrict corrosion to propellers (left) and brackets (right).*

Above: Imagine the wastage when your boat is carrying all this fouling with it!

connects up too, then the boats become electrically connected. This means that if the other boat is not properly protected from corrosion, your boat might suffer. Your anodes will be doing twice the work, and before you know it they will have corroded away, leaving your boat vulnerable. For this reason, some boaters fit a 'galvanic isolator' or isolating transformer.

If noble metals on your boat are corroding then that is more likely to be caused by electrolytic corrosion. A marine electrician may be required to discover the source of the stray current.

Antifouling

If replacing anodes sounds pretty easy, as maintenance goes, then let's move now to something that requires a little more elbow grease: antifouling.

Take a look at anything that has sat in the water too long, be it an old boat or the supports of a pier, and it is a reminder that our seas teem with life. Algaes, weeds and barnacles like a surface to grow on, and they will grow on almost anything they can find. The types of creature and the rate at which they grow vary from place to place, from surface to surface and even month to month, but the 'fouling' of surfaces by marine life happens virtually everywhere.

Clouds of green weed surrounding your boat do not look very pretty, but that is not the only reason for preventing fouling. Boaters don't have anything against marine life, they just don't like giving it a free lift everywhere they go. Fouling will significantly reduce your acceleration, your top speed and your fuel economy – and the effects really are drastic. Even a fairly light build up can reduce fuel economy by a third and top speeds by five or six knots.

The easiest way to prevent fouling is to keep your boat out of the water. However, if that is not an option, then you need protection.

Antifoul products typically work by deterring marine life from approaching too near, killing it or preventing it from latching onto your boat. Because the type and rate of fouling varies so much, so does the right product for you – but you will quickly develop a favourite, especially if you talk to fellow berth-holders at your marina.

THE TASK

Generally speaking, antifouling should be carried out every year. Some products promise to last two

Above: Applying antifoul to your boat will extend its life considerably.

or even three years, and some copper coatings claim to perform effectively for up to ten.

What you are doing, essentially, is painting – and like every painting job, the secret to success is in the preparation. Without proper preparation, the antifoul won't stick, and that means you will be carrying weed and barnacles all season.

If you have bought a new boat that has not been antifouled already, then the first task will be to scrape off that lovely gelcoat. With the boat in the water, use a marker pen to find the waterline. Make a succession of dots, and then join these up with masking tape (good-quality low-adhesion tape is best, so that it won't take half the boat with it when you pull it off). Now use coarse sandpaper to get rid of the gelcoat below the waterline. Apply a primer coat and then get cracking with the antifoul.

On an older boat, begin by pressure washing to get rid of the worst of the existing fouling. Now, do you need to remove last season's coat? Double check that the product you are using this year is compatible with whatever was used last time. Most paints are mutually compatible, but not all. If they are not, a barrier coat will be required. If they are compatible, what is the surface like? You need a solid layer to adhere to, so if the current antifouling is peeling off then it will need to be removed, again with coarse sandpaper. Once you are ready for the new coat, mask off the

Above: Your boat will need to come out of the water for maintenance work.

Above: A good jet-wash is essential before antifoul can be applied with a long-handled roller.

waterline, using last year's paint as a guide as you do so.

The best tool to use to apply the paint is a long-handled, small-headed mohair roller, which will give good accuracy and won't get too

clogged up. You will also need a paintbrush for awkward areas, as well as disposable gloves, overalls and goggles. Most antifoul works because it is toxic, so it is best not try it out on yourself.

Above: The hull needs to be properly cleaned before antifoul is applied.

Above: If a new boat hasn't been antifouled, the gelcoat will need to be removed first.

If there is one word that strikes fear into the heart of an owner of a GRP boat, it is 'osmosis'. This is the scourge of the older boat, and the reason it is so fearsome is because getting rid of it can be a hugely expensive process.

The root cause of osmosis is the fact that GRP is not actually 100 per cent waterproof. Over time, water will seep into the hull of a boat, forming acids and salts that break down the complex strings of molecules inside into GRP, gradually eroding the strength of the hull.

In reality, although boaters are petrified of osmosis, old salts are fond of saying that no boat ever sank from it. Instead, the usual symptom of osmosis is unslightly blistering in the gelcoat. And as the hull takes on more water, your boat will become heavier, slower and less efficient.

Above: Osmosis is caused by moisture in the hull.

When applying the paint it is always the thickness that counts. The manufacturer will give guidelines on how much paint you should need for your size of boat – and make sure you use at least that amount. If there is a little bit of paint left over, give an extra coat to the waterline, bow and chines – the areas where the new paint is most needed. Avoid your anodes, and make sure that any copper-based paint is kept well away from your sterndrive.

Two coats of paint will normally suffice. Remove the masking tape before the paint dries, and let nature take its course. As long as the weather is not below freezing and it is not raining, it shouldn't take too long for it to dry.

OSMOSIS

Osmosis is a vastly complicated process that scientists are only just beginning to understand. It is now believed that the root cause of osmosis is often the fact that although hulls are almost entirely hardened (known as curing) when they leave the factory, the complete curing process takes months or even years. Poor quality resin and contaminants in the GRP will further accelerate the process.

To prevent osmosis, it is necessary for the hull to be allowed to dry out regularly. Trailboaters and dry stackers should not suffer from osmosis; this is the preserve of the boat that sits on its marina berth all year long. Accepted wisdom has it that a boat should be lifted out for at least a month every year, or for several months every other year. It shouldn't be left in the water for a longer period than two years.

The usual 'cure' for osmosis is to strip back the gelcoat, dry out the GRP and then apply a new outer coat. It is an expensive process, so if you think your boat is suffering, examine those blisters very carefully. Are you sure they aren't just paint blisters or barnacles? Either way, before you dip into your pocket for hugely expensive remedial work, get the boat out of the water and let it dry out for several months. A moisture reader will tell you if the problem persists.

Above: Osmosis is unsightly rather than dangerous.

Above: Check blisters carefully before embarking on a costly anti-osmosis programme.

Above: Tough stains can be eradicated by lightly grit blasting your hull.

Above: Infra-red heaters are used to dry the hull in preparation for maintenance work.

Above: Clear epoxy being applied to bare laminate will help to protect your hull.

Cleaning and polishing

Without wanting to sound too much like a parent telling their children to tidy their rooms, regular attention to your boat's interior will prevent the build-up of really tough stains that will, ultimately, require much more work to remove.

As an example, one of the last jobs to do at the end of the season is to give the boat a proper wax polish. Fail to do this and the GRP will take on a dull finish by the start of the following season, and the only way to reverse this will be to take a cutting compound to the whole surface to bring back the shine.

Assuming the finish is generally all right, the bulk of the cleaning can be done with a pressure-washer, starting at the top of the boat and working your way down. Include a mild detergent mix, to break down tougher stains. Unfortunately, the pressure-washing won't clean the whole boat by itself; it will get you started, but you will still need to take a squirt-on wash and wax compound to get rid of the worst marks and bring out the shine of the hull. When you have finished, pressure-wash again to rinse it all off, this time using just water.

Apart from that, most work is pretty straightforward, if sometimes time-consuming. A chandler's will sell you a specific product for virtually all areas of the boat, including cockpit vinyl, glass or perspex windows and stainless steel fittings. There is now something available for every requirement.

Finally, a quick word on products. The chances are that any cleaners you use will end up in the water, so think about what you are doing. Your super-concentrated bathroom products might bring up your fenders a treat – but is it really responsible to allow toxic chemicals to flow into the water? Marinas may not be the healthiest of marine environments, but boaters, who gain so much joy from their natural surroundings, have a special responsibility not to cause unnecessary damage.

Above: Polishing the gelcoat will protect it in the long run.

Above: Learn to enjoy your maintenance.

Above: Applying antifoul and cleaning your boat can be a messy business!

Wooden boats

If your boat is made of wood, then good luck! The pay-off for a beautiful vessel that is the envy of all your friends is that your boat needs more maintenance than any other. Because most powerboats are made from GRP we won't go into too much detail here – seek out a book or magazine on 'classic' boats for more information.

However, most boats will have wood of some description onboard, in the form of teak decking and/or interior joinery, which can be made with anything from cherrywood to mahogany.

Beginning with teak, the worst thing you can do is to blast it with the power-washer. In fact, you have a decision to make to start with: do you wish to maintain the warm colour of a showroom finish, or are you happy for the wood to fade to

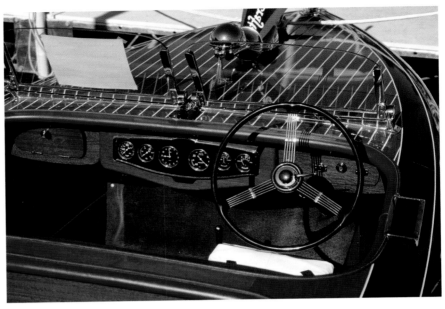

Above: *Wooden boats look beautiful, but they require constant maintenance.*

grey? Obviously the former is preferable, but it requires constant attention, or the colour will become patchy. If you are worried you won't be able to work at it, it might be best to let it fade.

If you do wish to preserve the colour, use an acid-based teak cleaner, applied to wetted decks with a stiff-bristled deck-scrubber. Then use an alkaline colour restorer, and lock the whole lot in with a

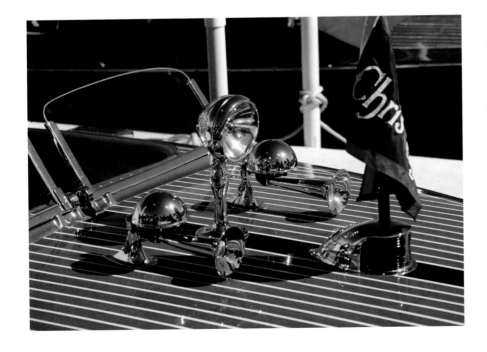

Above: *You won't find this kind of detail on your average 'plastic fantastic'!*

Left: *Anywhere where wood is punctured is a possible site of water ingress.*

non-slippery teak oil. It is this last job that is particularly likely to leave a patchy finish if you don't repeat the treatment regularly.

In the interior, make sure you know what you are up against before you attempt to make repairs or to considerably shine up the wood. What looks like a varnish finish might actually be a lacquer, which can be very difficult to colour-match if there is damage. In some cases it might be easier to buy a new locker door from the manufacturer, for example, than to attempt to repair one that has been damaged.

Bear in mind, also, that what looks like solid wood might actually be a veneer over a plywood base. Scrape or sand at the surface too vigorously and you could wear through the veneer.

WATER INGRESS

In normal circumstances, the point of a boat is to keep water on the other side of the GRP, away from you. If those circumstances change, you will have a problem.

In terms of maintenance, the place where you will find water that has entered the boat is in the bilges. These should be cleaned out twice a year, but checked far more regularly – every time you go to sea, in fact. If water is commonly collecting down here, then you need to find the source of it.

The two most common sources of water ingress are loose deckware and windows.

Above: *Maintaining teak is particularly difficult, but well worth the effort.*

You should periodically check your deckware – cleats, stanchions and so on – to ensure that they fit snugly into the deck. If there is some play, these need to be tightened urgently. Water that is getting in could be going anywhere and causing untold damage out of sight. Before long you could have a musty smell (which does you no favours when it comes to resale!) and rotting wood. If the latter takes hold, then your problem could rapidly become more widespread.

It may be more obvious if you have a leaking window, but even

Above: *Once your boat is out of the water, any areas of damage should be clearly visible.*

Above: *Lubricate all moving parts liberally.*

then the water could be flowing down the back of a lining, so it is invisible. If you go out in rough weather or in the rain, run your finger carefully around the inside of the windows when you get back, looking for traces of leaks and signs of wetness.

A common cause of windows leaking is that the run-offs on the exterior of your boat become clogged with leaves or other dirt. This means water cannot drain off, and the run-offs become little stagnant rivers. With the window seal constantly in contact with water, it is only a matter of time before at least some gets through.

SERVICING YOUR ENGINE

One of the main decisions of boat ownership is which maintenance and repair tasks to take on yourself, and which ones you pay someone else to do. There is a real sense of satisfaction in doing a good job and saving some money – but there is a very different feeling when you mess it up!

These days, engine servicing is moving away from something that the DIYer can do themselves. Boat engines are increasingly dominated by electrics and computer chips, and engine manufacturers are trying hard to dissuade us from working on engines.

If you do fancy servicing your engine – and it is certainly possible to do a good job, especially on an older unit – you will need to get hold of a workshop manual. Even if you don't want to take on the more complicated parts of servicing, it is perfectly feasible to take on certain tasks yourself – changing the oil, impeller and filters are three good examples.

Needless to say, if you have a new engine then it will need to be professionally serviced by a properly accredited marine engineer to keep within the conditions of its warranty.

Problems on the water

In general, peace and quiet on the water are beautiful things. One notable exception is the echoing silence of a sudden engine failure at sea. And while it is impossible here to give a complete guide to getting up and running again, we can at least explain the most common and easily rectifiable problems.

Firstly, remember that many engine breakdowns could have been prevented through proper maintenance or preparation. Never take any chances with running out of fuel, and check your impeller(s) and filters regularly for general wear and tear.

If your engine alarm sounds, or if you detect a problem with the engine while you are underway, act quickly. Check any warning lights to diagnose the problem and then turn the engine off before you cause more serious damage.

If you can, and you are not blocking a channel, drop your anchor. This means that you can concentrate on investigating the problem without drifting into danger. Now call the coastguard. Don't panic – a mayday is only required if you are in 'grave and imminent' danger, for example – but a Pan-Pan or Securité call will at least alert the authorities to a potential problem.

Now what? It is hard to generalize because different engine types will have different components that can or cannot be worked on while you are on the water but, in theory, there are three common causes of engine failure that you may be able to do something about: overheating, faulty electrics and fouled sterngear.

If your instruments indicate overheating then, if possible, reduce engine revs and check your exhaust outlet, if it's visible. If water is flowing out of the exhaust then it is not the raw water that is the problem, so it must be the freshwater circuit in your engine, probably a leak. You can try hunting for it, but this is a problem that is going to be hard to fix. Another potential source of difficulties could be if the freshwater pump has failed, which, in theory, might be replaceable on the water.

If water is not flowing from the exhaust then stop the engine immediately – you will kill the impeller, if you haven't already. Now the likely problems are a plastic bag or weed over the raw water inlet, which might be easily solved by lifting the outboard leg or poking around with a boathook. Next, check the strainers on your water filters, and replace them if necessary.

On an inboard engine, you can probably access the impeller to check and remove it if necessary. Remember, though, that if your impeller is not above the waterline then you will have to shut the stop-cock to stop the contents of the sea emptying into your boat! If the impeller is shredded then you can replace it, but before you start the engine again you will have to clear the debris of the previous impeller; if you don't, the system will block and you will lose another impeller.

Before you start up again, you might have to re-fill the freshwater cooling system. If you do, don't pour cold water into a hot engine, or you could break the whole thing.

Above: *On-water rescue services are available, and add to your peace of mind.*

The prevalence of electronics in the modern engine has many advantages for economy, responsiveness and safety, but when they fail, it is difficult to do much about it while you are on the water. In some instances you may be able to over-ride or reset the electronics alarm to limp back to port (not necessarily your home port); failing that, you could take a look at the battery to check for loose connections or corroded terminals, which could be fixed by some petroleum jelly and a bit of tightening. If you do work on the electrics, remember to isolate the battery, or you could be seriously injured by a short circuit in the system.

At some point in their lives, every boater will get something wrapped around the prop. If it is not a rope you have accidentally dropped overboard, it will be a lobster pot, a fishing net or particularly thick seaweed. Try gently reversing the engine to unwind it. On an outboard engine you can just lift up the leg and unwrap whatever's there, but on an inboard you may have to poke around with a boathook to solve the problem.

Winterizing

For some reason, lots of people don't like boating in the winter. Is it the rough seas, the biting cold or the darkness that falls in the afternoon that puts them off?

Seriously, boating in the winter can be a rare pleasure. Even the Solent is occasionally quiet, the light can be fantastic and – not to put too fine a point on it – you are paying for your marina berth, so why not enjoy yourself all year round?

However, if you do decide to give boating a rest for a few months, you will need to protect your vessel. Some tasks, such as putting antifreeze in your freshwater system, are required because of the potential for cold weather, and will have to be done whenever you leave your boat unattended in the winter. Some, such as removing the impeller, are good practice to prepare for any extended period of inactivity.

Your owners' manual will give you a general overview of what you need to do. Here, we will briefly run through some of the main tasks.

OUTBOARD ENGINES

The main area to attend to when winterizing an outboard is the fuel system. Fuel left in an outboard engine can evaporate into a powder, which will clog up the system for next season. To avoid this, drain off the fuel and, if you have it, squirt 'storage seal' into the carburettors and plug holes.

As with an inboard, cooling water will need to be replaced with an antifreeze/water solution. This is as easy as lowering the leg into a bucket of solution.

Make sure you apply liberal amounts of grease to the two pivot shafts and housings, the steering housing, plugs, electrics, fuel filter, carburettors (if any), fuel pumps and fuel lines and gearbox. The pivot shafts are the vertical pivot shaft and the horizontal tilt shaft, both of which should be fitted with grease nipples.

Above: *Before starting maintenance work, mark the waterline with low-adhesion tape.*

INBOARD ENGINES

Drain the oil

It is a tedious and sometimes difficult job pumping oil out of an inboard's sump, but it should be done at the end of the season, rather than at the beginning of the next. Make sure that before you do so, you run the engine for a little while. This will heat up and thin the oil and also mix up the impurities so that these can be removed rather than remaining in the system.

Replace the oil and filter. Replace the fuel filters, especially if it is a fuel-injected motor. If it is an older engine with a distributor, replace the points and condenser.

Cooling systems

On a fresh-water cooled system, the same water goes round and round the engine, so it may well already be a mix of antifreeze and water. If this job was not done last year, this will need to be replaced – drain off the water and pour the antifreeze/water solution in.

On raw water-cooled engines, it's a little trickier. The best way is to pour the solution straight into the raw strainer, while running the engine at the same time. The key is to keep the solution flowing through the engine while it is running; let the engine run dry and you will damage the impeller.

Once you have done all this, remove the impeller and check it for damage. Leave it out when

you are not using it, or it will become misshapen.

Wiring

Clean all the low-voltage ignition wire connections, for example, to the coil and distributor. Spray all electrical wiring with a good marine silicon spray.

Belts

Check your belts to the alternator, power steering pump, waterpump and any other auxiliaries your inboard drives. Remove them to save the tension while they are not being used, and inspect them for any cracking, in case they need to be replaced.

Linkages

Throttle and gearshift linkages need to be checked, cleaned, lubricated and adjusted. This applies equally to inboard and outboard engines. Always use the correct anti-corrosion grease.

GEARBOXES

Gearboxes need to be checked, too. Outboard boxes are simple mechanisms that can quickly be checked and topped up if necessary. It is tempting to leave the outboard gearbox unchecked, because to take a look involves removing the boat from the water. However, it is very easy for water to penetrate seals around the gearbox, which can contaminate the oil and cause costly damage over the winter.

Above: *Give your boat a good clean before you leave it for the winter.*

DOMESTIC WATER

Leave water in your domestic system and it could freeze over the winter, cracking pipes and causing serious damage. Run the taps until the tank is dry, not forgetting any taps that you do not normally use.

If you have a drain valve, you can blow air through with a dinghy pump to clear the system.

CLEAN UP

While you are working on your boat, this is a good time to give her a polish. It may seem strange to polish a boat before it takes the brunt of winter weather, but work now will make life much easier next season. Grime that has built up during nasty weather will be a real hassle to get rid of – and that probably isn't how you want to kick off your next season of powerboating.

Glossary

abaft – Aft of the beam of the boat and towards the stern.

adrift – Floating, usually out of control and unattached to shore or bottom.

aft – Towards the stern or rear of the boat.

aground – Touching or stuck on the bottom.

ahead – When the boat is moving in a forward direction.

alongside – Beside, e.g. next to another boat or dock.

amidships – Near or in the middle of the boat; halfway between the bow and the stern.

anchor – Device used to secure a boat to the bottom.

anodes – Zinc blocks used to prevent electrolytic corrosion eating away underwater fittings.

antifoul – Chemical composition used on underwater areas to prevent marine growth attaching to the hull.

astern – Direction the boat moves when it is in reverse, or the direction of an object approaching you from your vessel's stern.

auxiliary – Any secondary propulsion engine, used to give assistance or support to the primary power source.

beacon – A non-floating, fixed aid to navigation; anything that acts as a indicator for guidance or warning.

beam – The maximum width or breadth of a boat.

berth – A place to sleep on a boat, and also a location at a pier or marina.

bilge – The very lowest part of a boat's interior, located in the hull near the keel.

boat hook – A pole with a hook on one end, used to retrieve lines, etc.

bow – The forward or front end of a boat.

bow line – A line used at the bow end of the boat for tying up or making fast.

bridge – The navigation station on a boat that controls the speed and direction.

broach – The term used when a boat is broadside to the wind or waves, allowing possible capsizing.

bulkheads – Partition that divides up the interior of the hull into sections and helps to prevent the spread of fire or flooding.

buoy – An anchored floating device used as an aid to navigation; may also be used to mark a mooring. May carry a light, horn, whistle, bell, gong or combination of these.

buoyancy – The upward force exerted by a fluid on an object that is in that fluid. This upward force keeps a boat floating.

cabin – A decked-over living space on a boat.

capsize – To upset or overturn.

cast off – To undo all mooring lines in preparation for departure; to let go or unfasten a line.

channel – That part of a narrow waterway that is navigable, usually marked and having a known depth of water.

chart – A guide used for navigational purposes; would be known as a map if used on land.

cleat – Hardware or fitting with two projecting horns, used to secure the end of a rope.

cockpit – A sunken space or well in the deck that may contain the wheel in some boats.

COLREGs – Collision regulations, or International Regulations for Preventing Collisions at Sea.

compass error – The combined effects of variation and deviation on your ship's compass.

corrosion – The disintegration of metal due to weathering or galvanic action.

crest – The top of a wave.

current – The horizontal movement of water.

dead reckoning (DR) – Calculating a boat's position based on time, speed, distance and course direction from a previous position.

deck – The portion of a boat that covers the hull.

deviation – Compass error caused by a boat's own magnetic field, either influenced by metallic objects or electrical current in the vicinity.

dinghy – Small, open boat used as a tender.

displacement – The weight of water displaced by a floating vessel; therefore, the weight of the vessel itself.

drive system – A mechanical force or apparatus, by which power is supplied to the propeller to cause motion.

EPIRB – Emercency position indicating radio beacon – a satellite-linked emergency and distress beacon.

estimated position – The best estimate of one's position based on a dead reckoning plot and a single bearing.

fender – A protective shielding device placed between a boat and another object.

fly bridge – An elevated steering position located on top of the cabin of a powerboat.

fore – At, near or towards the bow (front).

foredeck – The deck of a boat located near the bow (front).

forward – At or near the front; moving toward a position in the front of the boat.

fouled – Jammed, tangled, snarled or hindered.

galley – A boat's kitchen.

gear – A name for non-permanent equipment on your boat, such as clothing, personal effects, supplies, etc.; also a round, toothed wheel that guides circular motion.

gelcoat – The outermost coat of a laminated fibreglass moulding.

give-way vessel – A term from the navigation rules used to describe the vessel that must yield when in a meeting, crossing or overtaking situation.

GMDSS – Global maritime distress and safety system.

GPS – Global positioning system – a satellite-based worldwide navigation system using simultaneous signals from three or more satellites to establish a highly accurate position reading.

ground tackle – Equipment such as anchors, chains or lines for holding fast a vessel to the bottom.

GRP – Glass-reinforced plastic – consists of fine strands of glass fibre impregnated with resin; better known as fibreglass.

gunwale – The upper edge of a boat at the deck or rail level.

harbour – A sheltered part of a body of water, deep enough to provide anchorage for boats.

head – The marine name for a toilet and its compartment.

heading – The direction in which a boat is pointing at any given moment.

headway – Forward movement.

helm – The steering wheel or tiller and related steering gear.

helmsman – The person who steers the boat.

hull – The basic structure or shell of a boat, minus any other features (cabin, deck, etc.).

hydroplane – A boat designed so that much of the hull lifts out of the water at high speeds, therefore skimming over it rather than through it.

inboard – Positioned inside the boat, towards its centreline

inboard/outboard – A propulsion system with an inboard engine connected through the transom to an outboard drive unit.

jet ski – Something like a waterborne motorbike – a very small boat with a seat and handlebar steering, propelled by a small but powerful engine and a waterjet drive system. Also known as a personal watercraft.

keel – The main centreline structural part of a boat; the backbone.

knot – A unit of speed based on a nautical mile.

latitude – A position north or southh of the equator, measured in degrees and minutes.

launch – The action of placing a boat in the water; also the name for a small boat used to ferry people betwen the shore and a moored vessel.

lee side – The side opposite the wind.

leeway – The sideways slippage of a boat through water caused by the wind.

line – A rope used for a specific purpose onboard a boat.

longitude – A position east or west of the prime meridian, measured in degrees and minutes.

marina – Any facility for berthing recreational boats.

mayday – A distress call – the number one priority term used to define an extreme emergency aboard a boat when calling for help and aid.

moor – To secure or make fast a vessel by means of anchor, lines, cables or other means.

nautical mile – A unit to measure distance that equals one minute of latitude.

navigation – To plan, control, steer a course and control the position of a vessel in order to reach a pre-set destination.

Navtex – Navigation teletext for forecasts and warnings.

osmosis – Blisters in the fibreglass laminate caused by water impregnation.

outboard – Positioned towards the outside of the boat.

outboard motor – An engine, with an attached propeller, designed to be fastened to the outside of the transom or stern of a boat.

pier – A structure that extends into the water from the shoreline to which you can moor a boat.

pile – A post or pole driven vertically into the bottom, used to support a pier.

piling – A group of piles often used to protect wharves and piers from damage that might be done by boats hitting the pier.

piloting – A means of navigating using reference points that may be seen or determined from information on charts, such as depths, heights, landmarks or ranges.

planing hull – A hull designed to climb towards the surface of the water as power is applied, thus reducing the amount of wetted hull surface and reducing the friction or drag and therefore increasing hull speed.

port – The left-hand side of a boat when facing the bow; an opening in a boat's dside, such as a port hole; a harbour.

position – Your location on the Earth based on latitude and longitude.

propeller – A screw-type device that drives or pushes a boat through the water.

PWC – Personal watercraft – a water-jet driven boat that a person sits, stands or kneels on, rather than in.

radio – Electronic equipment allowing communication from ship-to-ship or ship-to-shore.

rudder – A flat, wide shape made from various materials, which is hung on the stern and used to steer the boat.

rudder post – The shaft that connects the rudder blade to the boat.

runabout – A small outboard-powered boat used mostly for leisure or water skiing.

running lights – Navigation lights on a vessel, and the best way to determine another boat's size, type and direction of travel at night.

screw – An alternative name for the propeller.

sea anchor – A parachute-like, cone-shaped device deployed off the bow and usually used in heavy weather to keep the bow up into the wind.

seaworthy – A boat that is in a fit, sound condition, able to go to sea and survive.

shaft – A rotating cylindrical rod that connects the engine to the propeller, designed to transmit power from the engine to the propeller and provide movement either ahead or astern.

slipway – Sloping ground that runs into the water, in which to launch or recover boats. May feature railway tracks with a cradle in order to assist with this process.

stand-on vessel – A term from the navigation rules used to describe the vessel that stays on or continues its course, in the same direction and at the same speed, during a crossing or overtaking situation, unless a collision appears imminent

starboard – The right-hand side of a boat when facing forward.

stern – The aft or back end of a boat.

stern drive – An inboard engine with an outboard drive leg.

tender – A small boat accompanying a larger vessel, to be used as a service or work boat or a dinghy.

topside – Up on the open deck; wholly exposed to the elements.

transom – The portion of the hull at the stern that is perpendicular to the centreline of the boat.

underway – When a vessel is not attached to the bottom, shoreline or any other mooring device.

vessel – A term for all waterborne craft, regardless of size, shape or purpose.

VHF – Very high frequency – a frequency band of radio waves used on vessels within 25 miles of the shoreline.

wake – Visible turbulence of the water surface as a result of the vessel moving through the water.

Useful websites

www.mby.com
The website for *Motor Boat & Yachting* magazine, with reviews, news and all the powerboating information you could ever need.

www.ybw.com/ybw/power.htm
The best of motorboating news, reviews and features from *Yachting and Boating World*.

www.motorboatsmonthly.co.uk
Motor Boats Monthly website, with a full marine directory and listings of boats for sale.

www.powerboatmag.com
Features boat tests and articles as well as all the latest powerboating news from the US.

www.powerboating.com
The website for *Powerboating Canada* magazine, one of the most popular boating publications in the country.

www.sportsboat.co.uk
The website for the only magazine dedicated to mainstream sportsboats in the UK.

www.powerboat-reports.com
The independent product test report for powerboats.

www.rib.net
A great resource for those interested in RIBs, but equally for anyone interested in powerboating in any form.

www.powerboat.ie
Ireland's only virtual motor and powerboat club. Features forums for all classes of powered craft, as well as a central home where you can discuss general boating matters.

www.flpowerboat.com
The wesite of the Florida Powerboat Club, with details of events in the US.

www.powerboat-training.co.uk
Information on courses, powerboat schools and RYA training to help you further your powerboating and RIB-handling skills, and general information on sportsboats and RIBs.

www.splash.co.uk/powerboating
Powerboat hire and advice on all things water-based.

www.boatus.com
The website for the boat owners' association of the United States.

www.marineweb.com
Offers a variety of boating information including a bulletin board and information on marinas around the world.

www.landfallnavigation.com
Nautical charts and cruising guides, marine electronics, plotting and weather software and boating safety gear.

www.metmarine.com
Marine forecasts for the UK and Europe, including wind speed, trend and direction, pressure, visibility, weather and temperature.

www.ukho.gov.uk
The website of the United Kingdom Hydrographic Office, which has been charting the world's oceans for over 200 years. Information about tides, laws of the sea and much more.

www.nmwebsearch.com
A website that allows you to download Admiralty Notices to Mariners, which ensure that Admiralty charts and publications are fully up to date.

www.boatlaunch.co.uk
Online boating information, including details on slipways and marinas.

Index

PHOTOGRAPHIC CREDITS

The copyright of all the images used in this book rests with the photographers and/or their agents as listed below.
Key to locations: t = top; b = bottom; l = left; r = right; c = centre; fr = front cover; ba = back cover
(No abbreviation is given for pages with a single image, or pages on which all photographs are by the same photographer.)

ACR = ACR Electronics Inc
AJP = © Amet Jean Pierre/Corbis Sygma
AP = Andrew Pickthall/PPL
BEN = Bennett Marine
BM = Brunswick Marine
BP = Barry Pickthall/PPL
CBC = Century Boat Company/PPL
CC = Chris Caswell/PPL
C*C = Chris*Craft/PPL
CEC = Cobra Electronics Corporation
CL = Clipper
CMD = CMD Marine

DC = Don Carr/PPL
DK = Des Kilfeather/PPL
FB = Fairline Boats/PPL
GBY = Grand Banks Yachts
GF = Graham Franks/PPL
GJN = Gary John Norman/PPL
GL = Garmin Ltd
HL = Halyard Ltd
IC = Icom
ICS = ICS Electronics Ltd
JO = Johnson/PPL
JM = Jeff Mitchell/Reuters/Corbis
KM = Kawasaki Motors

KP = Keith Pritchard/PPL
LL = Lewmar Ltd
MDL = MDL Marinas/PPL
MM = Mercury Marine
MP = Mark Pepper/PPL
NB = Nimbus Boats
NJC = Nigel J Clegg/PPL
NL = Nordhavn Ltd
PB = Pearl Bucknall
PBE = Peter Bentley/PPL
PC = Powercats Ltd
PL = Plastimo
PML = Portland Marine Ltd/PPL
RB = Regulator Boats/PPL

RHD = Robert Holland/Dougherty/PPL
RL = Raymarine Ltd
RNLI = RNLI/PPL
RR = Roy Roberts/PPL
SB = Skeeter Boats
SC = Standard Communications
SH = Standard Horizon
SI = Sunseeker International Ltd/PPL
SL = Sealine International
SN = Ski Nautique
SR = Searex
SS = Stephen Saks/PCL

TM = Teleflex Marine
UKHO = Crown Copyright and/or database rights. Reproduced by kind permission of the Controller of Her Majesty's Stationery Office and the UK Hydrographic Office (www.ukho.gov.uk). **Not to be used for navigation.**
VP = Volvo Penta
WA = Whiteair.co.uk
WM = Walton Marine
YAM = Yamaha/PPL
YM = Yamaha Motors

Fr main ......CBC	14 (t) ....SB	41 (t) ....SS	69 (c) ....BEN	104 (r) ....PL	146 (t) ....RHD	165 (bl) ......BP
Fr (tr) ....YAM	14 (b) ....JM	41 (b) ....BP	69 (b) ....BM	106–11 ....UKHO	146 (b) ....SC	165 (br) ......AP
Fr (cr) ....BM	15 (t) ....PB	45................BP	70 (t) ....YM	112..............BP	147 (l).........SC	166 (t) ....BP
Fr (br)..........PML	15 (c) ....KM	46................LL	70 (b) ....VP	118 (l)..........JO	147 (r) ....ACR	167 (t) ....BP
Spine CC	16 (l)...........WA	47................SI	71................VP	118 (c) ....KP	149..............MP	167 (b) ....C*C
Ba (t) ....BM	16 (r) ....SN	48 (l+r).......BP	72 (l)...........VP	118 (r) ....BP	150..............CL	168 (l).........NJC
Ba (c) ....NB	17 (tl) ....NB	48 (c) ....DC	72 (r) ....CMD	119..............BP	151 (t) ....ICS	168 (c+r) ....GJN
Ba (b).........KP	17 (tr) ....WM	49–50..........BP	73 (b) ....SR	120 (t) ....RL	151 (b) ....BP	169 (t) ....KP
3..................BP	17 (b) ....SL	51 (t) ....PBE	77................YM	124 (t) ....BP	151 (l).........BP	169 (b) ....NJC
4..................C*C	18................BM	51 (b) ....BP	83 (b) ....YM	126–7..........BP	151 (c) ....RR	170 (t) ....NJC
6 (l).............BM	20................BP	52................GF	84 (t) ....YM	129 (t+br) ..KP	151 (r) ....PML	171 (t) ....BP
6 (c) CC	21 (t) ....TM	53 (t) ....DC	87 (b) ....HL	129 (bl) ......JO	153 (t) ....YAM	171 (b) ....NJC
6 (r) ....BM	21 (b) ....BM	53 (b) ....BP	88 (c) ....HL	130..............BP	153 (b) ....RB	172 (t) ....NJC
7 (l).............KM	22 (t) ....BP	54–60..........BP	90 (l+c) ......BP	131 (b) ....BP	154 (t) ....BP	172 (b) ....PBE
7 (c+r) ....BP	22 (b) ....BM	61 (t) ....GF	91 (br) ....MM	132 (b) ....BP	155 (t) ....GBY	173 (t) ....DK
8 (l+r)..........BM	26 (r) ....PL	61 (b) ....BP	97 (b) ....BP	135 (b) ....FB	155 (b) ....NL	173 (b) ....MDL
8 (c) ....KM	31 (tl) ....PL	62–3............BP	99 (tl+tr) ....BP	136 (l).........MP	156..............YAM	174–6..........NJC
9 (t) ....BM	31 (tc).........SH	64 (l)...........BM	99 (b) CC	136 (c) ....RHD	157..............BP	177 (t) ....PBE
9 (b) ....SL	31 (tr) ....TM	64 (c) ....GJN	100 (l+r)......PL	136 (r) ....BP	158 (b) ....PML	177 (bl) .....GJN
10–11.........BM	31 (b) ....BM	64 (r) ....SI	100 (c) ....BP	137 (t) ....BP	159 (t) ....BP	177 (br) ......MP
12 (t) ....BM	32................BP	65................CC	101..............PL	137 (b) IC	160..............RR	178–9..........CC
12 (c+b)......SL	33................BM	66 (t) ....GJN	102 (t) ....PL	138 (t) ....CEC	161–2..........BP	180..............BP
13 (tl, tr, cr +bl).......SL	37 (t) ....AJP	66 (b) ....BP	102 (b) ....GL	140 (t) IC	163 (t) ....BP	181..............RNLI
13 (br) ....VP	37 (b) ....BP	67 (t) ....SI	103 (b) ....SH	140 (b) ....SH	164..............BP	182..............MP
	39 (b) ....BP	69 (tr) ....YM	104 (l)..........RL	145..............IC	165 (t) ....PC	183..............GJN